UNFINISHED BUSINESS

Revised Edition of
THE NEW REFORMATION

UNFINISHED BUSINESS
RETURNING THE MINISTRY TO THE PEOPLE OF GOD

Greg Ogden

ZONDERVAN™

GRAND RAPIDS, MICHIGAN 49530 USA

ZONDERVAN™

Unfinished Business
Copyright © 1990, 2003 by Greg Ogden

Requests for information should be addressed to:
Zondervan, *Grand Rapids, Michigan 49530*

Library of Congress Cataloging-in-Publication Data

Odgen, Greg.
    Unfinished business : returning the ministry to the people of God / Greg Odgen.
    — Rev. ed.
        p.   cm.
    Rev. ed. of: The new reformation. c1990.
    Includes bibliographical references and indexes.
        ISBN 0-310-24619-9
        1. Priesthood, Universal.   2. Clergy—Office.   3. Lay ministry.   4. Pastoral
    theology.   I. Odgen, Greg. New reformation.   II. Title.
    BT767.5 .O37 2003
    262'.15—dc21

                                                                        2002156683

Interior design by Tracey Moran

Printed in the United States of America

---

03 04 05 06 07 08 09 /❖ DC/ 10 9 8 7 6 5 4 3 2 1

To my wife, Lily, and daughter, Aimee,
whom I deeply love

Contents

Contents

Preface

SINCE THE RELEASE OF *The New Reformation* some thirteen years ago, much has happened to confirm the prophetic message of this book that we are living in the time when we would see the promise of the Reformation fulfilled. It has been broadly observed that the first Reformation of the early 1500s placed the Bible in the hands of the people and that the Second Reformation will place the ministry in the hands of the people. I thought I was being daringly prophetic in my predictions that we were in the midst of a new Reformation. In retrospect, I see that I greatly *under*estimated the change that was happening in the church, which is in major part a reflection of the shift that is taking place in Western culture.

What I now see is that this shift to a people-centered ministry is part of the seismic Western drift from a Christendom to a post-Christendom model of the church. For some 1,600 years, from the reign of Constantine in the early fourth century to somewhere in the 1960s, Christianity existed at the very least in a supportive and favored place in those nations with European roots. Though the climate has been changing slowly over the last two to three hundred years, only in the last decade has it dawned on church leaders and Christian academics that we are now in a new missional environment. The church of Jesus Christ has been largely marginalized and rendered powerless. We no longer enjoy a respected and favored position in Western culture.

This relatively recent setting has caused us to ask: Who are we as the church of Christ? What is our identity? How are we to navigate these waters where the surrounding culture is now a mixture of some indifference, some supportiveness, and some hostility? In many ways this new context makes an updated version of this book all the more relevant. We live in a time of transition, in the overlap of paradigms. The Christendom paradigm viewed the pastor primarily as the chaplain or caregiver. It assumed a maintenance setting. The task of the church was to pass on the faith intact from one generation to the next in a church supported by a friendly culture.

Over the centuries, the roles of pastors in the Christendom model were finely honed. The pastoral office was highly regarded and clearly understood. The people of God knew what a pastor was supposed to be and do. The pastoral role under Christendom was to be a *teacher/caregiver*. To be successful as a pastor you needed to fulfill four roles fairly effectively, and the people of God would be content.

1. **Teacher of doctrinal tradition**—There was a time in the not-too-distant past when pastors chose to be ordained into a denomination based on its distinctive theological heritage. It was the pastor's responsibility to keep those distinctives alive through their teaching and preaching ministry. This was the time when denominations had a theological heritage of which they were proud and clear. Presbyterians had a Reformed tradition; Lutherans looked to Luther as their theological father figure; Methodists were Wesleyans; Baptists and other Anabaptist groups were proud that they truly saw the implication of the Reformation.

Not only did pastors do an effective job in preserving their theological and worship distinctives, but people actually identified with their tradition. So if a Lutheran family moved, the first thing they did was to look for a Lutheran church in their new community. Not just any church would do, but a Lutheran church was where they felt comfortable. They would leave their tradition only under dire circumstances. It sounds like a quaint holdover to institutional loyalty, but this was not too long ago. It was the job of the pastor to bear the weight of that tradition.

2. **Caregiver**—Being a pastor is associated with pastoral care. Pastors are to be present in people's lives at the times of crisis—illness, grief, and quality-of-life-threatening incidents such as unemployment or divorce. God's people have come to expect that there is no one like the pastor who can tend to their needs when life turns south. If there is an emotional contract that people have with their

pastors, it is that they show up in times of crisis. Only the pastor is qualified to meet their caregiving needs. God's people can help, but they do not match up to the pastor.

3. **Public symbol of the sacred**—The clergy represented the institution of the church in public life. They were public symbols of the sacred. Loren Mead writes about the symbol of being an Anglican priest in England just a generation ago:

> In the Christendom Paradigm, the role of clergy was clear. It was strong, central and unquestioned. It was high-status role, carrying authority. Clergy were *the ministry*. Clergy were chaplains and guarantors of community life, with power far beyond the walls of the church. As a thirty-year-old Episcopalian priest walking the streets of a village in southern England, I often had mayor and street-sweeper alike defer to me as "Rector." Their deference was not to me, but to the power that the pastor carried in Christendom. For many people in churches today, that remains a very attractive idea. For many people the problem would be solved if we could return to that strong, hierarchical model, when Herr Pastor was Herr Pastor and the rector was truly "ruler" (which is what the word means in Latin).[1]

4. **Presider over rites of passage**—Central to each tradition are rites of passage that mark a person's incorporation into them. Pastors were and still are the ones who preside over these markers in life. They baptize, confirm, marry, and bury. The most visible expressions of being a presider are the weekly responsibility of leading the people of God in worship and acting in the priestly role as the celebrant behind the communion table.

If pastors fulfilled these four roles effectively under Christendom, the esteem of the pastor was intact. However, today the cultural context in which these roles were refined does not exist in the same way. It is difficult to make generalizations regarding the surrounding culture of a church because even in the United States there are widely varying settings. New England and the Western states in America are worlds apart from Peoria, Illinois, or the heart of the Southern Bible Belt. Yet certainly we would agree that the assumed supportive environment of the Christian church as a respected and consulted institution has greatly diminished. The church I served in Saratoga, California, from 1988 to 1998 was set in a professional community in the Silicon Valley. Santa Clara County, dominated by San Jose, had a church-going population of all faiths of approximately 13 percent. I said regularly to our congregation, "This means that 87 percent of the people surrounding us have voted with their feet that they think we are irrelevant to the well-being of their lives."

All of this is to say that we need to be and do church in a drastically different way, because the mission of the church is now on the doorstep of the church. Mission is not just a hundred people providing the support to send one person to a far-off land. We live in a time of transition, in the time of the overlap of Christendom and the post-Christian world. We need bridge strategies that help us make the shift from the denominational, institutional expression of the first Reformation to the second Reformation where the church is a living organism. If ministry was identified with the clergy under the Christendom model, then in this new post-Christian setting, ministry will become the province of the people of God. If maintenance marked the church under Christendom, then mission will be in the forefront in a new apostolic context. The question is, how do we get from here to there?

Now, twelve years after the first edition, I view the purpose of this book in a little different light than when it was first written. The theological vision contained here serves as a guide to making the transfer to ministry into our postmodern context. The church of Christendom, trapped in an institutional mind-set, equated ministry with a few professionals. Now in the new-paradigm churches, it is generally assumed that ministry is the province of the *laos,* the whole people of God. Undergirding this shift in conception of who does ministry is a biblical image of the church as the extension of the life of Jesus on earth. A key to all of this transition is the role of the pastor. If the teacher/caregiver model that was carefully refined within Christendom (and is still being taught by many seminaries) is no longer relevant, then what is an appropriate and dignifying role for pastors that actually empowers the people of God for ministry? I believe we need to shift from the *teacher/caregiver* to an *equipping leader* model of pastor. Whereas the teacher/caregiver inadvertently tended to foster dependency of the congregation on the pastor, the equipping leader model assists the people of God to grow into full adulthood as disciples and ministers of Jesus Christ.

During transition periods confusion reigns. This is especially true when it comes to the pastoral role. What makes it difficult to be in leadership today is the conflicting expectations of pastors that come from the representative voices of Christendom and post-Christendom in our churches. Those schooled in Christendom expect their pastors to be the primary caregiver. Others speak the voice of post-Christendom. We don't need the pastor to take care of us, but we need the pastor to be a visionary and mentor. In teaching pastors today, I say to them that they have only two choices when it comes to conflicting expectations: they can manage you, or you can manage them. Without a theological vision for ministry, pastoral leaders are left with the pragmatism of the moment or living out the expectations that others have of a pastor's responsibilities. But with the backing of a theological vision of the pastor as equipping leader, you can begin to articulate the role you will play. That does not mean everyone will salute, but the more clearly you can define who you are vis-à-vis the body of Christ, the greater clarity and role definition will ensue. Over time a new consensus can be built.

With this in mind, I have written in a style I like to call "accessible," or popular theology. In other words, theology written by a practitioner. I trust that the theological analysis and biblical exposition would pass academic scrutiny, yet it is presented in a way that always moves toward implementation of ministry. Interwoven with the theological framework is the story of my experience as a pastor trying to live out of his theology. We pastors and church leaders need to be guided by a clear theology of ministry in the daily practice of ministry. All too often books written about the church tend to be either a successful model with little theological vision or a theological treatise that has little to do with the realities of ministry in the local church. It is my hope that this book bridges that gap.

Any theological vision for ministry that has a ring of truth comes out of real-life community. I have been a blessed man. The first writing of this book took place when I was an associate pastor at the St. John's Presbyterian Church in West Los Angeles. Before this congregation I "sang" my song ad nauseum that all God's people are called to ministry and that they needed to demand that their pastors equip them. They responded, not with patronizing smiles, but with motivated desire to be God's ministers. Not only did they affirm my gifts and delight in what I had to offer, but I had to try to keep up with their energy for ministry. An equipping ministry is not possible unless it is shared with a staff team of similar vision. My dearest friend, Darrell Johnson, senior pastor and trusted colleague; Joan Stock, fellow associate pastor; and I were privileged to hold each other in highest regard and share a common vision.

This ministry as an associate pastor was followed by an equally challenging and gratifying ten years as senior pastor at the Saratoga Federated Church in the city of Saratoga adjacent to San Jose, California. This independent church was prepared to see the people of God mobilized for ministry. I was blessed to be able to share ministry with a staff team and committed elders who partnered together to address the issues of an every-member ministry. In those ten years we saw the staff shift from being doers of ministry to being equippers of others: small groups became the basic unit in the life of the church; an expanding network arose from reproducing discipleship groups; ministry teams formed to address the needs of the community and world; worship styles changed to embrace youth and families; and the people of God discovered their spiritual gifts and took on ministries that expressed the passions of their hearts. I observed two major movements during those ten years. The first movement was internal: we moved from a fairly traditional program-based church life to an organism ministry done in teams and small groups. The second was external: we moved from a self-consumed maintenance ministry to mission, giving our lives away in compassionate service and evangelism.

During my tenure as a pastor at Saratoga Federated Church, I co-taught an annual, two-week intensive course, *Empowering God's People For Ministry,* in Fuller Theological Seminary's Doctor of Ministry Program. My teaching partner was Bob Slocum from Dallas, Texas, who has a Ph.D. in physics. We would share and dialogue with eager pastors about the need and know-how to make the shift from fostering dependency to equipping people for ministry. It was for me an annual opportunity to see the progress we were making in my local church. But it was also a continuous window into the state of pastoral ministry.

As much progress as we have made over the last decade, the reports trickle in from the front lines that resistance is firmly in place. Pastors are still acting as chaplains or caregivers, rushing off to meet the needs of the bleating sheep. This leaves the people of God in a continuously dependent position, unable to fully grow up and assume full responsibility as disciples of Jesus. Pastors tell me that as much as they would like to share the ministry with God's people and act as coaches and equippers for the ministry of others, many people still want the pastor to be the paid professional who is identified with "the ministry."

As far as we have come, there is still much to do. Unfortunately, the re-release of this book is an indication that the need for a New Reformation is still in process and we are not fully there yet.

As *Unfinished Business* is released in this expanded and updated form, I owe a debt of gratitude to many. Bob Slocum, my teaching partner and now dear friend, and I have been joined at the heart in our desire to see the people of God find their voice. I am privileged to count as colleagues in this field of lay equipping friends such as Sue Mallory, Bruce Bugbee, Paul Ford, John and Nancy Ortberg, and Gilbert Bilezikian. Paul Engle at Zondervan convinced me that an update of this work would be helpful to leaders in the church. And finally, and always, to my best critic and life traveling partner, my wife, Lily, thanks for believing in me.

NOTES

[1]Loren Mead, *The Once and Future Church* (New York: Alban Institute, 1991), 3.

Introduction:

Transforming People from Passive to Active

E LIVE IN A GENERATION when the unfinished business of the Reformation may at last be completed. Nearly five hundred years ago Martin Luther, John Calvin, and others unleashed a revolution that promised to liberate the church from a hierarchical priesthood by rediscovering "the priesthood of all believers." But the Reformation never fully delivered on its promise.

When Luther made such explosive statements as, "Everyone who has been baptized may claim that he already has been consecrated a priest, bishop or pope"[1] and "Let everyone, therefore, who knows himself to be a Christian be assured of this, and apply it to himself—that we are all priests, and there is no difference between us,"[2] he envisioned the priesthood of all believers on two fronts.

Within Protestant circles we are fully acquainted with the first aspect of the priesthood of all believers since it is a part of our Christian practice. It is in the Protestant air that we breathe that all believers have direct access to God through Jesus Christ. The Reformation released us from the stultifying practice of going through a human mediator to plead our case before God. The one high priest, Jesus Christ, has opened the way to God by presenting himself as the sacrifice for our sin, and he sits at the Father's right hand to make intercession for us continually (Heb. 7:23–26). A special class of priests representing us to God and God to us has been superseded in Jesus

Christ. We are all drawn into the priesthood in that we represent ourselves before God through the one intermediary, Jesus Christ.

The unfinished business and the unkept promise that has the power to unleash a grass-roots revolution in the church is the logical corollary to the priesthood of all believers: *not only are all believers priests before God, but we are also priests to one another and to the world.* Wallace Alston captures our priestly role of representing God to each other:

> The priesthood of all believers, therefore, does not only mean that each person is his or her priest. . . . In very personal terms, it means that the minister is your priest and that you are the minister's priest; that you are my priest and I am your priest; that we are God's representatives to each other, and that we are each other's representatives before God. It means that we are to speak to each other about God, calling each other to repentance and faith. It means that we are to speak to God about each other, interceding before God for each other, and seeking God's guidance and blessing. It means that we should try to become increasingly responsive to one another, tending to each other in God's name and offering each other practical and constructive help for Christ's sake.[3]

Nearly five hundred years after the Reformation, there are rumblings in the church that appear to be creating a climate for something so powerful that we can call it a New Reformation. *The New Reformation seeks nothing less than the radical transformation of the self-perception of all believers so that we see ourselves as vital channels through whom God mediates his life to other members of the body of Christ and to the world.* What are these rumblings of renewal in the church that now create the climate to complete the unfinished business of the Reformation? What has been occurring over the last four decades to transform people from being passive recipients of others' ministry to being active ministers in Christ's name?

Over the last generation the face of Protestantism, especially in the evangelical world, has changed dramatically. Lyle Schaller, considered by many as the most astute observer of the American church scene, stated at a Leadership Network Conference that the most important development in the church over the last forty years has been the rise of the ministry of the laity.[4] Evidence for this statement can be traced both through significant publications and through renewal movements centered in the ministry of the laity. Elton Trueblood, a Quaker lay theologian and a voice ahead of his time, wrote two influential and prophetic volumes, *Your Other Vocation* (1952), on the role of laity in the workplace, and *The Incendiary Fellowship* (1967), where he proposed the seminal image of the pastor as "player-coach" as the best modern equivalent of an equipping pastor. Hendrik Kraemer released his often-referenced *A Theology of the Laity* (1957), as a reminder of our constant tendency to fall back into clericalism. On a more popular level, Keith Miller's *A Taste of New Wine* (1965) spoke to fresh discovery of the lay community, while Ray Stedman's *Body Life* (1972) was accessible theology and practice for the church as the body of Christ.

But beyond these important works, there have been eight renewal movements over the last generation that have changed our understanding of the Christian life, of ministry, and of the character of the church. These are:

- Charismatic Movement
- Small Groups Movement
- Worship Renewal Movement
- Spiritual Gifts Movement
- Ecumenical Movement
- Church Growth Movement
- Seeker Church Movement
- New Paradigm Church Movement

The golden thread that runs through them all is the recovery of the ministry of the whole people of God. In tracing the conditions that make our day ripe for the return of the ministry to the people of God, I lace into my observations the contribution that these renewal movements have made.

CHARISMATIC MOVEMENT

Though the roots of the modern charismatic or Pentecostal movement can be traced to the Azusa Street revivals in Los Angeles in 1906, it did not begin to truly affect the mainline Protestant and Roman Catholic churches until the 1960s. The charismatic movement has reshaped our understanding of the way God speaks to us, of the nature of the Christian life, and of the church as people indwelled by the Spirit and has transformed our experience of corporate worship. The charismatic movement reintroduced to us the hidden member of the Trinity, the Holy Spirit. Experience-starved people came to realize that a direct encounter with a living God was possible, that the Christian life was more than ethical respectability. It is living with Christ from the inside out. The church was not simply an institution keeping alive the memory and legacy of Jesus but the living extension of Christ on earth. The worship life of the church has been changed from a predictable routine and a performance carried out by clergy to a people-focused, participatory expression of our personal response to a loving God. In sum, the charismatic movement has opened up the faith to ordinary believers.

The Holy Spirit Has Been Rediscovered as the Means of Direct Encounter with the Living God

The Holy Spirit as Hidden Member of the Trinity

Figure 1.1

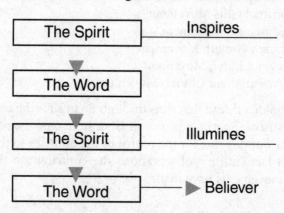

Over the last generation the Christian church and the nature of the Christian life have been deeply affected by a renewed understanding of the role of the Holy Spirit. As recently as the early seventies when I was a seminary student, I was taught what I would call a "rationalist" approach to the work of the Holy Spirit. From this perspective, the person of the Holy Spirit had little independent identity and was hidden in the shadow of the written Word of God. According to the "rationalist" view, the Spirit has three roles to play in relationship to believers, the first two tied to the Word: (1) the Holy Spirit is the *inspirer or source* of the Word. The Word of God can be trusted as the rule of faith and practice because it has its origin in the Holy Spirit. (2) The Spirit takes the written Word and applies it to our hearts. Reformed theology speaks of the *illuminating* work of the Spirit. Our minds are perfectly able to grasp what the Word says, but our hearts need to assent and bend before the Word. So the Spirit both *inspires* and *illumines* the written Word. (3) The third brief appearance of the Spirit occurs at conversion, when "our hearts are strangely warmed" and turned to trust in Christ alone for our salvation.

I call this the rationalist approach because in it the Christian life is conceived as the passionate study of, and conformity to, the Word of God. Except for conversion, the Spirit's work is solely related to the Scriptures. Transformation occurs by filling our minds with biblical content. If we want to encounter God, we do so in his Word. The Holy Spirit's job is to point to the written text and create a love for the Word of God. In this scenario, the Christian life is comprised of grasping propositional truth and assimilating sound doctrine. The mark of being an orthodox believer is holding to the historic truths of the faith.

The fear that lurks behind the rationalist approach is that religious experience apart from the Word of God can lead to doctrinal and behavior error. Therefore, I was taught to distrust any emotional or spiritual experience because it could and probably would lead to heresy or bizarre conduct. Nonrational occurrences such as dreams, visions, healing, and direct inward impulses of the Spirit were suspect. These were the seedbed for error. The only reliable source of truth was the Word of God, never experience. After all, how can we test whether an experience is true or false? It is better to stick with the objective standard of the Word and not go beyond it. All that is needed is fully revealed in the Word. So for me—and I believe for many others—the Holy Spirit was the forgotten member of the Trinity.

The Holy Spirit as Encounter with the Living God[5]

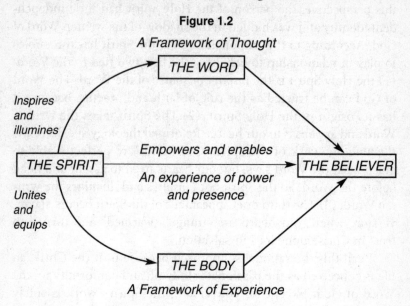

Figure 1.2

A Framework of Thought

THE WORD

Inspires and illumines

THE SPIRIT

Empowers and enables

An experience of power and presence

THE BELIEVER

Unites and equips

THE BODY

A Framework of Experience

Over the last generation, one of the spin-offs of the charismatic movement has been a paradigm shift. The Holy Spirit has stepped out from behind the shadows of the Word to have an identity as a full-fledged member of the Trinity. The rationalist approach was not wrong; it was merely incomplete. The charismatic understanding of the Holy Spirit incorporated everything the rationalists affirm about the Holy Spirit's work and more. While there is inseparable connection of the Holy Spirit and the Word, at the same time it is asserted that the Holy Spirit also has a direct relationship to the church and to the individual believer. The Word must remain the objective standard by which we measure truth and therefore serve as the test of whether the claims of the Spirit's work are valid; yet the Spirit also speaks directly to the church today and not solely through the written Word of God.

The rationalistic approach can leave God's people inwardly starved. It fills the mind without satisfying the heart. It can create a formal and distant relationship with Christ. To fill this void of the heart, the Holy Spirit is being rediscovered as the means of a direct encounter with the living God. The work of the Spirit includes mediating the direct presence of God to the life of the believer.

"What did the early believers experience that so fired them to action?" we ask. "How can we have the same inner filling?" The apostle Paul writes, "God's love has been poured into our hearts through the Holy Spirit that has been given to us" (Rom. 5:5). Paul is speaking of more than grasping propositional truth; he describes being grasped by the God who encounters us.

We are not only experiencing a revitalization of our faith in our day, but we are also rediscovering that God continues to speak a direct word to the church through the Holy Spirit. This can occur through inward impression or an immediate word of guidance. The way the Lord spoke to the apostle Peter in Acts 10 provides a biblical paradigm for this work of the Spirit. Peter was informed by messengers sent from Cornelius, a centurion in Caesarea, that an angel had appeared to this God-fearing man, saying that he should send for Peter to come to him. Yet before these messengers from Cornelius arrived, Peter fell into a trance on his rooftop at noon in Joppa and had a vision of a sheet coming down from heaven full of creatures heretofore considered unclean.

"Get up, kill, and eat," Peter is told. Three times he refuses because the vision does not fit his rationalistic interpretation of the Old Testament law. He later comes to understand this image as both a literal and figurative symbol. All foods are clean and so are the Gentiles. While he is pondering this picture, the Spirit speaks directly to him (how we are not told), saying that there are messengers at his door and that he should go with them. Peter goes to the house of Cornelius, preaches the goods news, and watches the Holy Spirit come upon these Gentiles just as he had graced Jewish believers. What Peter could not have fathomed a couple of days earlier, because it violated the core of his theological conviction, was now his new reality.

Yet when Peter later defends his actions to legalistic Jewish Christians, he does not simply ground his discovery in experience; he goes back to "the word of the Lord" as his final anchor: "I remembered the word of the Lord, how he had said, 'John baptized with water, but you will be baptized with the Holy Spirit. If then God gave them the same gift that he gave us when we believed in the Lord Jesus Christ, who was I that I could hinder God?" (Acts 11:16–17). In summary, the Holy Spirit spoke in a variety of ways: (1) through an angel to Cornelius, (2) in a trance or vision, (3) in a direct message to Peter, (4) through Peter in the retelling of the gospel, and (5) in bringing to remembrance the words of the Lord. The Holy Spirit definitely has a ministry of his own apart from the Word, but not disconnected from the Word.

God also speaks to the church through gifted people who are channels for the immediacy of the Holy Spirit. This ranges from those who have a prayer ministry for physical healing in Jesus' name; to those who are led by the Spirit through inner healing prayer as Christ releases people from the debilitation of past hurt or sin; to prophets who speak a timely, confrontive message to a local body or to the church universal; to those with gifts of discernment who pray for those under the bondage of spiritual addiction or demonic oppression.

The Holy Spirit as Separated from the Word of God

Figure 1.3

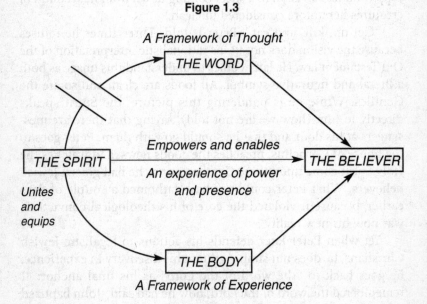

Let me anticipate an objection. Isn't it possible for those who believe they have direct messages or leadings from God to be misled? Doesn't this contribute to the megalomania we have witnessed in some who set themselves up as mouthpieces of God? It certainly can—and does. The work of the Holy Spirit can be falsified and counterfeited. Therefore, there must always be two tests in place:

1. *The Word of God must always be the ultimate test of truth.* We should be suspicious whenever we hear people make claims such as, "The Holy Spirit is saying something different in our day than he has ever said before." Any theology that drives a wedge between Word and Spirit is cultic. How can the Spirit who inspired the Word now say something contradictory to the very Word he brought into being?

2. *The Spirit of God is the Spirit of the community of believers.* The Holy Spirit in the New Testament is almost without exception portrayed as the One who indwells the corporate assembly of believers. The New Testament knows nothing of an individualized Spirit operating apart from community. Therefore, anything spoken to an individual must be tested by the church. Autocratic leaders who claim to have a direct pipeline to God and who set themselves up as spiritual potentates accountable to no one else are outside the New Testament view of the relationship between the Holy Spirit and the church.

The rediscovery of the ministry of the Holy Spirit has allowed the ordinary believer to have a direct encounter with the living God. If the New Reformation is about people coming to understand that they are priests, then they must see themselves as channels of the Holy Spirit's work.

At least three direct natural consequences came with the rediscovery of the work of the Holy Spirit. First, the Christian life shifted from a life of simple conformity to ethical standards, to an experience of the indwelling Christ. Second, the church shifted from a maintenance institution passing on a historical faith, to a living body of Christ. Third, worship shifted from a performance or routine done in front of a congregation, to a people whose hearts were engaged in worship of the One who was present among them.

The Christian Life Is Christ in You

The Christian Life as Ethical Respectability

A generation ago a person with high moral standards who supported the institution of the church might have been the common definition of a Christian. In the decade following World War II, the United States experienced a religious boom: build a church edifice, open the doors, and watch the people stream in. A respectable family with three children and a station wagon would be found in church on a Sunday morning. What did this routine mean? It was the "right" thing to do. The church was seen as the disseminator of religious values for the family and society. Going to church was as American as apple pie, since the church provided the moral glue for the community and the national spirit. Commenting on this 1950s faith, Joseph Triggs and William Sacks write:

> Loyalty to the churches seemed to be the natural comple-ment to respect for the nation. President Dwight D. Eisen-hower captured the spirit of the time when he said in 1954, "Our government makes no sense unless it is founded on a deeply felt religious faith—I don't care what it is."[6]

But being a part of the fifties church did not generally mean its people had a vital, living encounter with Christ. In fact, if you asked average churchgoers to explain the nature of their relationship with Christ, they probably would have been personally offended. The church was for respectable citizens, not broken, needy, or hurting people. Respectability meant distance. The idea of gathering face-to-face with other believers to discuss how following Christ inter-sects daily struggles was alien to the church atmosphere. People had a kind of institutional faith. They believed in what the church as an institution represented. The church was a moral pillar of the American way.

The Christian Life as Being Alive in Christ

In the 1950s Herberg identified a void in personal religious experience that was a clue to renewal: "The bland, homogenized force of secular American culture could not satisfy any genuine hunger for holiness."[7] Starved for an internal reality, the Christian life moved away from being defined in terms of the ethical norms that the institutional church represented and toward an encounter with the living Christ. Formerly the Christian life was character-ized by acquiring behavior that was consistent with the way "a good Christian" acted. Ethical rectitude, do's and don'ts, and acting in a generous, loving manner made one a good Christian.

Properly understood, being a Christian is not simply being good, but being alive—alive in Christ. Though goodness and holiness are outward expressions of the Christian life, they are not its essence. Genuine faith means knowing God in Christ—repenting, receiving forgiveness, and beginning a new life under Christ's lordship. Triggs and Sacks describe "conversion" as the means of entry into a relationship with God: "It is dramatic, decisive, and individual, a conscious form of religious experience with the potential for far-reaching changes in a person's life."[8]

We pile up adjectives like "born-again" or "Spirit-filled" before "Christian" as a way of saying that Christianity means knowing God. Each person can have a relationship with a loving God with whom he or she communes daily. We speak of "walking in the Spirit" or "abiding in Christ" as a way to capture the moment-by-moment, direct guidance of the Holy Spirit and the truth that God through Christ resides in our hearts.

We seek more than dry, institutional faith; we hunger for a God-reality at the center of our being. We are more than rational beings; we are also emotional and spiritual beings who need to be filled with God's presence, to encounter the living God, and to know and be known. And by God's grace, this relationship has become a transforming reality to many today.

If the ordinary believer has the capacity to be the container of the Holy Spirit, is this not the very definition of what it means to be a priest? A priest is a vehicle in whom God lives and through whom God works to bring his presence to others. The ground is being laid for the priesthood of all believers.

SMALL GROUPS MOVEMENT

The Church Is a Living Organism, the Body of Christ

If the Christian life is experienced as Christ in the believers, what happens when all those believers get together? This then makes the church, fundamentally, the community in whom Christ dwells. This understanding of the church is a direct consequence of the ministry of the Holy Spirit. Over the last generation we have witnessed a fundamental shift from a pastor-centered to people-centered ministry.

The Church as Pastor-Focused

Historically, the church has been entrapped in institutionalism. The institutional church resembles a corporation with the pastor as its head. Locked into a hierarchical structure, the clergy are ensconced at the pinnacle of the pyramid. They are the "experts" in religion. As a separated, elevated class, the clergy have occupied a spiritual realm not open to the ordinary believer. The clergy as a distinct caste have supposedly received a special unction and calling that enable them to have a closeness to God unattainable by average church members. This theology of ministry has more in common with the Old Testament priesthood than with New Testament peoplehood.

Appropriating another image, we can describe the pastor as a solo performer or a one-person act on the theater stage, while the church members serve as the admiring audience. Laypeople passively warm a pew and place money in the offering plate to create the context for pastors to perform their ministry.

The Church as People-Focused

As we rediscover the church as a living organism, the body of Christ, church members have been called out of the audience to become players on the stage. Everyone has a part in this play. Every believer is a necessary part of the drama God is producing, the drama of salvation history. We are on stage together, pastors and people alike. There is no longer a select, professional union of actors. In the body of Christ, all the "actors" have a direct connection to the Producer, the Creator, and the Choreographer of History. The debilitating class distinction between clergy and laity is breached. The pastor no longer plays all the parts but acts more like a director who draws out the hidden talents of a myriad of actors and encourages them to perform according to their skills.

The small groups movement over the last generation has provided a means to express the organic nature of the church. Stimulating the early stages of this movement were Keith Miller's classic *A Taste of New Wine* (1965) and Lyman Coleman's *Serendipity* small-group ministry. Small groups are a visible microcosm of the church as the body of Christ, sharing life and ministry together in face-to-face relationships. Here Christians gather to encourage each other in spiritual growth, Scripture study, intercessory prayer, and neighborhood outreach. All this occurs in the context of warmth and intimacy without dependence on, or expectation of, pastoral participation. Honest, noncondemning community put relationship at the center of the church. This was living water for parched souls.

Since those early days of the small groups movement, we have discovered how many of the purposes of the church can be fulfilled in these groups of eight to twelve persons. They provide a context for mutual care, belonging, expression of ministry gifts, lay leadership development, evangelism in the context of community, accountability, and discipleship. From the initial sharing and Bible study groups have come an explosion in various types of groups found in churches today: *recovery groups* for the addicted or victims of the addicted; *support groups* for those with a common need, such as cancer or chronic pain; *discovery groups* for those seeking to understand the Christian message; *study groups* for those wanting to go deeper in Christian doctrine and practice. In the last decade, we have also seen the rise of cell-group churches, where the basic unit of the church is a reproducing cell. Carl George, Ralph Neighbor, and William Beckham have been instrumental in giving us both the vision and the structure for this totally integrated model.[9] Randy Frazee's *The Connecting Church* promotes the neighborhood group as the place to experience the elements of biblical community.[10]

More than any other structure, small groups call people out of the audience and onto the stage to live together as the body of Christ. Small groups commonly proliferate when the church is being renewed. We can look at the first-century house churches, the Wesleyan class meetings, and the seemingly endless variations of cell groups today and affirm with Triggs and Sacks, "It is the small group experience, grounded in appreciation of the early church, that has been the most visible feature of spiritual movement today."[11]

WORSHIP RENEWAL MOVEMENT

Worship Is the Defining Event in the Church

We might not make a conscious connection between the charismatic movement's focus on the immanence of the Holy Spirit and the transformation that has occurred in corporate worship, yet the links are unmistakable. Our experience of worship has probably undergone more change since the 1950s than any other aspect of the church's ministry. This mark of renewal should perhaps be at the top of the list, because what happens in worship leaves its imprint on every other aspect of ministry.

Worship as Performance

Institutional worship is something done to you, in front of you, or for you, but not *by* you. The congregants come as passive recipients, unconsciously thinking, "I hope this is good today." People arriving for corporate worship in this frame of mind can leave worship as unmoved as when they arrived. After all, pastors are paid to put together the order of worship, exude charisma, insert moving musical selections, and then preach a stirring message. Since the dynamic is essentially a performer-audience relationship, the worshipers are put in the position of being critics of the latest pastoral effort.

Somehow we don't think it unusual for the remarks at the door after a church service to focus on evaluating the morning message or worship service. This audience-performer mentality had become so much a part of our mind-set that George Plagenz, who wrote a weekly column for a Cleveland newspaper, took to rating the quality of worship. Churches dreaded this clandestine reporter sneaking in and slipping out of worship, for the next day a review of their service would appear in the local newspaper.

Worship as Participation

In contrast, there has been a profound shift over the last generation to worship as participatory. The new face of worship has been driven by two major factors: (1) pressures from within the church to address a deadly routine, and (2) pressures outside the church from a changing culture that had declared the church irrelevant. Driven by the desire for new life and relevance, mainline churches especially, have attempted changes in their worship life that have led many into what has been dubbed "the worship wars." This battle has been fought around worship forms and musical styles in particular. In my ten-year tenure as senior pastor at Saratoga Federated Church from 1988 to 1998, we lived through the two factors identified above. When I arrived, unbeknownst to me, the church had a worship order that had remained unchanged for well over thirty years. The doxology, Gloria Patri, and Lord's Prayer were formatted exactly in the same place in each printed order of service. In addition, there were the unspoken worship rules: worship dare not go over an hour, and one should never do anything in worship that one cannot control. I stumbled into making changes in worship that thrilled some and disturbed others. Some said, "Thank God, you are throwing open the windows to the fresh breeze of the Spirit." Others said, "How dare you touch what has become my sacred way of connecting with God?"

At the same time, living in the Silicon Valley where 87 percent of the population had no church involvement, we had to question whether our form of worship had any relevance to the lives of those around us. An enormous gap had grown between the liturgy and language of the church culture and the culture of the surrounding community. We became aware that we were asking people to step into a subculture about which they knew little and which was like a foreign language to them. We needed to change our forms to connect both in message and style with the world in which we existed. This story has been retold in untold numbers of churches across this land. I have said to pastors, "If you haven't experienced the worship wars in some form, you are either dying or you are a new church plant."

Underlying much of worship renewal is the shift from performance-centered to people-centered worship. It matters little whether the worship is highly structured or spontaneous. The difference is that people are prepared to give of themselves in song, prayer, praise, and response to the Word of God. The presence of the Holy Spirit is the only sure variable to vital worship. It makes no difference whether it is lead by a multirank organ or a contemporary praise band. The X-factor is the prepared hearts of the people. Worship is an expression of the community, not something done to the people by worship leaders. Søren Kierkegaard pointed us back to the image of the theater when he wrote that in worship the people are the actors, the worship leaders are the prompters, and God is the audience.[12]

We have been resourced in worship renewal through the works of Robert Webber and Sally Morgenthaler.[13] We have learned from the models of Willow Creek Community Church, Saddleback Community Church, Church of Joy, Church on the Way, and many others. I have often joked that there has been a full employment plan in place for all the Christian musicians with all the worship bands, orchestras, ensembles, and so forth that now grace the front of our worship settings. But equally we are rediscovering the place of tradition in worship. There is a revival of the observance of the Christian year as our culture has become increasingly secularized. Gen X worship can just as often have the raw edge of contemporary music as the feel of ancient liturgy with lighted candles. This is a time of great worship experimentation and eclecticism. Yet still at the heart of it all is the issue of community: How can we as the whole people of God live in the midst of the presence of the God who "resides in the praises of his people"?

SPIRITUAL GIFTS MOVEMENT

All God's People Are Ministers

Ministry as Tasks Done for the Church

If the pastor is the star on center stage, what roles are left for God's people? In the institutional church, there is a clear line of demarcation between spiritual and nonspiritual matters. The clergy are qualified to handle the spiritual (e.g., preaching, teaching) and people (e.g., pastoral care, counseling) ministries. The laity are left with odd jobs as stage hands, lighting technicians, and custodians. They carry out support or temporal functions so that the play can go on.

In the past, laity too often have performed tasks for the church but have not been allowed to exercise ministry gifts to build up the body of Christ. They have been given tasks such as overseeing budgets and devising systems for pledging, collecting, and accounting for the monies. For laity, maintaining the church facility consumes an inordinate amount of time, along with straightening up the pew racks and setting up and putting away the communion elements. The only legitimate spiritual ministry generally entrusted to the laity a generation ago was the teaching of children in Sunday school. While we must not demean these tasks or deny them as legitimate areas of service, we have to recognize that they define a limited realm in which laity have heretofore been allowed to serve.

Ministry as an Expression of the Giftedness of the Body

As the reality of the church as an organism has been reclaimed, we have discovered that all new creatures in Christ are gifted for ministry. Ministry is not to be equated with what professional leaders do; ministry has been given to *all* God's people. Therefore, the pastor's role is not to guard ministry jealously for him or herself, but instead to turn the spotlight on this multigifted body. In the process, God's people are discovering that in fact they are gifted to serve.

Christianity is essentially a lay movement. Over the past generation specialized parachurch ministries have arisen for the particular purpose of equipping laity to find their place in building up the body. Today a person can be trained to provide pastoral care as an under-shepherd; lead a small group of almost any kind; share faith through friendships; act as lay counselor, touching the hurts and wounds in people's lives; teach the Bible to adults; or start a mission team to the homeless. These parachurch equipping organizations fill a gap for training people in ministry that the church has long neglected.

We are also rediscovering that ministry is not confined to the church building. We are just beginning to see the church as a base of operations called to support and equip people to live out their Christian witness in the work environment. The broken world in which we live needs a *called army* to address the enormous pain that is the result of sin. Only people who know they are ministers can be compassionate tools of God's healing work.

This emphasis on the gifted body has been fueled by an explosion of resources and ministries that have assisted in helping God's people discover their spiritual gifts and passions for ministry.[14] Many denominations have their own versions of these programs particularly crafted for their theological tradition.

The fundamental assumption underlying the spiritual gifts movement is that anyone in whom the Spirit dwells has been gifted and called to ministry. We are to be stewards of the unique design and motivation that God has placed on our hearts. Instead of filling a church slot as defined by the institution, an organism seeks to have each person play the part for which he or she was created. A church's ministry takes the shape of the gifted people instead of forcing the people into preexisting niches that act like a confining straitjacket.

To me, the clearest expression of body ministry's becoming a reality has been the influx of able and gifted women into service. When we begin to view ministry as what God performs through *all* persons, the doors are flung open to women. In the two thousand years since Christ affirmed the equality of all through the cross, there has never been a time when the opportunities for women in ministry have been greater. And this has happened largely in the last thirty years. When I graduated from the largest interdenominational seminary in the country in 1973, there were no more than four women among the 350 students in the master of divinity program. Today about fifty percent of that seminary's students are women. I believe one of the main reasons for this remarkable change is the realization that all God's people are ministers.

AN ECUMENICAL MOVEMENT

An Ecumenism of the Spirit Transcends Denominational Loyalties

Ecumenism as Structural Unity

Two kinds of ecumenism have been running on parallel tracks over the last generation. One is an ecumenism of structural union. The other is an ecumenism of the Spirit that is uniting believers across former denominational divides.

Over the last generation we have witnessed the consolidation of structural union within denominational groups such as the union of the southern and northern versions of the Presbyterian Church into the Presbyterian Church, U.S.A. and within the Lutheran tradition to create the Evangelical Lutheran Church of America (ELCA). Other conversations continue, such as those between the ELCA and the Episcopal Church of America. The Church of Christ Uniting was formed as a consultative body among many mainline churches with the goal of creating a megachurch. The driving force behind these ecumenical movements is the desire for the church to be one, uniting across former divides. It is a scandal to have Christ so divided.

All of this effort at consolidation has been occurring as the loyalty to denominational brand names has declined to such an extent that it is common to speak about being in a "post-denominational" era. A case could be made that the basis for many of the mainline denominations has so eroded that the future of the church will no longer be in the form that we currently know it. For the past four centuries, post-Reformation Protestants have lived up to their name. We have protested against one another and fractured into untold numbers of denominations. The basis for denominational life is now in question. It appears that the foundations have already crumbled, and denominational life as we know it is perhaps fifty years from extinction.

What is the evidence for this? (1) Denominations existed to keep alive a theological tradition. Roots could be traced to founders driven by theological conviction. Clarity of theological heritage appears to be hard to find among Methodists, Presbyterians, Lutherans, Episcopalians. They have for all intents and purposes ceased to be confessional traditions. (2) With heritage came a commitment to a style of worship. There was a day not long ago that you could tell what denomination of church you were in based on the worship form. Given the influx of new styles and the melding of new and old, it would be difficult to find such distinctives today. (3) People under sixty have little loyalty to a denominational heritage. The same is true of pastors. (4) Many denominational churches find it more of a liability than an asset to be associated with their denomination. I have asked pastors in the classes I have taught in recent years what help they receive from their denomination to resource the ministry and mission of their local church. Beyond the denominational mission program and pension plan, they have been hard-pressed to state the benefits. (5) A final sign of the weakening position of denominations is the common practice of churches to remove the denominational name from their church title. Instead of Calvary Baptist Church, it is simply Calvary Church. In a post-Christendom culture, where the church has negative baggage, one simple way to jettison some of it is to minimize these associations.

Ecumenism as Spiritual Unity

In contrast to organizational union and denominational life, a sign of renewal in recent years has been an ecumenism of the Spirit that transcends denominational loyalties and has nothing to do with structures. Denominational distinctions become blurred when Christians connect with each other through the Spirit. People are not as exercised over the theological debates and precision that marked previous divisions between Christians. People are more concerned about heart connections that cut across former barriers.

Since I serve in an interdenominational seminary, I have the privilege of witnessing people coming together in the Spirit of Christ across denominational and nondenominational lines. In Fuller's Doctor of Ministry Program, it is common to have pastors and missionaries from across the spectrum from classical Pente-costal to high church Episcopalian. It is rare that we flare in dis-agreement over denominational doctrinal distinctives. The usual comment from leaders is appreciation of the rich diversity they experience as they rub shoulders with those from traditions differ-ent from their own. But the primary reason that the debates don't degenerate into theological squabbles is that we are working hard together to see the mission of Jesus Christ come alive in our min-istry contexts.

So an ecumenism of the Spirit shifts our focus of loyalty. We are loyal first to the movement of God's Spirit, wherever his work is being accomplished, and loyal only secondarily to structures.

CHURCH GROWTH MOVEMENT, SEEKER CHURCH MOVEMENT, AND NEW PARADIGM CHURCHES

The entire flow of the last forty years has been to wake the sleeping giant of the priesthood of all believers. In the latter half of these forty years, the waves of the Church Growth Movement, Seeker Church Movement, and New Paradigm Churches[15] have washed over us.

The Church Growth Movement identified the ministry of the laity as one of the seven vital signs of healthy churches. In Peter Wagner's 1976 classic, *Your Church Can Grow,* his second vital sign was "a well-mobilized laity."[16] The genius of the Seeker Church Movement has been to create the vehicle of a "seeker service" as the means to mobilize all believers for witness. The seeker service, which is done in an attractive, contemporary fashion, is a tool that assists every believer to be an inviter. New Paradigm Churches just assume that the ministry is what the people of God do: "The extensive network of home fellowships in new paradigm churches is part of a strategy to deprofessionalize religious functions, returning the priesthood to the people."[17]

CONCLUSION

Although this overview of the signs of renewal has been brief and selective, we get the impression that we live in a historical moment of enormous opportunity. The very foundation of the church of Jesus Christ is reverberating with renewal. *God is raising up at the grass roots a Spirit-filled people who see themselves as ministers, spiritually gifted ecumenists who see worship as the center.*

What appears to be the common element that gives sparkle to this multifaceted gem of renewal? Simply put, from one viewpoint, we could say that we are rediscovering the ministry of the Holy Spirit. When this period of church history is written, it may well be labeled the Age of the Holy Spirit. It may also be called the New Reformation. Either way, through all these elements of renewal runs the radical transformation in the *self-perception* of every believer. Followers of Christ in this age will see themselves as Spirit-filled ministers who are a part of the ministry given to all Christians. In a word, Christians are priests, ministering the presence of God on behalf of the people of God and the lost world.

These individual transformations are possible only because the church is again being perceived fundamentally as an organism. Only an organism can complete the unfinished business of the Reformation and return the ministry to the people of God.

This book is an attempt to sketch the shape of the sails of the church in order that we might catch the new winds sweeping over us. For us to skim the seas at full clip, the sails must be set. There are three sails that need to be hoisted in order for the church to be propelled by the gale of the New Reformation. In these pages I will attempt to shape a biblical view of these sails: the church, pastoral ministry, and leadership in the New Reformation.

NOTES

1. Martin Luther, "An Appeal to the Ruling Class" (1520), quoted in Lewis W. Spitz, *The Protestant Reformation* (Englewood Cliffs, N.J.: Prentice-Hall, 1966), 54.

2. Martin Luther, "The Babylonian Captivity of the Church," *Works of Martin Luther* (Philadelphia: Westminster, 1943), 282–83.

3. Wallace M. Alston Jr., *Guides to the Reformed Tradition: The Church* (Atlanta: John Knox, 1979), 47.

4. The Gathering of Church Champions, Dallas, Texas, January 11, 1999.

5. Chart used by permission of William Tibert, associate pastor of Glendale (California) Presbyterian Church.

6. Joseph W. Triggs and William L. Sacks, *Of One Body: Renewal Movements in the Church* (Atlanta: John Knox, 1986), 11.

7. Quoted in Triggs and Sacks, *Of One Body*, 37.

8. Triggs and Sacks, *Of One Body*, 15.

9. Carl George, *Prepare Your Church for the Future*; Ralph Neighbor, *Where Do We Go From Here?*; William Beckham, *The Second Reformation*.

10. Randy Frazee, *The Connecting Church* (Grand Rapids: Zondervan, 2001).

11. Triggs and Sacks, *Of One Body*, 43.

12. Søren Kiekegaard, *Purity of Heart* (New York: Harper and Bros., 1938).

13. Robert Webber has been the most prolific author bringing to bear the insights of historical theology to our postmodern context. Sally Morgenthaler has written the highly influential *Worship Evangelism* (Zondervan, 1995) in which she develops the thesis that unbelievers can encounter God in vital worship. She challenges the assumption that you must separate evangelism and worship services.

14. For example: Peter Wagner, *Your Spiritual Gifts Can Help Your Church Grow*, 15th Anniv. Ed. (Ventura, Calif.: Regal Books, 1994); Bruce Bugbee, *Network* (Grand Rapids: Zondervan, 1994); Sue Mallory, *The Equipping Church* (Grand Rapids: Zondervan, 2001); Sue Mallory et al., *The Equipping Church Guidebook* (Grand Rapids: Zondervan, 2001); Paul Ford, *Discovering Your Ministry Identity* (Church Smart Resources; www.churchsmart.com; and Saddleback Community Church's *SHAPE* (Spiritual Gifts, Heart, Abilities, Personality, and Experience), a resource used in the CLASS 301 gifts discovery process around the purpose of ministry.

15. Donald E. Miller, *Reinventing American Protestantism: Christianity in the New Millennium* (Berkeley: University of California Press, 1997).

16. C. Peter Wagner, *Your Church Can Grow: Seven Vital Signs of a Healthy Church* (Glendale, Calif.: Regal Books, 1976), 69.

17. Ibid., 138.

Part 1

THE CHURCH IN THE
NEW REFORMATION

Chapter 1

The Church as Organism: Together We Have It All

I N THE INTRODUCTION I made the bold assertion that we live in a moment of history when the ministry is being returned to the people of God. This assertion is undergirded by the eight movements in the church over the last forty years that have been largely driven by the emergence of the ministry of the whole people of God. Yet the return of the ministry to all of God's people can only become a reality if we understand and experience the fundamental biblical vision of the church as a living organism. The church is emerging from its cocoon of institutional entrapment to the liberty of organism life. We are in the midst of a paradigm shift.

What do I mean by organism? The church in its most fundamental essence is nothing less than *an interdependent, life-pulsating people who are indwelled by the presence of a resurrected and reigning Christ*. A host of biblical images for the church point to this reality. In the New Testament the church is variously described as the household of God, the people of God, the bride of Christ, and a fellowship of the Holy Spirit. In fact, ninety-six word pictures of the church have been identified.[1] Yet the image that permeates the New Testament understanding of the church and serves as an umbrella for all these metaphors is that of the church as *the body of Christ*.

I have never heard a better summary of the interdependent nature of the church as the body of Christ than the words of one of the leaders at my former church. Speaking at our annual adult retreat, Mike said that we tend to put inordinate pressure on ourselves to be complete, multitalented, thoroughly well-rounded individuals. The trouble comes when we compare the ideal of what we think we should be to our real selves with all our deficiencies in character and limitations in talent. Fortunately, he said, his self-flagellation led to a breakthrough. It dawned on him that we were never intended by God to be paragons of self-sufficiency: *We don't have it all together, but together we have it all.*

Mike has given us the backdrop against which to explore three questions that are implicit in the phrase "body of Christ":

1. What is Christ's relationship to the church?
2. How does the church as the body of Christ become a living reality?
3. What undermines the living reality of the church as the body of Christ?

Our responses to these questions provide the biblical vision for the church as a ministering community. To address these questions we turn to the *locus classicus* for the image of the church as the body of Christ—1 Corinthians 12—though we will not be restricted to it.

WHAT IS CHRIST'S RELATIONSHIP TO THE CHURCH?

The apostle Paul addresses Christ's relationship to the church by using the human body as an analogy: "For just as the body is *one* and has *many* members, and all the members of the body, though *many*, are *one* body, so it is with Christ" (1 Cor. 12:12). Two repeated words stand out: *one* and *many*.

The image of the body conveys the two poles on which Paul builds his understanding of a healthy church—oneness and "manyness," unity and diversity, individuality and corporateness. These poles are inseparable. The human body could not be a better picture of diversity within unity.

First, the body displays oneness or unity. At first glance, one is impressed with the functional integration of all the parts of the body into one. Under the central control of the head, all the body parts work together for the health of the whole body. Each part does not have a will of its own. The hand doesn't say to itself, "I don't care what the head says, I am going to do as I please." Can you imagine being picked up for shoplifting in a department store and using as your defense: "Your honor, I am innocent. My head said not to steal that leather jacket, but I just couldn't get my hand to go along." The body is healthy when the parts respond in oneness to the coordinating impulses of the head.

Second, the body is a perfect expression of diversity. Upon closer examination of the body, one is impressed with the unique function of the individual parts and the necessity of each part for the health of the whole. The hands serve a very different function from the feet, the eye does what the ear cannot, and vice versa. For the body to thrive, every part must operate according to its design. We know all too well that when our bodily parts cease to function in the way they were supposed to our health is impaired. The same is true in the church.

Paul affirms that a balance of oneness and "manyness" is what the body of Christ is to be.

Metaphor or Literal

Yet is Paul's choice of the human body simply to be a nice analogy for the way the church is to function? Is Paul only saying that just as the body is an organic picture of interdependence, so the church is supposed to be? Or is there something deeper than metaphor that Paul has in mind? Paul does not stop at the level of metaphor but points us to a deeper mystical reality. What is the difference between metaphor and literalness? A metaphor is a symbol that points to a deeper reality, but the symbol is not the same as the reality. For example, when Jesus held up the bread at the Passover meal before his disciples and said, "This is my body broken for you," we Protestants do not believe Jesus was speaking literally. The bread was not in actuality his body, but it was a symbol that pointed to his broken body. However, in contrast, when it comes to referring to the church as the body of Christ, I believe Paul is intending more than just an appropriate word picture.

How does Paul conclude 1 Corinthians 12:12, and how does that differ from what we might expect? "For just as the body is one and has many members, and all the members of the body, though many, are one body, *so it is with the church.*" What is wrong with that? What I have highlighted is the way we *expect* Paul to conclude this sentence. I had read this verse perhaps a hundred times before I realized that this was not Paul's actual phrasing. I read *church* into the text because this is what I expected, since the church is Paul's subject. But this is not Paul's concluding phrase. He says, "so it is with *Christ*," not *the church*. By interchanging Christ with the church, Paul is telling us that the church is nothing less than the living extension of Jesus here on earth. The church and the resurrected, reigning, and living Jesus are inseparable. Jesus mediates his life through the church. Is the "body of Christ" metaphor or reality? "The body is a reality," writes Arnold Bittlinger. "Christians are not like members of any body but are according to their very nature members of a specific body, the body of Christ."[2]

The church is not a human organization that has contracted by common consent to keep alive the memory of a great man, Jesus Christ. On the contrary, the church is a divine organism mystically fused to the living and reigning Christ, who continues to reveal himself in a people whom he has drawn to himself. Ray Stedman puts it this way in his book *Body Life:* "The life of Jesus is still being manifest among people, but now no longer through an individual physical body, limited to one place on earth, but through a complex, corporate body called the church."[3]

Where did Paul get such a radical notion as to associate the church as the people in whom Christ dwells? I believe he understood it from the moment of his first encounter with Jesus. Before he was Paul, an apostle, he was Saul, a Pharisee, who expressed his loyalty to the God of Israel by persecuting the church. Saul had received authority from the Sanhedrin to arrest Christians in Damascus. As he and his entourage were making their way to the city, Saul was stopped in his tracks. Suddenly a light flashed from heaven, and Saul was knocked on his backside. While on the ground, he heard a voice, "Saul, Saul, why are you persecuting me?" Knowing that he was in the presence of a power far greater than himself, Saul replied, "Who are you, Lord?" Note the response, "I am Jesus, whom you are persecuting" (Acts 9:4–5). Now, wait a minute. Saul isn't persecuting Jesus, he is persecuting the disciples of Jesus. Yet here is the truth that sank into Saul's consciousness from the beginning. If you touch Christians, you are touching Christ. There is such a close identification between Jesus and his followers that to touch them is to touch him. You could go so far as to say that Jesus continues his incarnation through his people. True, he sits at the right hand of the Father in power, but through his Spirit, the Spirit of Jesus, he indwells his people. Jesus continues to manifest his life through us.

What is the relationship between Jesus and the church? Jesus dwells in them; the church is the aggregate body to whom Jesus has given his life. Christians are a *sacramental* people. A sacrament is a means of grace; it is a symbol that mysteriously bears the presence of Christ through which believers encounter Christ. It would then be fair to say that *the church is a sacramental people* who are corporately and individually the conduit of Christ to the world.

The church as the living organism of Christ is further underscored in Paul's cosmic statement in Ephesians about the place of the church in God's eternal scheme. Paul concludes with a flourish: "And he [God] has put all things under his [Jesus'] feet and has made him the head over all things for the church, *which is his body, the fullness of him who fills all in all*" (Eph. 1:22–23).

The key interpretational question is: What is the relationship of the phrase "fullness of him" to "his body"? Does Jesus fill the body, or does the body fill out Jesus? The Greek word *pleroma* (fullness) is most often used in an active sense in the New Testament to mean the content (body) that *fills* some container (in this case, Jesus). For example, the pieces of the loaves of bread in the feeding of the five thousand are described as *filling* the baskets (Mark 6:43). In Ephesians 1:23 *pleroma* taken in the active sense would mean that the body fills Christ. In other words, the church as the body of Christ fills out, or completes, Christ. Christ is in some way incomplete without the church. Jesus is the head, but a head is no good without a body. Some theologians, such as Armitage Robinson, go so far as to say, "In some mysterious sense the church is that without which Christ is not complete, but with which He is and will be complete. Christ is waiting to find completion in His body."[4]

I believe it is more consistent with the message of the New Testament to interpret fullness in a passive sense: "that which is filled." The church is that which is filled by Christ. *The church is the container, and Jesus is the one who fills it with his life.* Jesus is the content who indwells the form. Nowhere else in the New Testament are we given the sense that Jesus is incomplete. Jesus' existence and sufficiency do not rely on us for completion. Jesus gives his life to us, not out of an unfulfilled need, but out of his sovereign and gracious freedom. He desires to share his very being with the creatures he has made; he wants us to enjoy the love that overflows from the triune God.

What makes the church different from every other way humans have chosen to relate to each other? It is different because the church is not of human origin but is a divine creation. Thomas Oden has captured this uniqueness:

> Christianity is distinctive as a religious faith in that it understands itself to be living as a continuing community through the living Christ. . . . Its uniqueness lies in its particular relationship with its founder. . . . It is the resurrected presence of the living Lord that continues to be the sole basis of the present reality of the church. Jesus is not merely the one who founded the community and left it, but rather the one who is present to the community now and in each historical period as the vital essence of the church.[5]

We do not understand the core nature of the church until we grasp the inexpressible truth that Jesus extends his life on earth through a corporate people that can literally be called "the body of Christ." Frank Laubach poignantly summarizes Christ's relationship to the church:

> When Christ was here on earth, He was limited to performing His ministry in one place and at one time. He was one man, walking beside one sea in one little corner of the earth. He healed whoever He touched, but His touch was necessarily limited by time and by space. Now, does it make sense that the Father would send His Son for this limited ministry? I don't think that is tenable. He made provision to carry on the work through the Holy Spirit: we are to complete His mission. We are His multiplied hands, His feet, His voice and compassionate heart. Imperfect and partial to be sure, but His healing Body just the same. And it is through the Holy Spirit (Christ's love which is everywhere at once) that we receive the power to carry on the work of the apostles. It is a challenging and sobering thought: when we

receive the Holy Spirit into our lives, we receive the same urgent and life-giving force that led our Master.[6]

A friend of mine, Jeff Cotter, a pastor at the time, spins a story that playfully illustrates the organic nature of the church. Jeff provided a seatmate on a plane an unforgettable ride. Returning from a job interview wearing jeans, Jeff was not at all looking the part of a pastor. The man next to him was quite a contrast. He was the image of GQ in his Brooks Brothers suit, designer shirt, and tie. Quite full of himself, he waxed eloquent to Jeff, his captive audience. His business was women's fitness, and he had plans to establish his salons throughout California. Once that territory was conquered, he would expand the empire by going nationwide. His goal of being a millionaire by age thirty, he thought, was quite within reach. After dominating the conversation, the man finally turned to Jeff and, looking askance at Jeff's casual attire, said, "And what is it that you do?"

As only Jeff can, he thought he would have a little fun with this man, while making a point about the nature of the church. "It's interesting that we have similar business interests," said Jeff. "You are in the body-changing business; I'm in the personality-changing business. We apply basic theocratic principles to accomplish indigenous personality modification." Not wanting to appear ignorant, Jeff's companion said, "You know, I've heard of that. But do you have an office here in the city?"

"Oh, we have many offices. We have offices up and down the state. In fact, we're national; we have offices in every state including Alaska and Hawaii." The listener was searching his mind for the Wall Street listing of this company. Jeff continued, "As a matter of fact, we've gone international. And management has a plan to put at least one office in every country in the world in this business era." Jeff paused for dramatic effect. "Do you have that in your business plan?"

"Well, no, not yet," admitted the young man. "You mentioned management. How do they make it work?"

"It's a family concern," said Jeff. "There's a Father and a Son . . . they run everything."

"They must have a lot of capital," Mr. MBA said longingly.

"You mean money? Yes, I suppose so. No one knows exactly how much it takes, but we never worry because there's never a shortage. The Boss always seems to have enough. He's a very creative guy. And the money is, well, just there. In fact, those in the organization have a saying about our Boss, "He owns the cattle on a thousand hills."

"Oh, he's into ranching too."

"No, it's just a saying we use to indicate his wealth."

Now totally hooked the man said to Jeff, "What about with you?"

"The employees? They're something to see. They have a 'Spirit' that pervades the organization. It works like this: The Father and Son love each other so much that their love filters down through the organization so that we all find ourselves loving one another too. I know this sounds old fashioned in a world like ours, but I have people in the organization that are willing to die for me. Do you have that in your business?"

"What about the benefits?" This guy was ready to abandon his measly plan and hire on. "They're substantial. I have complete life insurance, fire insurance—all the basics. You might not believe this, but it's true: I have holdings in a mansion that's being built right now for my retirement."

"You know one thing bothers me. I've read journals, and if your business is all that you say it is, why haven't I heard about it before now?"

"That's a good question," Jeff said, "After all, we have a two thousand-year-old tradition—it is called the church."

This is the body in whom Christ dwells. Through his guidance, the church has and is penetrating every part of the globe all under the management of the triune God. We have an employee training manual that has been translated into thousands of languages. We gather in cathedrals, modest buildings, houses, basements—and Jesus is present to all.

HOW DOES THE CHURCH AS THE BODY OF CHRIST BECOME A LIVING REALITY?

Jesus Intends to Run His Church

What is Christ's relationship with the church? He not only indwells it, but he intends to run it. The church as the "body of Christ" is not just an awesome thought; it has very practical significance. Paul means us to understand our identity as a people indwelled by Christ in operational terms. The intent of his teaching in 1 Corinthians 12 is quite functional and day-to-day. Christ extends himself through us as the body of Christ and is its chief executive officer. Jesus can immediately run the church because all the parts are connected to the head and therefore can turn to the head to know their assigned part. Paul Stevens writes in his book *Liberating the Laity,* "There is a direct and living connection between the Head and every member of the body.... No church leader in the New Testament is ever called the head of a local body. That title is reserved for Jesus. The head does not tell the hand to tell the foot what to do. The head is directly connected to the foot. Therefore, people find their ministries not being directed by the leaders but by being motivated and equipped by the Head."[7]

So how does the body function, in operational terms, under the orchestration of the Spirit of Christ so that Jesus is actually mediating his life through the church? Paul goes on to tell us. When each of us understands our value and place in the body of Christ and seeks to know from the head of the body the part we have been assigned to play, then Jesus is given the freedom to run his church. Though Paul never uses the word *value* in this passage, I believe that this is the concept that dominates Paul's thinking. In the church we are to *value* all the parts. We are all needed, because we are only the body of Christ as we function together. We are designed as incomplete so that I have something to give to you and you have something to give to me. Instead of being these well-rounded, multitalented, thoroughly complete, and independent people, God has designed his church in such a way that we all are needed. We were never intended to be islands of self-sufficiency, as our culture might idealize. Remember, "*We don't have it all together, but together we have it all.*"

We Are to Value Our Part

We all have ministries: "To each is given the manifestation of the Spirit for the common good" (1 Cor. 12:7). It is through our ministry or spiritual gifts that we make our contribution to the health of the whole. Our ministry is prescribed by the gifts God has given to us.

Now there are varieties of gifts, but the same Spirit;
and there are varieties of services, but the same Lord;
and there are varieties of activities, but it is the same God
who activates all of them in everyone. (1 Cor. 12:4–6)

The word *variety* should not be overlooked. When we use this word, we think of the options from which we get to choose. Yet in this context *variety* is not meant to connote choices available to us, but the diversity of gifts bestowed by God. A more accurate word here would be "apportionments." The Lord is the one who doles out the gifts, and we find our part in the body of Christ based on what we are given. Paul repeats this in verse 11: "All these [gifts] are activated by one and the same Spirit, who allots to each one individually just as the Spirit chooses." Lest we miss who is running the church, Paul says again in verse 18, "But as it is, *God arranged* the members in the body, each one of them, *as he chose.*"

Paul uses a number of synonyms to capture what he means by spiritual gifts:

◆ "Gifts" (1 Cor. 12:4). The Greek word for "gifts" is *charismata,* from which we get our word *charismatic.* The root of *charismata* is *charis,* which means "grace." Add the *ma* ending and you get *charisma,* or "gift." So charismata are literally "grace-gifts" that come with the package of salvation, or our new life in Christ. We have been given a bonus. I like to look at spiritual gifts as the tangible, manifest expression of the love of God for us. In verse 7 Paul has said that each of us is given a "manifestation" of the Spirit. A manifestation is something that is clear, visible, or observable. Each of us has a basic need to make a contribution, to know that our lives have added to the common good. The grace-gifts are the tangible means God has provided for us to make this contribution.

◆ "Services" (1 Cor. 12:5). The Greek word translated "services" is derived from *diakonia* from which we get the word *deacon.* It could just as easily be translated as "ministries." *Service* captures the attitude in which we make our contribution. Jesus is our model. He said, "For the Son of Man came not to be served but to serve, and to give his life a ransom for many" (Mark 10:45). The way we give our lives

away is through the proper stewardship of our gifts. We all
have a service to give the body.

♦ Gifts are not for self-advancement but "for the common
good" (1 Cor. 12:7). Barrett translates verse 7 "with a view
to mutual profit." Gifts are community property, given to be
given away. I confess that in my early years of ministry I had
the secret desire to become a great orator. People would
come from far and wide to hang on my every word as sweet
words imbued with wisdom flowed from my lips. This motivation was the opposite of service; it was self-inflation. Gifts
are for the community.

♦ "Working" (1 Cor. 12:6 NIV). The term "working" also has a
familiar derivation, coming from the Greek word *energematon*, from which we get our word "energy." In other words,
gifts energize, charge, or make a positive impact on the body.
Each gift operates in its particular way to strengthen the
body. Evangelists bring in new babes in Christ, pastors help
create a nurturing atmosphere, mercy-givers reach out in
compassion, servers identify and meet basic needs, and so
on. Each one strengthens in his or her own way. Therefore,
a spiritual gift is an ability to minister that is given by God
to strengthen and upbuild the body of Christ.

Each of us is given a ministry through the spiritual gifts we
have been assigned. No gradation or hierarchy of value or importance is placed on the members of the body. That does not mean
we are equally gifted, but it does mean that we refuse to place
degrees of status on the members of the body. For every part is
needed in ministry if the life of Jesus is to be manifested on earth.

Scott Peck captures so well the value we are to afford to ourselves and each other through a story entitled "The Rabbi's Gift."[8]
A monastery had fallen on hard times. It used to be a very vital
place, but twentieth-century secularism and self-sufficiency had
eroded its power. Now only five monks remained to occupy a
decaying motherhouse. All were over seventy; clearly it was a dying
order.

The abbot of the monastery went to visit the rabbi who lived in
a hut in the nearby woods. The abbot told him how the spirit had
gone out of the monastery. The rabbi commiserated, *"I know how*

it is." The abbot and the rabbi wept together over the diminishing interest in spiritual things. The abbot was hoping for some bit of advice that would help him save his dying order. The rabbi said, *"I have no advice for you. The only thing I can tell you is that one of you is the Messiah."*

When the abbot returned to the monastery, the other four brothers gathered around. But the abbot reported forlornly that the only thing he could say was that one of us was the Messiah— I don't know what he meant by that. They all began to ponder what the rabbi might mean by one of them being the Messiah. Could it really be that one of us monks at the monastery was the Messiah? Who could it be? Was it the abbot? Maybe brother Thomas. He is a holy man. Perhaps brother Elfred, because he sure is wise. As they contemplated who might be the Messiah, they began to treat each other with extraordinary respect in the off chance that each might be the Messiah. As people visited the monastery, they were drawn to the aura of respect that radiated and permeated the atmosphere. There was now something attractive and strangely compelling about the monastery. People came back to the monastery frequently to play, picnic, and pray. They brought their friends to show them this special place. All because of the rabbi's gift, the monastery became a vibrant center of light, and a thriving order was born out of death.

In order for the priesthood of all believers to be a reality, we must experience the church as a living organism. The church that is a living extension of Jesus values all the parts of the body without any hierarchy of status given to the parts. Jesus is free to run his church, and it comes alive to the indwelling presence of Christ when all the parts of the body seek to know their valued place in the body of Christ.

WHAT UNDERMINES THE LIVING REALITY OF THE CHURCH AS THE BODY OF CHRIST?

According to Paul's body image, all the parts are interdependent and necessary for the body's health. Robert Banks says, "God has so designed things that the involvement of every person with his special contribution is necessary for the proper functioning of the community."[9] No individual part can function without a connection to the other parts. A hand disconnected from the wrist is useless. "Indeed, the body does not consist of one member but of many" (1 Cor. 12:14).

Attitudes That Undermine Value

But why is it that all too often we fail to see the church operating as a ministering community? Why don't we experience the church as a place where Christ is orchestrating the ministry and all the people of God are engaged? Why is there more of a spectator mentality than a ministry mentality in our churches?

If the church functions as an organism when we recognize the value of each other in Christ and ourselves, then it is *devaluing* that undermines the organic reality of the church. Paul warned the Corinthians about two devaluing attitudes that would cut the heart out of organism. It is these devaluing attitudes that have crippled the church and turned it from organism to institution. In fact, these attitudes have become so much a part of our church systems that we don't even recognize their crippling impact and how they have become normative.

Inferiority (vv. 15–16)

First, Paul surfaces the negative attitude of *inferiority* or a low self-esteem as detrimental to a healthy body. Some remove themselves from participation in the body of Christ because they feel unimportant to the overall scheme. To capture this, Paul personifies the body parts and places them in conversation with each other. The extremities speak first: "If the foot would say, 'Because I am not a hand, I do not belong to the body,' that would not make it any less a part of the body." Then the senses enter into dialogue with each other: "If the ear would say, 'Because I am not an eye, I do not belong to the body,' that would not make it any less a part of the body" (1 Cor. 12:15, 16). Some compare themselves with the highly gifted and conclude that they have nothing to offer. As Bittlinger put it, "They say: 'I am only a foot'—now if I were a hand then I would be something. A hand is much better than a foot and much more useful to the body."[10]

Why would the foot and the ear feel like they are not worth much in comparison to the hand and the eye? My guess is that the

Corinthians suffered from the same malady we do in the church today. They exalted some gifts as higher than others. They placed gradations of value on gifts. The church today is in part sick because we have so exalted the clergy/pastors and preaching that no other gift can match that level of importance. Hear this statement from Martin Luther as the legacy of the importance of the preacher in the body of Christ: "A Christian preacher is a minister of God who is set apart, yea, he is an angel of God, a very bishop sent by God, a savior of many people, a king and a prince in the Kingdom of Christ and among the people of God, a teacher, a light of the world. There is nothing more precious or nobler on earth and in this life than a true, faithful parson or preacher."[11]

Protestant churches have been just as priest-ruled as Roman Catholic churches; we just call it by a different name. Within Roman Catholicism, a sacramental priest presides over the Lord's Supper or Mass, whereas in the Protestant realm the gifts of the preaching pastor are elevated higher than the other parts of the body.

How does this express itself? The phrase "I am just a layman" has so worked itself into our psyches that we have developed quite clearly first- and second-class Christians in the kingdom. First class are those in full-time Christian service, especially cross-cultural missionaries or pastors. Then there are the rest who do filler roles because the paid professionals can't do it all. We have developed a hierarchy of worth. I overheard the following exchange among participants at a Christian conference. A denominational executive asked one of the attendees, "Are you a pastor?" The immediate response was, "No, I am *just* an elder." Inferiority.

As soon as you set up a hierarchy of gifts in the body, two undermining effects are set in motion: comparison and copying.

1. **Comparison**—We compare our gifts to others and declare ourselves deficient. We begin to play what I call the "if only" game. "If only" I could be like so and so, then I would have significance and value. There is not a person alive that has not secretly envied the gifts of someone else and thought that he could have worth and value "if only. . ." As a teacher of the Word, I catch myself in secret envy: "*If only* I could tell stories like Chuck Swindoll; *if only* I had the passion of Bill Hybels; *if only* I had the sense of humor of Rick Warren; *if only* I had the intellect of——." As soon as we begin to compare, we always come out second best.

A hierarchy of gifts creates a practice of comparison. We have assumed that real ministry is what the ordained do. Therefore, any other kind of ministry is secondary to that. The mother of Lester Pearson, the former prime minister of Canada, had always hoped her son would be ordained and become a minister of the Church of Canada. Instead, he went into politics as his sphere of service. The day he was admitted into the cabinet, he telephoned his mother and said to her, "Mother, I'm a minister now." She replied, "I'm delighted even if it is a second-class kind."

George Peck tells the story of his father, who spent forty years of his life as a coal miner in Australia but whose secret disappointment in life was that he was never able to fulfill his desire to become an ordained minister. Yet during those years as a coal miner he was a committed Christian who served his church as a preacher, as a teacher in the Sunday school, and in leadership roles. He served his family by raising three children, two of whom became ordained pastors and a third a missionary. He served the world by the way he lived out his faith among his fellow miners, and he was deeply involved in issues of justice on their behalf. Peck concludes, "He ministered if anyone did, to individuals, to the structures of society, to his community. . . . Yet neither he nor his church ever thought of him as a minister or his service as ministry. . . . He ministered without ever being able to say with clarity, 'I am a minister of Christ.'" What a tragedy!

Upstairs—downstairs. Split-level valuing. To the extent that this exists, it undermines the organism nature of the church.

2. **Copying**—The second natural response when we have a hierarchy of gifts, is to try to copy those we admire. Instead of being ourselves, we mimic someone else and cease to be the unique creation we were made to be. Paul says that copying is a sin against our brothers or sisters and a sin against God. It was the Lord who designed you the way you are, and you are just the one needed in the body: "But as it is, God arranged the members in the body, each one of them, as he chose" (1 Cor. 12:18). To try to be someone else is to be a pale imitation and to miss seeing the glory of the unique way God has designed you. You are needed as you are.

Paul makes this point with humor. "If the whole body were an eye, where would the hearing be? If the whole body were hearing, where would the sense of smell be? . . . If all were a single member, where would the body be?" (1 Cor. 12:17, 19). Can you imagine a six-foot eyeball? What a monstrosity! When we limit the body of Christ to a few parts, we have created a dysfunctional organism. For the biblical message is that all parts are needed. Paul carefully avoids any sense of hierarchy or valuing some gifts over others. When we build the church around a hierarchy of gifts, we have blasphemed God's design. Inferiority disrupts a healthy body. You are valued just as you are.

Superiority (v. 21)

If the first devaluing attitude is *inferiority*, then the second devaluing attitude is *superiority*. In verse 21 Paul selects higher parts of the body that look down from above and treat the lower as lesser: "The eye cannot say to the hand, 'I have no need of you,' nor again the head to the feet, 'I have no need of you'" (1 Cor. 12:21). What are you in comparison to me? I am more important than you. We don't express that attitude overtly. We are much more subtle than that. We have worked the attitude of superiority into a primary American character quality that we call independence and self-reliance.

American individualism, self-reliance, and independence have cut the heart out of the community and the interdependence that are integral to the body of Christ. Robert Bellah and his research team went in search of what is distinctive about the American spirit or character. In their landmark study entitled *Habits of the Heart*, they state that the defining quality of the American character is "radical freedom from obligation." Americans have a skewed view of freedom. It is not a freedom *to*, but a freedom *from*. This is expressed as: "I want to do what I want to do when I want to do it. And no one is going to tell me otherwise." The self has become the basic unit of society. Not the community, not the family, but the self. The self is autonomous.

Paul Stookey of the folk group *Peter, Paul and Mary* does a humorous routine in their concerts where he traces the evolution of our society toward the individual through the magazine titles of the last few decades. "What was the most popular magazine a generation ago?" he asks. The crowd, being mostly baby boomers, shouts back knowingly, *"Life!"* Stookey spreads his arms out wide, indicating that Life is as large as the world. He continues, "Then we moved from *Life* to *People*." His outstretched hands move closer together. "From *People* we went to *US*." Again the distance between his hands narrows. "Then we went from *US* to *SELF*." Now the hands are about an inch apart. He concludes, "I am waiting for the next magazine to appear. It will be simply entitled *ME*. You open it up, and it is made up of page after page of aluminum foil reflecting your image back to yourself." Robert Bellah draws the conclusion that the individualism at the heart of the American identity is hardly the stuff from which to build either lasting relationships or enduring community. When it is all about *me,* eventually you can get fairly lonely.

Attitudes of superiority can work against the sense of belonging and mutual service that is integral to the church as the body of Christ. There is a common belief that being integrally involved in the church is not a necessity for Christian living. Some time ago, my wife and I worshiped at a well-known Southern California church the Sunday after Easter. On Easter Sunday a considerable number of people had responded to the invitation to commit their lives to Christ. The object of the Sunday-after teaching was to help these new believers take their first steps toward following Christ. The teacher of the morning asked the congregation a rhetorical question, "Is it necessary to go to church or be a part of the church to be a Christian?" His answer was "No, it is not necessary." I had to do everything I could to keep myself in my seat. I wanted to stand up and scream, "Yes, it is absolutely necessary." Some people have come to the smug conclusion that they have graduated from organized religion, that spirituality is separate from any corporate connection or regular practices of joining with others in worship or intertwining our lives with fellow believers. Today we often hear: spirituality "yes," but church "no." Paul tells us that "I don't need you" attitudes will tear the heart out of the church as a community of the living Christ.

Instead of being self-reliant, Paul is telling us to value each other's gifts. To help me do this, I periodically put myself through a personal exercise. I try to visualize those in the body toward whom my underlying attitude might be "I have no need of you." Because their tastes and opinions differ from mine, there are people in my life that I wish were not. I am tempted to call the pastor down the street and offer, "I'll trade you so and so for a future draft choice." To deal with my elitist attitude, I place that person in the presence of God in prayer and say, "I need you. My life benefits because of you. You have gifts and a perspective I need to hear. If I let you into my life, I will grow because of it."

No hierarchy of value exists in the body of Christ because Christ values all of us equally. Any hint of devaluing our own importance or the importance of others undermines the oneness of the body and our celebration of diversity.

I have a dream. I am praying for the day when every member of this body will know that they have a valued role based on the ability to name their spiritual gifts and take responsibility to use them. This body will reflect the presence of the living Christ when we can affirm this statement by Gordon Cosby: "Christ makes each of us something unlike any other creation fashioned by God— something wonderful, exciting, unique; something specifically needed in the total body of Christ. This uniqueness, this very self that is so hard to describe, this charismatic person is the gift of the Holy Spirit. It is the primary gift we bring to the body, and without it the body is immeasurably impoverished."[12]

Interdependence (v. 27)

The middle ground between inferiority and superiority is *interdependence*. Interdependence means that the Lord has created each of us with something of immense value to contribute to the health of the body of Christ, while at the same time realizing that we are completed by our connection to others in the body of Christ. None of us is complete in and of ourselves. We are whole only in relationship to other parts of the body. Jesus makes himself known more fully corporately than he does to isolated individuals. For example, evangelism done in the context of community is more powerful than individual witness. I cannot illustrate this better than by quoting the words of a college student in a note I received thanking me for the impact of this ministry on her life. She describes what drew her to Christ: "I was so impressed with the few times I heard you teach, but more than anything I was drawn into the love that the fellowship had for you and each other. To an outsider at the time, like myself, one saw such a deep love that I now know was prayerfully developed. The term 'discipleship' was living."[13]

We are created for relationship from the beginning. Before creating Eve, the Lord said: "It is not good that the man should be alone" (Gen. 2:18). None of the living creatures could be a "helper," or better yet, a "counterpart" to Adam. When the woman was presented to him, Adam exulted, "This at last is bone of my bones and flesh of my flesh" (Gen. 2:23). He was no longer alone. The Hebrew language reflects this completion. Until the creation of woman, the word for "man" was *adam,* meaning "mankind." When woman was created, the word for man became *ish,* meaning "male" as contrasted to *ishah,* "female." In other words, Adam, or "mankind," did not become male until there was his counterpart, female.

To be created in the image of God means to be created for relationship. "In the image of God he created them; male and female he created them" (Gen. 1:27). But sin marred the image of God in man and thereby shattered relationship. The church of Jesus Christ is meant to be a reflection of the corporate restoration of the broken image. Christ, "the image of the invisible God" (Col. 1:15), called a people out who would be the visible expression of the image of God being restored. The church is not simply a good idea, convenient when it is needed. The church is essential to God's redemptive plan. Jesus reflects his presence to the world through an interdependent people. We need each other.

The purpose of this chapter has been to sketch in broad strokes the shape of the biblical vision of the church as an organism. For the ministry to return to the whole people of God and not be restricted to a clerical caste, an organism view of the church must take precedence over the institutional view. If the fundamental reality of the church is the body of Christ, then we are affirming that the resurrected Jesus continues his ministry by indwelling a new humanity called the church. Jesus intends to run his church and does so if each person is seeking to know from the head what is his or her God-assigned part. The church lives as an organism when persons sense their value and equally value and need the other parts to make them whole. "We don't have it all together, but together we have it all." Paul offers his own summary: "Now you are the body of Christ and individually members of it" (1 Cor. 12:27).

Snapshots of Organism

In conclusion, let me share some snapshots from the photo album of the Saratoga Federated Church in Silicon Valley, California, as a way to be able to "see" the church as organism come alive. The church as organism is

◆ a community of people who are encouraged to seek answers to the heart question "What difference would it make if you knew the purpose for which God created you?"

◆ the loving and patient life in a small group that creates the supportive atmosphere to enable a couple to move from a distant, formal, institutional understanding of faith and church, to a warm relationship with Christ.

◆ a woman who comes to a Spiritual Gifts Discovery Workshop thinking that God had bypassed her in the distribution process, only to discover that her gift of helping others says that she has a ministry after all.

◆ a man with a guarded heart who goes on a mission team to Romania only to have his heart broken for AIDS children. He then builds another team and takes the lead to establish a nonprofit organization that now operates the orphanage that has become a light in the darkness.

◆ person after person who discover that the kingdom of God is inclusive of the workplace and that ministry is as much about what God does there as what he does in the church.

◆ a healthy foment of desire within members of the body to worship in new and fresh ways that leads to the birthing of corporate worship styles that bring the body of Christ alive.

◆ reproducing discipling groups where one person invites two others into a year-long commitment to study, pray, and grow together while equipping the participants to disciple others. These little triads reproduce year after year until the whole body is infused with transformed people.

When the church is receiving the infusion of life from its head, the body grows organically. People are added to the body, and new ministries arise spontaneously from within the body. Ministry takes on a sense that God is doing something that is bigger than could ever be engineered by human ingenuity. God's people are being led to see that the church is primarily and essentially defined as the living organism whose life is created by, and dependent on, the living Christ.

Yet sadly, this beautiful picture of the church as organism tends not to be our normative experience by and large. The priesthood of all believers remains largely a doctrinal ideal with little correlation to the reality in the church culture. What is it that gets in the way of releasing the organism life that is its essence? The Reformation promised the return of the ministry to the whole people of God, yet it failed to deliver on the promise. What got in the way? In the next chapter we will explore the relationship of institution to the organism side of the church and will see that the church has been trapped in an institutionalism that is antithetical to the priesthood of all believers.

NOTES

1. E. Best, *One Body in Christ* (London: SPCK, 1955).

2. Arnold Bittlinger, *Gifts and Graces* (Grand Rapids: Eerdmans, 1967), 55.

3. Ray C. Stedman, *Body Life* (Glendale, Calif.: Regal Books, 1972), 37.

4. J. Armitage Robinson, *St. Paul's Epistle to the Ephesians, With Exposition and Notes* (New York: Macmillan, 1903), 42–43; as quoted by John R. W. Stott, *The Message of Ephesians* (Downers Grove, Ill.: InterVarsity Press, 1979), 64.

5. Thomas C. Oden, *Agenda for Theology* (New York: Harper & Row, 1979), 117.

6. As quoted by Bittlinger, *Gifts and Graces,* 56.

7. Paul Stevens, *Liberating the Laity* (Downers Grove, Ill.: InterVarsity Press, 1985), 44.

8. M. Scott Peck, *A Different Drum* (New York: Simon & Schuster, 1987), 13.

9. Robert Banks, *Paul's Idea of Community: The Early House Churches in Their Historical Setting* (Grand Rapids: Eerdmans, 1980), 64.

10. Bittlinger, *Gifts and Graces,* 59.

11. Martin Luther: as quoted in H. Richard Niebuhr and Daniel D. Williams, eds., *The Ministry in Historical Perspectives* (San Francisco: Harper & Row, 1983), 115.

12. Gordon Cosby, *Handbook for Mission Groups* (Waco, Tex.: Word Books, 1975), 72.

13. Personal note received from a student who was a freshman in the college ministry that I pastored.

Chapter 2

The Institutional Entrapment of the Church

HENDRIK HART LEVELS THE FOLLOWING indictment against the Reformation: "Even though the leaders of the Protestant Reformation sincerely intended to break with the traditional Roman Catholic conception of the church, nevertheless the tradition arising from the Reformation did not succeed in making the break."[1] In this chapter we will explore the reasons why the Reformation did not make the break from a clerical conception of ministry and deliver on the promise of the priesthood of all believers.

Before embarking on this historical analysis, however, let's review the images of the church as organism and the church as institution that serves as our contrasting filter through which to view the church. In chapter 1, I stated that for the ministry to return to the people of God, our fundamental understanding and experience of the church must be as an organism. I made the claim that we are in the midst of such a radical refocus that we could call it a paradigm shift. The church is being released from its institutional entrapment and is rediscovering its primary identity as a living body. The church as organism suggests that God's people are indwelled with the presence of the living Christ.

I have already referred to *the church as institution* without clearly defining what I mean by that phrase. A clear definition is necessary in order to grasp the Reformation's inability to realize what it means for the body of Christ to be priests to one another. The term *institution* as applied to the church can be understood two ways. The first meaning is benign. Every organism also needs order. Therefore, *institution* refers to the need for organization within the organism of the body of Christ. The second meaning is pejorative. Here I am using the word *institution* interchangeably with *institutionalism,* which equates ministry with a professional caste. In institutionalism the ministry of the church is viewed from the top-down perspective of its office holders rather than from the bottom-up vantage point of the whole people of God.

THE NECESSITY OF INSTITUTION

By emphasizing the primacy of organism, it could appear that I am promoting anarchy or suggesting the dismantling of all institutional or structural elements of the church. A parody of my position might be: "It sounds like you are saying to just let Jesus run the church and therefore do away with all structures, offices, committees, policies, or anything that has an institutional tinge." However, this would misstate my position. As I said above, there is a need for order within the organism or organization within the church as the body of Christ. The issue is, which is primary, or the essence of the church?

Although the church as institution does not describe its fundamental reality, the church must have an institutional aspect. The human body illustrates the need for order within the organism. There are four life-support systems that are essential to the body's health. The *skeletal structure* serves as the frame on which all the vital organs hang, and it gives a shape distinctive to each person. The *nervous system* is the body's internal communications network that harmoniously integrates the whole. Running through every extremity are hundreds of miles of nerves that carry electrical impulses sent from the head to activate the individual body parts. The *digestive system* takes in food as fuel, breaks it down, and replenishes life for the body's survival. The *circulatory system* carries this fuel in the form of oxygen and nutrients to every cell and also cleanses the body's waste. The human body demonstrates a harmonious relationship between organism and order. Its internal structure provides the means for the proper flow of organic life.

To apply this analogy to the church, the institutional aspects should similarly serve the organism of the church to facilitate its life-flowing energy. It should come as no surprise, therefore, that in the same context where Paul defines the essential nature of the church as organism, the body of Christ, he also affirms the necessity of institution or order. If 1 Corinthians 12 were read in isolation, we might conclude that there is no need for a defined leadership structure or policy guidelines within the church. After all, Jesus is the head of the body and thus arranges the members of the body directly through the impulses of the Holy Spirit.

But Paul makes it clear that there must be order within the organism. He seems to anticipate the potential for an anti-institution bias that could be drawn from the organism nature of the church. In 1 Corinthians 13 and 14 the principles of order are delineated in order to address the chaos created by the Corinthians' abuse of freedom and mismanagement of spiritual gifts. For the Corinthians, the Christian community had become a stage on which to display their spiritual gifts—a platform for self-absorbed performance and "look-what-God-gave-me" display. Their motivation was to build up themselves rather than to edify the body. Paul was compelled to remind the Corinthians that unless the gifts are motivated by love, they lose their value. To paraphrase Paul: "If I speak in tongues, prophesy, understand all mysteries, exercise phenomenal faith, or give generously, but have not love, I am nothing" (1 Cor. 13:1–3).

Paul continues his emphasis on order in 1 Corinthians 14 by dealing with two problems that surfaced in the worship gatherings of the Corinthian community: the misuse of speaking in tongues and prophecy. First, some were speaking in tongues without interpretation into the *lingua franca*. Paul had previously affirmed the value of addressing the mind with an intelligible word from God rather than speaking in an ecstatic manner in an unknown language. While underscoring the legitimacy of the gift of tongues, Paul stated that tongues in a public setting must be interpreted into a meaningful message. In this context Paul laid down an operational principle: "If anyone speaks in a tongue, let there be only two or at most three, and each in turn; and let one interpret" (1 Cor. 14:27). This is the kind of statement that would be appropriate for the church bylaws.

The second problem related to governing prophecy. One way that the gift of prophecy expressed itself was through spontaneous messages under the prompting of the Holy Spirit. If more than one prophet at a time was speaking, there was cacophonous confusion. To bring control and restore order, Paul wrote, "Let two or three prophets speak, and let the others weigh what is said. If a revelation is made to someone else sitting nearby, let the first person be silent. For you can all prophesy one by one, so that all may learn and all be encouraged. And the spirits of prophets are subject to the prophets, for God is a God not of disorder but of peace" (1 Cor. 14:29–33). Paul concluded this section with a statement of his overall concern: "All things should be done decently and in order" (1 Cor. 14:40).

All this is to say that in spite of the absolute priority we must give to the church as organism, there is a real need for the institutional elements of leadership, policy, and structure.

THE ENTRAPMENT OF INSTITUTION

From here on, I will be using the phrase "church as institution" in the pejorative sense of institutionalism. Institutionalism equates the ministry of the church primarily with its ordained or official leadership. In many historic churches ministry is equated with top-down leadership.

Thomas Gillespie, president of Princeton Seminary, quotes from the *Form of Government* of the Presbyterian Church, USA, in a paper entitled "Our Ministerial Roots." This denomination adopted the following statement as its understanding of ministry:

> The ministry is one, but specific forms of ministry may emphasize special tasks and skills such as proclamation, celebration, teaching, ordering, or deeds of love and justice.

At first glance it might appear that the phrase "the ministry is one" could imply that the subject is body ministry and that the specific ministries listed belong to the whole body. But on further examination it becomes clear that ministry here is associated with the ordained offices. The ministries outlined above are subsumed under one of three offices in the church:

> The ministry is characterized by an essential unity within a functional diversity. This diversity is honored, on the basis of a division of labor, in the ordering of the ministry into three church offices (the tasks of "proclamation, celebration, and teaching" *being assigned primarily to the "ministers,"* the task of "ordering" [i.e., governance] *being undertaken by the "ministers" and "ruling elders" conjointly*, and the tasks of "deeds of love and justice" *being the special responsibility of the "deacons"*).
>
> The three offices together constitute the *one ministry of the Church in its wholeness.* (italics added)[2]

In other words, it is through the offices of the church that the ministry of the church finds its expression. These offices represent the entirety of the church's ministry. The conclusion is that ministry is accomplished through the set-apart, top-down leadership in the body. Therefore, when I use the term "institutionalism," it is akin to clericalism. The starting point for defining ministry is through its offices.

Ironically, it was this very institutionalism of the Roman Catholic Church that the Reformers attacked and attempted to change. The Reformers confronted a church that was hierarchical, sacerdotal, and clerical.

Hierarchical

Roman Catholicism was locked into a rigid hierarchy that reflected an institutional understanding of the church. In Roman Catholic theology the church was viewed as a repository of grace. Grace could only be received if one was within the institution of the church; therefore, to be outside the institution was to be beyond the bounds of grace. Within the institution those in the leadership hierarchy were the ones set apart to be the dispensers of grace. Grace was mediated through the divine offices. The priest, as a representative of the institution, could grant or withhold absolution since he was set apart to mediate the grace given to the church.

Sacerdotal

Since God dispensed grace through the church by means of a holy order, this meant that the priest bore a *sacerdotal* function.

Priests acted as intermediaries between God and the people. As the exclusive celebrants of the Mass, the reenactment of the sacrifice of the Christ, the priests stood behind the sacrificing altar as the set-apart, holy representatives who could dispense the sacraments to the people. A holy order was necessary in order to handle the holy sacraments. Only a priest, changed by ordination, was consecrated to hold the sacred elements.

Clerical

The sacerdotal understanding of the priest's role led to an increasing split between priesthood and people. This was the explosive issue addressed by Martin Luther in his *Open Letter to the German Nobility*. The Roman Catholic Church had come to divide people into the "spiritual" and "temporal" estate. The *spiritual estate* consisted of those who went into the church and chose a holy vocation, while those occupying the *temporal estate* were the vast majority of people—princes, lords, artisans, farmers, and so forth. It was believed that those who went into the spiritual estate had chosen a superior way of life because the spiritual was over the temporal in terms of both authority and value. This distinction between the spiritual and the temporal led directly to the belief that there were two kinds of people, clergy and laity. Ordination was viewed as a kind of second baptism that lifted the clergy into a higher stage of Christian achievement, while the laity lived a compromised life.

THE REFORMATION CONCEPTION OF MINISTRY

It was this hierarchical, sacerdotal, and clerical order that Martin Luther confronted with his rediscovery of the evangelical gospel. So explosive was the doctrine of justification by faith that it held the promise of new wine bursting old wineskins. Luther's rediscovered gospel put all people on an equal footing: an individual is made right with God through a personal response to the saving grace of Christ. This marked a radical shift from the institutional church being the dispenser of grace to the proclamation of the gospel as the means of salvation.

Hierarchy Undermined in the Gospel

In principle, the doctrine of justification by faith was to have a marked effect on the view and practice of ministry. Ministry under Roman Catholicism was conceived in hierarchical terms because receiving grace and being within the realm of the church institution were one and the same. There was no grace apart from the church. This made those in leadership the dispensers of grace and the guardians of church order. The Reformation, by contrast, linked the reception of grace with the gospel message and the response of the individual to Christ. Being made right with God is not mediated through the church institution, but directly through Jesus Christ. Neither pastors, bishops, archbishops, cardinals, nor the pope can represent an individual before God. Jesus Christ alone has that function. A hierarchical conception of ministry is therefore undermined by the gospel.

Sacerdotal Role of the Priesthood Removed

The sacerdotal function of the priest was also eliminated by the Reformed understanding of the gospel. To the Reformers, the idea of the continuous sacrifice of Christ in the Mass was an abomination. Christ died for sinners once and for all. The Lord's Supper could not be a resacrificing of Christ. If the nature of the Lord's Supper was no longer the actual sacrifice of Christ, then this had tremendous implications for the nature of the priesthood. Thomas Gillespie concludes, "For if the Lord's Supper is not a sacerdotal ('sacrificing') act, then those who administer it serve no sacerdotal function and they have no sacerdotal character or status. The ground was thus cut from beneath the ministry as a separate priestly office."[3]

Clergy-Laity Split Dashed

The implication of the doctrine of justification by faith alone leads directly to the belief in the priesthood of all believers. Luther's conviction that every believer in the gospel is by nature a priest, mediator, and intercessor between God and man had revolutionary potential for the conception of ministry. The obvious consequence of the priesthood of all believers is the elimination of the difference in status between clergy and laity. The rediscovery of the priesthood of all believers "signaled the end of the distinction within the Church between clergy and laity."[4] According to the universal doctrine of the priesthood of all believers, as articulated by Luther, every Christian should be a minister of the Word of God.

Luther was deeply disturbed by the qualitative gulf that had arisen between those who pursued a monastic life as a "higher calling" and the ordinary Christian, viewed as tainted by worldly-mindedness. Luther attacked this hierarchy of callings. Instead of there being a superior calling sanctioned by God, Luther said that because of the gospel, the call of God comes to all in our ordinary stations of life:

> God has placed his Church in the midst of the world among countless undertakings and *callings* in order that Christians should *not* be monks but live with one another in social fellowship and manifest among men the works and practices of faith.[5]

As a sign of the change from a sacerdotal and priestly conception of ministry, clerical vestments were replaced by the academic gown for preachers of the Word. The Reformation scholar Wilhelm Pauck has written, "Henceforth, the scholar's gown was the garment of the Protestant minister. It symbolizes all the changes that were wrought by the Reformation in the nature and work of the ministry."[6] In other words, instead of there being a qualitative distinction between pastor and people, the distinction is one of function and training.

A Promise Unfulfilled

Although the rediscovery of the gospel promised a reversal of the Roman Catholic conception of ministry and in principle laid the groundwork for it, this has seldom been realized. In spite of the Reformation, clericalism has more often than not held sway. Pauck explains, "Clericalism tends to identify the church with the priestly-sacramental clergy to such an extent that it is no longer, in fact or conception, the people of God."[7] David Watson observes,

> Most Protestant denominations have been as priest-ridden as the Roman Catholics. It is the minister, vicar, or pastor who has dominated the whole proceedings. In other words, the clergy-laity divisions have continued in much the same way as in pre-Reformation times, and the doctrine of spiritual gifts and body ministry have been largely ignored.[8]

The question that screams for an answer is, Why didn't the new wine of the gospel produce the new wineskins of body ministry? What kept the Reformers from returning the ministry to the people of God?

Hendrik Kraemer intensifies our inquiry:

> "His [Luther's] attack, fully justified, implied the abolition of all clericalism, and the most emphatic vindication or rehabilitation of the laity ever uttered. And yet it must frankly be stated that neither this new conception of the church nor this strong vindication of the laity ever became dominant. To this present day it rather fulfills the role of a flag than of an energizing, vital principle."[9]

The Reformed Church: Institutionally Bound

Why was the Reformation unable to deliver on the promise of the priesthood of all believers? I have identified seven reasons why it did not become a reality. The first three of these relate in some way to the Reformed definition of the church.

1. The Reformed definition of the church was trapped in institutionalism. The Reformers were concerned to establish a working definition of the true church. The seventh article of the Augsburg Confession summarizes the essential Reformed tenets as "the congregation of the saints in which the gospel is rightly preached and the sacraments rightly administered." Calvin wrote, "Where the Word is heard with reverence and the sacraments are not neglected there we discover . . . an appearance of the true church."[10]

To the Reformers, the true church was distinguished by two qualities: (1) the Word of God rightly proclaimed, and (2) the sacraments rightly administered. Some would add a third quality, (3) the proper exercise of discipline.

Why would I claim that this is a definition trapped in institutionalism? When one observes the characteristics of the true church, all one needs to ask is: Whose duty is it to make sure that the Word of God is rightly proclaimed and the sacraments are rightly administered? Answer: The clergy. The true church, then, becomes equated with the way its ordained leadership performed these two tasks. The essentials of the Reformed understanding of the church were solely in the hands of the clergy. Thus we have in most Reformed churches the title of Minister of the Word and Sacraments as the way to state the call of those who hold the ministerial office. It has been sarcastically observed that "the new preacher is just the old priest, writ large."

2. The Reformed definition of the church was formed against the backdrop of polemics and protest. It was a reaction against the corruption of the Roman Catholic Church. It was as much an attempt to say what it was not as to affirm what it was.

The true church is the place where the Word of God is *rightly* proclaimed, as opposed to wrongly. Proclamation of the word was the way to inspire saving faith. "But how are they to call on one in whom they have not believed? And how are they to believe in one of whom they have never heard? And how are they to hear without someone to proclaim him" (Rom. 10:14)? The preaching of the true gospel was a sign that the true church existed. The content of the proclamation was further informed by the core doctrinal watchwords that served as the theological formulation of the Reformation: *sola Scriptura* (by Scripture alone), *sola gratia* (by grace alone), *sola fide* (by faith alone), and the priesthood of all believers. That is, the Reformers focused on the power of God to save based solely on the completed work of Christ as proclaimed in the gospel versus the church being a repository and dispenser of God's grace.

The true church is the place where the sacraments are rightly administered, as opposed to wrongly. By "rightly administered," the Reformers meant at least two things. First, the number of sacraments was reduced from seven to two. Therefore, a redefinition of what constituted a "means of grace" was of central concern. This was especially true since the church did not dispense grace. Second, the Mass was removed from the list of sacraments. The sacraments do not save; they are a means whereby we are nourished with the presence of Christ. It is Christ who saves through faith in him.

Again we see a reinforcement, perhaps unwittingly, of a clerical caste who alone are given the authority to be the guardians of the marks of the true church. It was the Reformers' burden to take the church back from its Roman Catholic expression. By focusing the definition of the church around this historical moment, it limited the full expression of what is the essence of the church.

3. The Reformed definition of the church was absent of any concept of body ministry. What is the implied role of the whole people of God in the Reformed definition of the church? The people of God play a passive role. It is their part to receive the word of God rightly and take the sacrament rightly. The clergy carry out the marks of the true church. It is as if the concept of the people of God was overlooked in the desire to distinguish between the true and false church.

These observations about the Reformed definition of the church lead to the obvious question: Did the Reformers have an organic or an institutional understanding of the church? I have defined institutionalism as the tendency to equate ministry with top-down leadership. Therefore, the Reformed definition of the church is thoroughly rooted in an institutional mind-set. On the other hand, the priesthood of all believers assumes an organic vantage point from which to understand church. *The Reformation was never fully able to realize the fullness of the priesthood of all believers because it attempted to wed this organismic doctrine to an institutional definition of the church.* The priesthood of all believers cannot be grafted onto the root of the institutional understanding of ministry. It was the institutional understanding of ministry that prevailed.

4. **There was ambivalence about the priesthood of all believers within Reformed teaching.** As radical as Luther could be on the one hand, with statements about all being priests, bishops, and popes, he could just as quickly take it away with the other hand by affirming a priesthood within a priesthood. He wrote, "We are all priests insofar as we are Christians, *but* those whom we call priests are ministers selected from our midst to act in our name, and their priesthood is our ministry."[11] It seems as if Luther is speaking out of both sides of his mouth. On the one hand he affirms all to be priests. In the next breath he is saying that there are some who are selected to be priests, whose ministry is representative of the whole. As long as leadership is conceived in mediatorial and representative terms— one group doing for another—then the doctrine of the priesthood of all believers is undermined. It was affirmed in theory and denied in practice. As soon as you make a few representative of the whole, then the rest will gladly relinquish responsibility to the few and become passive recipients of their ministry. You can't have it both ways.

5. **The Reformers exalted the office of preaching.** The old priesthood was simply replaced by the new preacher. Instead of the

minister of the sacraments, you have the minister of the Word as the most important part of the body. Exaltation of the office preaching above all others has had a debilitating effect. It has created passivity by turning the church into an audience. Luther, in fact, called the church the *Mundhaus,* mouth or speech house. People gather to listen to the word of God spoken.

As we observed in the last chapter's exposition of 1 Corinthians 12, as soon as one part becomes elevated over the other parts of the body or one is valued more than others, the organic nature of the church is gutted. John Calvin wrote about the value of preaching: "Neither the light and heat of the sun, nor any meat or drink, are so necessary to the nourishment and sustenance of the present life, as the apostolic and pastoral office is to the preservation of the church in the world."[12] Clearly the centrality of the pulpit is a legacy of the Reformation. The exalted office is held by the preaching pastor. All other contributions pale in comparison.

The final two reasons for the Reformation's inability to make the break with institutionalism have to do with the interweaving of a replicable leadership structure and the intermingling of church and state.

6. The church was enmeshed with the civil structure. The principles of Reformed church order can be traced to Ulrich Zwingli's introduction of the Reformation in Zurich, Switzerland. A fundamental principle of church government is that its purpose is to secure a sustaining, faithful obedience to Christ as the head of the church.

Church government, it must be remembered, was conceived in this Swiss context as a union of church and state, not the separation of the two as we are accustomed to in North America. Ecclesiastical and governmental authority were completely intertwined. From the time of Constantine's rule over the Roman Empire at the turn of the fourth century to the ratification of the U.S. Constitution, it was an unchallenged assumption that the church needed the coercive power of the state to disseminate its teaching in order for there to be a stable social order. Therefore, Zwingli instituted in Zurich a new church order supported by the coercive power of the government. Every citizen and subject in Zurich was required by law to conform to this new evangelical religion preached by Zwingli. Faith as free association was not part of the Reformation mind-set. There was little distinction between congregation and society. All were a piece.

Wilhelm Pauck explains, "The evangelical churches were thus formed as territorial or state churches. Each of them became a closed unit, subject to the political authority of its own government, the prince, or the city council."[13] To be a part of the city or state was to submit to the established religion. The Protestant faith was often introduced to a city or new territory by a prince or dignitary. The emperor of a nation ruled by divine fiat in an "unholy alliance" with the religious power structure, known as "the vicar of God." Church and state were hopelessly intermarried. The catch phrase was "He who reigns, his religion."

7. **The Reformers were obsessed with a Reformed church order that could be replicated where the Reformed church held sway.** When church order was refined by Martin Bucer in Strasbourg and further refined by John Calvin in Geneva, it consisted as of four divinely appointed offices; ecclesiastical authority was interwoven with the city government. Calvin adopted in Geneva what he saw practiced in Strasbourg. He believed the Scriptures taught that there should be preachers, teachers (doctors), elders, and deacons. The function of pastors was to carry out the marks of the true church by preaching, teaching, and administering the sacraments. They shared the responsibility of enforcing church discipline with the city council, made up of twelve elders who also had the authority to appoint and discipline its ministers.

Structuring church government into four ecclesiastical offices was intended to be the practice not only in Geneva but in all Reformed communities (France, Holland, and Scotland in particular). After Calvin returned from Strasbourg, the Geneva city council adopted his *Ecclesiastical Ordinance:*

> There are four orders of offices that our Lord instituted for the government of his church: first the pastors, then the teachers, after them the elders, and fourthly the deacons. Therefore if one would have the church well ordered and maintained in its entirety, we must observe that form of rule.[14]

By conceiving these offices as a sacred law instituted by Christ, Calvin made this order of the church rigid. The Reformers seemed fixated on the right structure more than on developing body ministry.

All this is to say that even though the liberating doctrine of the priesthood of all believers was rediscovered and its radical implications at times clearly seen, yet the institutional definition of the church and subsequent obsession with proper church order blurred the vision and stifled its expression. The focus of ministry was top-down.

A NEW STARTING POINT

For ministry to be returned to the people of God, we must have a bottom-up view of the church. James Dunn calls for a reversal of our methodology and a new starting point:

> The attempt to graft a concept of ministry of the people of God onto the root of ordained ministry has not really worked. Now it is time to reaffirm the root of all ministry as the charismatic Spirit given variously to the members of the body, to recognize our starting point as the New Covenant of the Pentecostal Spirit, and not the old covenant of priesthood.[15]

An organism view of ministry begins with the people of God as the place where ministry resides, and it conceives of leadership from within the one body. In contrast, an institutional view of ministry defines the territory occupied by its ordained leadership and then attempts to tack on a role for lay ministry. The Reformation operated from an institutional mind-set that tried to fuse an institutional conception of ministry with an organismic doctrine of the priesthood of all believers. It did not work.

The lens through which we look at the essential nature of the church and ministry will inevitably lead to diametrically opposed understandings. Figure 2.1 below summarizes this chapter's discoveries.

If institutionalism is your starting point, it will necessarily lead to the belief that there are two kinds of people (clergy/laity) and therefore two ministries. But the genesis of the organism view is the whole people of God, which leads to the conclusion that there is one people and one ministry.

Before we examine the radical implications of viewing the church through the lens of organism, we must deepen our understanding of the institutional entrapment of the church. If a revolution is to be unleashed that sets God's people free, we must first see how thorough our bondage is to institutionalism. Liberation does not come easily. For the church to be unleashed, we must engage in spiritual warfare. In the next chapter we will assess the strength of the enemy.

Figure 2.1

┌──────THE CHURCH──────┐

Organism	Institution
1. Starting point: The body of Christ. The church is the whole people of God in whom Christ dwells.	1. Starting point: Leadership offices in the church. The true church is found where (a) the Word of God is rightly proclaimed; (b) the sacraments are rightly administered.
2. Bottom-up: The church's ministry is shaped by the gifts and callings distributed by the Holy Spirit to the whole body of Christ.	2. Top-down: The ministry is the province of the ordained offices of the church.
3. All ministry is lay ministry.	3. Lay ministry supplements and is secondary to ordained ministry.
4. Conclusion: One people/one ministry.	4. Conclusion: Two people (clergy/laity)/two ministries.

NOTES

1. Hendrik Hart, *Will All the King's Men* (Toronto: Wedge Publishing Foundation, 1972), 30.

2. Thomas Gillespie, "Our Ministerial Roots: The Historical Origins of the Presbyterian Doctrine of the Ministry" (Unpublished paper, Princeton Theological Seminary), 1.

3. Ibid., 5.

4. Ibid., 6.

5. Martin Luther, "On the Ordering of Divine Service in the Congregation," vol. 4, Weimar ed., *Luther's Works,* 62.

6. Quoted by Gillespie, "Our Ministerial Roots," 6.

7. Wilhelm Pauck, "The Ministry in the Time of the Continental Reformation," in *The Ministry in Historical Perspectives,* ed. Richard H. Niebuhr (New York: Harper & Row, 1963), 114.

8. David Watson, *I Believe in the Church* (Grand Rapids: Eerdmans, 1978), 253.

9. Hendrik Kraemer, *A Theology of the Laity* (Philadelphia: Westminster Press, 1958), 62.

10. John Calvin, *Institutes of the Christian Religion* (Philadelphia: Westminster, 1936), 4.1.10.

11. *Luther's Works*, Weimar ed., 6:564.

12. Quoted in H. Richard Niebuhr and Daniel D. Williams, eds., *The Ministry in Historical Perspectives* (San Francisco: Harper & Row, 1983), 115.

13. Pauck, "The Ministry in the Time of the Continental Reformation," 121.

14. Gillespie, "Our Ministerial Roots," 10.

15. James Dunn, "Ministry and the Ministry: The Charismatic Renewal's Challenge to Traditional Ecclesiology" (Unpublished paper), 10.

Chapter 3

Unveiling Our Institutional Mind-Set

THE NEW REFORMATION IS IN part about the transformation of our self-understanding. If ministry is to be returned to the people of God, then the people of God must have a makeover. The apostle Paul says that transformation has to do with our thinking: "Be not conformed to this world, but be *transformed by the renewing of your minds*" (Rom. 12:2). It is a matter of putting off an old way of thinking and in its place having our thinking renewed. In other words, transformation is about reclamation.

Growing up in Southern California, I watched a transformation take place in a stinking landfill. Throughout my elementary school years, Scholl Canyon was the place where trash trucks emptied their loads of rotting garbage and household discards. In my twenties I played golf on the top of this same landfill. Once the gorge had reached capacity, someone had the grand idea that this refuse depository could become a new creation as a place of recreation. Scholl Canyon is now a beautifully manicured, green playground overlooking the San Fernando Valley.

As nice as this sounds, the creators of this golf course failed to follow the biblical pattern of transformation. To be truly transformed in biblical terms, means that you must "put off" before you can "put on." It is not just a matter of covering over what is already there so that it looks good on the outside. I only played golf once on this course that on the surface appeared so attractive. Emanating from below the topsoil was a nauseating stench. As I stood on the greens, I had the sense that just below the surface of ground was a bubbling, gaseous chemical caldron.

What is it that we must put off or clean out before we can put on a new way of thinking? We must put off an institutional way of thinking and replace it with an organism understanding of the ministry of all God's people. So entrenched has the institutional mind-set become that we have taken wonderfully inclusive biblical words that refer to the whole people of God and turned their meaning inside out so that they refer to an exclusive few. The filter through which we have passed the words *saints, minister, priest, clergy,* and *laity* is institutional. They go into the filter as inclusive and come out as exclusive. The ministry of all has become the ministry of a few.

In this chapter I want you to see how thoroughly corrupt our thinking has become by examining the common or vernacular usage of these terms. The way we use words reveals the categories in which we think. Then I want to reclaim the biblical meaning of these inclusive terms as a way to transform our identity. Paul locates transformation in the "renewal of our minds." Right thinking can lead to right living.

I love the *Peanuts* cartoon where Linus and Lucy are involved in substantive dialog. Lucy is worried because it has been raining so hard for so long. She wonders whether there will be another worldwide flood as in Noah's day. Linus informs her that this won't happen. Referring to Genesis 9, he reminds her that God promised never to flood the earth again. Lucy says, "Well, that takes a load off my mind." Linus, while sucking on his blanket, says, "Yes, sound theology will do that."

Let's do some sound theological thinking. We will look at the garbage that needs to be "taken out" so that we can "put on" a biblical mind-set. Institutionalism needs to be replaced by the organism perspective of Scripture.

SAINTS

Popular Image of "Saints"

We use the term *saint* in many ways, but common to each ascription is the idea of a person who is spiritually elite. Saint is most commonly used as a formal designation, a title. In the Protestant tradition, saints are the apostles or authors of Scripture, labeled "St. Mark," "St. Paul," and so on. The Roman Catholic and Eastern Orthodox Churches have expanded this list by canonizing selected exemplary Christians who meet certain criteria such as performing verifiable miracles.

In a less formal sense, we consider people "saints" who have demonstrated their commitment by giving their lives to God in a religious order or full-time Christian service. The implication is that these people are willing to forego worldly pleasures and enter into heroic work with little earthly reward. Mother Teresa was placed in the category of a saint because of her devotion to the poor and dying in the streets of Calcutta. We hear people say reverently, "Oh, she's a saint," referring to someone who seems to be on a first-name basis with God or for whom self-sacrifice is a way of life.

The most evident clue that we use "saint" in a restrictive sense is the personal embarrassment we experience when this term is applied to ourselves. "Me, a saint? Be serious!" We associate saint-hood with those who have achieved a certain level of holiness or piety. In fact, we may shun the designation of saint, for it implies an other-worldliness that comes with unattractive overtones that are dull and unexciting.

The Biblical Usage of "Saints"

When we examine the biblical use of the term *saints,* we find the word always applied to the whole body of Christ, not to some select group that have achieved spiritual stardom. Saints (Greek, *hagios*) are the ordinary, garden-variety Christians in a particular time and place whose only distinction is that they are chosen by God, claimed by Jesus Christ, and convened by the Holy Spirit as the church.

It is instructive to note the apostle Paul's salutations to the churches with whom he corresponds. Paul always addressed the church as the whole; he never addressed his letters to the leaders. The church is *all* the people of God, not a representative group such as pastors, elders, or deacons. In six of the nine letters addressed to churches, Paul's salutation is to the "saints" (Rom. 1:7; 1 Cor. 1:2; 2 Cor. 1:1; Eph. 1:1; Phil. 1:1; Col. 1:2). The one time when the leaders are mentioned in the salutation is Philippians 1:1, but only after referring first to the saints: "To all the saints in Christ Jesus who are in Philippi, with the bishops and deacons." The term is used sixty-two times in the New Testament and never in the singular. Never is an individual designated as a saint, only the body of believers corporately.

The clearest indication of Paul's usage occurs in his greeting to the Corinthians: "To the church of God that is in Corinth, to those who are sanctified in Christ Jesus, called to be saints, together with all those who in every place call on the name of our Lord Jesus Christ, both their Lord and ours" (1 Cor. 1:2).

Even though "saints," according to common usage, implies personal holiness, Paul's focus is not on our personal purity, but on God's holiness. To be saints means to be set apart and called out. To be a saint is to come within the realm of God's holiness. We are holy, not because of our purity, but because we have been made holy or declared right before God based on the work of Christ.

The phrase that precedes "called to be saints" is the key to the meaning of the word. We are saints because of what has been done for us—"sanctified by Jesus Christ." "Sanctified" means we are made holy by Christ and not through our own effort. The designation is all the more startling when we remember who the recipients of this letter are. The Corinthians would be the last congregation in the New Testament whom we would endow with sainthood if "saints" refers to keeping one's ways pure. The Corinthian church (1) was marked by party spirit (1 Cor. 1:12); (2) was described as carnal because the people were spiritually still drinking milk when they should have been eating meat (1 Cor. 3:2–3); (3) allowed the pagan immorality of a man consorting with his stepmother (1 Cor. 5:1); and (4) profaned the Lord's Supper because of the divisions between rich and poor (1 Cor. 11:27). But Paul can still describe the Corinthians as saints because he understood that God viewed them from the standpoint of the completed work of Christ on their behalf.

Paul demonstrates the all-encompassing scope of sainthood by calling the Corinthians "saints together with all those who in every place call on the name of our Lord Jesus Christ." You cannot get more inclusive than that. How far we have strayed from the biblical usage by narrowing saints to a restrictive group who supposedly excel in godliness!

We need to return to the Reformed doctrine of the communion of the saints, which views all God's people—past, present, and future—as a part of an eternal fellowship linked by our common life in Jesus Christ. The hymn "For All the Saints" by William H. How leads us in the right direction.

> For all the saints who from their labors rest,
> Who Thee by faith before the world confessed,
> Thy name, O Jesus, be forever blessed:
> Alleluia! Alleluia!
>
> O blest communion, fellowship divine!
> We feebly struggle, they in glory shine;
> Yet all are one in Thee, for all are Thine:
> Alleluia! Alleluia!

MINISTER

Popular Image of "Minister"

Who is a "minister," according to common usage? A person who goes into *the* ministry. We all know for whom the ministry is reserved; it is for people who have heard a call from God to enter into the ranks of the ordained. A magazine advertisement by a well-known seminary uses this tag line, "When you get *the* Calling, call 1–800." Our universal usage tends toward a hierarchical class distinction. We distinguish between two kinds of people: those who have stepped behind the veil into the aura of holiness, and those second-class citizens who have not been called to a "holy order." "Going into the ministry" is associated with a certain honor, and "leaving the ministry" leaves a mark of shame.

We give titles such as "reverend" that set apart "ministers" into a spiritual realm unattainable by those who have chosen a "secular" way of life. Michael Green, an Anglican pastor, observes this tendency toward class distinction:

> One cannot but help feeling that the whole gamut of ecclesiastical courtesy titles, "The Venerable," "The Very Reverend," "The Most Reverend" and so on, are a hindrance rather than a help in the work of *the* ministry [sic]. They tend to build an invisible wall between their bearer and the

world at large; much more important, they tend to make him just a little proud, just a little pleased with himself, just a little further removed than he was before from the role of servant.[1]

You may not come from a tradition that uses such flowery designation, but you have your own ways, perhaps subtly, of reinforcing the class distinctions. Numerous pastoral "perks"—from clerical garb, to reserved parking spaces, to the exclusive right to preside at Communion—underscore the qualitative difference between pastor and people.

The Reformed tradition has expanded the definition of ministry beyond pastors to include elders and deacons. To be sure, each office has an assigned biblical role, but the whole ministry is defined only in terms of these functions.

Yet if the ministry is associated with and summed up by the offices of the church, we must ask what is left for the whole people of God. If the ministry is for the initiated and ordained, by definition it is not for the rank and file. I have said on many occasions, "If the minister is called into *the* ministry, what is left for everyone else?" The laity are often viewed as those who supplement the ministry of pastors because, after all, they cannot do it all. Under this theology, the people of God are at best adjuncts to the true ministers and have no real ministry identity of their own. This restrictive view of ministry seen through the lens of institutionalism leads directly to two peoples of God (clergy and laity) and two ministries (*the* ministry for first-class Christians, and what's left for second-class Christians).

The Biblical Usage of "Minister"

Nowhere in the New Testament does the term "ministry" or "minister" refer to a particular class of people set apart from the rest of the church. The noun *diakonia* is variously translated "service," "ministry," or "mission." The personal form of the noun *diakonos* is translated "servants," "ministers," or "deacons," depending on its context. It appears that these terms are used in the Bible in three ways:

1. "Service" or "ministry" captures the spirit in which our ministry is to be rendered on behalf of the whole body. Jesus embodied

the model of servant when he said, "For the Son of Man came not to be served but to serve, and to give his life as a ransom for many" (Mark 10:45). In Paul's description of the ministry, motivated abilities have been distributed by the Holy Spirit to the entire body. One synonym for "spiritual gift" is "service" or "ministry" ("And there are varieties of services [ministries], but the same Lord," 1 Cor. 12:5). "Service" captures the manner in which ministry is to be exercised. Ministry is to be performed for the common good (1 Cor. 12:7), not to promote the ego of the doer. Ministry inherently means giving one's life away on behalf of others.

2. Ministry is also the particular task or call we have been set apart to perform. Since the term *ministry*, translated "service," is here a synonym for *charismata* (grace-gifts), Paul wants us to understand that our gifts are also the means or channel through which we exercise our ministry. Paul evidently has the entire body in mind, not a select few, when he writes, "To each is given the manifestation of the Spirit for the common good" (1 Cor. 12:7).

Since the institutional ministry mind-set is so pervasive, it should not be surprising to find it infiltrating the translation of Scripture. From the Revised Standard Version's rendering of Acts 6:4, one might think that the apostles are the only ones set apart as a class by themselves to perform ministry. The apostles were drawn into a dispute between the Greek-speaking and Hebrew-speaking widows. Concerned that they might become deflected from their primary call, the apostles reaffirm that "we will devote ourselves to prayer and the *ministry* of the word" (Acts 6:4 RSV). One could conclude that it is the apostles who are called to ministry. Yet the exact same word translated "ministry" in Acts 6:4 is translated "distribution" in Acts 6:1: "The Hellenists complained against the Hebrews because their widows were being neglected in the daily distribution [ministry]." Did a translator's bias infiltrate the text? The apostles do ministry, while those involved in caring for widows "distribute" food. I would assert that distributing food to the widows was as much of a ministry as the apostles call to preach the word. Both have a ministry. The apostles were called to a particular function of prayer and proclamation, whereas the seven were appointed to give oversight to a ministry among the widows. Both are ministries without a qualitative distinction.

3. Ministry is the province of the entire body of believers. An unfortunate error in punctuation has sometimes been used as the basis for claiming that the Bible teaches a distinct class set apart for ministry. The 1946 edition of the Revised Standard Version of Ephesians 4:11–12, inserts a comma after the word "saints," leading one to conclude that those with particular gifts are to do all the ministry. The passage reads, "And his gifts were that some should be apostles, some prophets, some evangelists, and some pastors and teachers to equip the saints, for the works of ministry, for the building up of the body of Christ." With the comma included it would appear that these gifted individuals have three tasks: equip the saints, do the work of ministry, and build up the body of Christ.[2]

Almost all scholars agree that the comma after "saints" should be removed. This deletion changes the entire flavor of the statement. The passage now reads, "to equip the saints for the work of ministry, for the building up of the body of Christ" (RSV 1971 edition; NRSV).

The saints (Paul's designation of all God's people) are to do the work of ministry with the empowerment of apostles, prophets, evangelists, and pastor-teachers. The role of these gifted ones, as we shall see in chapter 6, is to bring the ministry of the whole body to its fullness, not to guard the ministry for themselves. Far from ministry being associated with a few, it is coterminous with the entire body. There is only one ministry—the ministry of the people of God.

PRIEST

Popular Image of "Priest"

Let's play a word association game. What immediately comes to your mind when you hear the word *priest?* Your answer probably is the designation for clergy in the Roman Catholic or Orthodox tradition, unless you happen to be Episcopalian. The immediate association most of us make on hearing the word *priest* is a person, addressed as "Father," who is qualified to hear our confession and offer absolution. A priest is one who has a mediator role, representing the people before God and God to the people. The priest enters the realm of a holy order to be set apart through taking vows.

Even in the Protestant tradition the minister has a "priestly" aura. Ministers are persons who, because of their office and ordination, carry with them the sacramental presence of Christ. Jesus is somehow more available or nearer to a minister than to ordinary Christians. Since it is assumed that the pastor's prayers have a more direct access to the ear of God, I as a pastor am often asked to pray for a particular need. All pastors have experienced a sense of being treated differently because of their priestly position. A Dutch colloquialism captures the holy aura of a pastor: When there is an awkward and uncomfortable lull in a social conversation, someone may interject the expression, "A minister walked by." The implication is that we cannot have our usual dialogue in the presence of ministers because of their priestly "purity." There is nothing that kills a party more than the presence of the "priest." The same reality can be turned into a sense of privilege. Many times I have heard people pronounce themselves blessed because a pastor was sitting at their table for a meal.

I believe the function that reinforces more than any other the priestly role of a pastor is the administration of the sacrament of the Lord's Supper. As the Old Testament priest offered up sacrifices on behalf of God's people, so the contemporary priest stands behind the ornate table, breaking the bread and holding up the cup as the people's representative before God. James Dunn adapts Milton for our purposes: "Today's minister is but the old priesthood writ large!"[3]

The Biblical Usage of "Priest"

There is a startling contrast between the Old Testament and New Testament views of the priesthood. Under the old covenant there was a group clearly demarcated as priests and Levites, who were descendants of Aaron. They were so distinctively set apart that when the Israelites entered the Promised Land, the priests and Levites received no inheritance of land as did the other eleven tribes. They were to dedicate themselves to the service of the religious cult and be supported from the people's sacrifices, tithes, and offerings.

The priest's role under the old covenant was generally twofold: (1) he represented God to the people; he was a mediator of sorts who communicated the word of God to the people, for the people were considered holy only when they heard the Word and responded; and (2) he represented the people before God. Since the people could not come directly before a holy God because of their sin, the guilt of sin had to be dealt with through offering sacrifices. The role of the priest as the mediator for God's people is most clearly demonstrated in the high priest's entering the Holy of Holies annually on the Day of Atonement to offer an atoning substitute of a bull or lamb.

But there is a radical reorientation in the New Testament. The office of priest is eliminated as it pertains to a select group of people. This is based on the physical sacrifice of Christ, the ultimate high priest. Jesus fulfilled and completed the role of priest in his substitutionary death. "Unlike the other high priests, he [Jesus] has no need to offer sacrifices day after day, first for his own sins, and then for those of the people; this he did once for all when he offered himself" (Heb. 7:27).

Here we encounter a profoundly moving convergence of images. Not only is Jesus the high priest who *offers* the sacrifice, but he himself *becomes* the blameless, spotless sacrifice for our sin. In other words, as the perfect high priest, Jesus offers himself as the atoning sacrifice. Since Jesus' work is complete and he makes intercession for us continually before the Father, any human who claims for himself that priestly role would be denigrating the work of Christ. David Watson writes, "[Jesus] is now the eternal high priest in the heavens. All earthly and human priesthood has now once for all been fulfilled and finished by that unique, final and unrepeatable sacrifice of our great high priest who 'is a priest forever' (Heb. 7:24)."[4]

Marjorie Warkentin, quoting Michael Green, draws attention to the radical departure that the New Testament writers made with the Old Testament understanding of priest:

> "It is simply staggering in view of the background these New Testament writers, steeped as they were in the priestly system of the Old Testament, that never once do they use the term *hierus* [priest] of the Christian minister. The Aaronic analogy for their ministry lay obviously at hand. But they refused to use it. It is hard to overrate the significance of this point when they did use it of the whole Christian community."[5]

In fact, the New Testament idea of "priest" has so radically departed from the Old Testament that the entire body of believers is now described as by nature a priesthood (1 Peter 2:5). By ascribing to the church the images formerly applied to the nation of Israel, the apostle Peter makes it clear that the new priesthood is the church: "You are a chosen race, a royal priesthood, a holy nation, God's own people" (1 Peter 2:9).

The Reformers clearly understood the revolutionary implications of the transfer from the select Old Testament priestly office to the New Testament priesthood open to all believers. The first implication is that we all have direct access to God through Jesus Christ, the great high priest. Calvin wrote,

> Now, Christ plays the priestly role, not only to render the Father favorable and propitious to us by an eternal law of reconciliation, but also to receive us as His companion in this great office (Rev. 1:6). For we are defiled in ourselves, yet are priests in Him, offer ourselves and our all to God, and freely enter the heavenly sanctuary that sacrifices of prayers and praise that we bring may be acceptable and sweet-smelling before God.[6]

This first aspect of the priesthood of all believers we have affirmed and incorporated into our Reformation practice.

The second aspect of the believers' priesthood is one that the Reformers clearly envisioned but that we have yet to appropriate fully. Yet God is unleashing upon us in our day a power that I believe will usher in the New Reformation. We are priests to each other. We are God's representatives to each other. No one had keener insight into the logical conclusions of this doctrine than Luther himself. He foresaw the explosive possibilities of the doctrine of the priesthood of all believers. The return of the ministry to all of God's people was in sight. Commenting on 1 Peter 2:9, Luther wrote,

> Therefore we are all priests, as many as are Christians. . . . The priesthood is nothing but a ministry as we learn from 1 Corinthians 4, "Let a man so account of us as of the ministers of Christ, and the dispensers of the mysteries of God."[7]

Even though this truth never came to fruition in the Reformation, as we have seen it was captured in the theological vision of the Reformers.

CLERGY

Popular Image of "Clergy"

"Clergy" is another term, along with "minister" and "priest," that formally designates a leadership caste. The word *clergy* is almost impossible to use without contrasting it to its counterpart. It has come to mean those who stand over against "laity." Clergy conjures up reverse collars and the institution of righteousness.

When someone introduces me as a member of the clergy, I immediately sense that I am considered a part of a third gender—there are men, women, and clergy. I have suddenly become a holy man who does not experience the struggles and temptations of the rest of the human race. As a pastor I take care of things spiritual so that the rest of the church can enjoy the temporal.

I fear that many participants in the church view their pastors as specialists in the things of God, so they need not be bothered with that realm. As a result, clergy are held in both respect and contempt. The layperson's respect is derived from the clerical devotion of one's whole life to God—something the laity considers beyond their grasp. At the same time, however, there is contempt based on the clergy's supposedly cloistered lives that separate them from the rough-and-tumble matters of the real world. The underlying assumption is that religion does not fully work where it matters.

Even though the Bible knows no distinction between clergy and laity, the separation of the classes developed relatively early in the history of the church. The first hint of a professional ministry that became synonymous with the ministry of the church occurred in the writings of Ignatius of Antioch (between A.D. 98 and 117). In some personal correspondence, Ignatius defined the church as "one eucharist, one body of the Lord, one cup, one altar, and *therefore one* bishop together with the presbyterium and the deacons, my fellow servants."[8]

The distinction between clergy and laity did not become full-blown until the fourth century, when the church adopted a secular model. In the Greco-Roman world, the Greek word *klēros* referred to municipal administrators and *laos* to those who were ruled. As the gulf between these two grew, the *klēros* in the church became associated with the sacred, the *laos* with the secular. Since the lives of the *laos* were consumed with temporal affairs, they were perceived to be on the low rung of the saintly ladder.

By the twelfth century, the partition between clergy and laity was fixed to the point where Hugo Grotius could speak of two kinds of Christians: the *klēros*, who have devoted themselves to the divine office, marked by contemplation and prayer with freedom from earthly things; and the rest, called "laity," who have compromised the authentic Christian life by marrying, possessing worldly goods, and making other concessions to human frailties.

The Biblical Usage of "Clergy"

How far all this has strayed from the New Testament meaning of *klēros!* John W. Kennedy summarizes the irony of our inversion of the meaning of clergy: "Through some strange etymological perversion, from a word which indicated the great unity and privilege of the church as a whole, there has been derived a word which means practically opposite, and is used to denote a class of people with special privilege within the church itself."[9]

The word *klēros* means "lot" or "inheritance." It can mean a share or a portion or that which is allotted. It is used in Acts 1:17 to refer to Judas: he "was allotted his share [*klēros*] in this ministry." The replacement for Judas was chosen by casting lots, and the lot *(klēros)* fell to Matthias (Acts 1:26).

Klēros more richly refers to the inheritance all the saints receive in Christ. Paul concluded his prayer for the Colossians with gratitude, "giving thanks to the Father, who has enabled [us] to share in the inheritance [*klēros*] of the saints in the light" (Col. 1:12). Recounting God's call to him to carry the message of the gospel to the Gentiles, Paul stated Christ's promise to them "that they may receive forgiveness of sins and a place [*klēros*] among those who are sanctified by faith in me" (Acts 26:18). It would be hard to imagine a more dramatic inclusive use of the word *klēros*. The Gentiles, who were considered cut off from the covenant people of God, are now fully included in Christ. Far from *klēros* ever carrying the distinction between an upper and lower class in the kingdom, the word conveys the full inclusion of the Gentiles as equal partners in the benefits of the gospel.

Inheritance can refer to what we receive from being adopted into the family of God, but it can also refer to what God receives. The Scripture affirms that God has an inheritance. What could God possibly inherit? Us. The Lord considers us his prize. The riches God bestows on himself are his people. In Ephesians 1:18, Paul says that we are to have the eyes of our hearts enlightened that we may know "what are the riches of his glorious inheritance among the saints." This same message is affirmed in the Old Testament: "The LORD's own portion was his people, Jacob his allotted share" (Deut. 32:9).

Kraemer summarizes our discoveries: "In the New Testament the word *klēros* when it is used in regard to the new community in Christ is always meant as the body of men and women who share in God's gift of redemption and glory, which is their 'inheritance.' There is not a shimmer of an idea of a definite body, called clergy."[10]

LAITY

Popular Image of "Laity"

To this point we have examined the terms "saints," "minister," "priest," and "clergy," which have all become associated with a particular set-apart class, often designated as the ordained. On the other side of the ledger is "laity," used for the vast majority of the church. In common speech "layperson" and "laity" have largely negative connotations. The Oxford English Dictionary defines laity as "the body of people not in orders, as opposed to clergy." Kathleen Bliss captures this sense of nonentity of laity well: "For these [the laity] have a strong element of 'over-againstness' toward the clergy—the clergy are, the laity are *not*, the clergy do, the laity do *not*. Nobody wants to be an is *not*."[11] John Stott illustrates further how the word "lay" has been debased: "'Lay' is often a synonym for 'amateur' as opposed to 'professional,' or 'unqualified' as opposed to 'expert.'"[12]

The Biblical Usage of "Laity"

The same term "laity" that in contemporary usage has a pejorative ring, is filled with dignity and honor in the Scripture. *Laos* exudes a sense of specialness. God designates Israel as his special people, selected from among all the peoples of the earth to be his possession. Speaking to the gathered nation, Moses conveyed God's covenant heart: "For you are a people holy to the LORD your God. The LORD your God has chosen you out of all the peoples on earth to be his people, his treasured possession" (Deut. 7:6). God said, "I will . . . be your God, and you shall be my people" (Lev. 26:12).

As we have already noted, this special covenantal relationship is transferred to the church, which was purchased at the price of Jesus' blood. Peter said, "You are a people of God's own possession" (1 Peter 2:9 NASB). Out of all the peoples (*ethnos*) of the earth, there is a special people (*laos*) who are God's called-out people. The *laos* of God are nothing less than a new humanity, the vanguard of the future, the prototype of the kingdom of God not yet completed, a people of the future living in the present. Next time we hear someone say, "I'm just a layperson," we can say, "That's more than enough."

THE INSTITUTIONAL MINDSET

From this survey of the common biblical designations for leaders of the church, we can see that a thoroughly institutional mindset has been all too dominant in Christian history. The damage to the church of defining God's people from a top-down perspective has been catastrophic. Robert Munger writes,

> In our time it may well be that the greatest single bottleneck to the renewal and outreach of the church is the division of roles between clergy and laity that results in a hesitancy of the clergy to trust the laity with significant responsibility, and in turn a reluctance on the part of the laity to trust themselves as authentic ministers of Christ, either in the church or outside the church.[13]

The institutional model of the church leads us to a two peoples/two ministries bifurcation. Richard Lovelace points to the very issue that the New Reformation addresses:

> It is still true that the model of congregational life in the minds of most clergy and laity is one in which the minister is the dominant pastoral superstar who specializes in

the spiritual concerns of the Christian community, while the laity are spectators, critics, and recipients of pastoral care, free to go about their own business because the pastor is taking care of the business of the kingdom.[14]

This institutional legacy has quenched the release of the Spirit. But a new vision is arising in the church today of a living organism in whom Christ dwells. Therefore, the whole people (laos) of God are called to the ministry, which means exercising their function as priests to each other and to the broken world. When we come to realize that there is only one people and therefore one ministry, God's people will be released to fulfill their callings.

In the next chapter we will get specific about the radical changes the church will need to undergo if it is to experience an organism reality.

NOTES

1. Michael Green, *Called to Serve* (London: Hodder and Stoughton, 1976), 16.

2. John R. W. Stott, *The Message of Ephesians* (Downers Grove, Ill.: InterVarsity Press, 1979), 166.

3. James D. G. Dunn, "Ministry and the Ministry: The Charismatic Renewal's Challenge to Traditional Ecclesiology" (Unpublished paper), 9.

4. David Watson, *I Believe in the Church* (Grand Rapids: Eerdmans, 1978), 248.

5. Marjorie Warkentin, *Ordination: A Biblical-Historical View* (Grand Rapids: Eerdmans, 1982), 161.

6. John Calvin, *Institutes of the Christian Religion* (Philadelphia: Westminster, 1960), 2.15.6.

7. Martin Luther, "An Open Letter to the Christian Nobility," *The Works of Martin Luther* (Philadelphia: Muhlenberg, 1941), 279.

8. Quoted in Watson, *I Believe in the Church,* 275.

9. John W. Kennedy, *The Torch of Testimony* (Auburn, Maine: Christian Books Publishing House, 1965), 54.

10. Kraemer, *A Theology of the Laity,* 52

11. Kathleen Bliss, *We the People: A Book About Laity* (London: SCM Press, 1963), 69.

12. John R. W. Stott, *One People* (Downers Grove, Ill.: InterVarsity Press, 1968), 29.

13. Robert Munger, "Training the Laity for Ministry," *Theology News and Notes* (June 1973): 3.

14. Richard Lovelace, *Dynamics of Spiritual Life* (Downers Grove, Ill.: InterVarsity Press, 1979), 224.

Chapter 4

Shifting from Institution to Organism

THE FRESH WIND BLOWING in the church today is being felt wherever the doors of ministry are thrown open to include all of God's people. We live in a day when the shift from institution to organism is taking place. We are on the verge of recapturing the biblical vision of the church as a ministering community with a full employment plan.

Before we consider the shifts that need to be made for the organism reality to take hold, let's review what we have discovered thus far:

- The church as organism understands itself to be the living extension of Jesus' ministry.
- This biblical perspective causes us to shift our starting point for defining ministry from the institutional view of the ordained clergy to the organism perspective of the entire body.
- The ministry of the people of God cannot be tacked onto the root of ordained ministry; ordained ministry must find its place within the whole people of God.
- The New Testament knows of only one ministry, the ministry of the one people of God.

If we are to capture the wind of the Spirit, the question before us is: What is the shape of the sails that can catch this fresh breeze? What are the contours of the canvas if the ship of the church is to skip through the high seas of organism ministry? Or to put it neg-atively, what old, tattered sails need to be discarded because they will only tear under the force of the new wind? Movements of the Holy Spirit are replete with opportunities seized and squandered. We are being presented with the choice of catching the gale and skimming the seas or resisting and watching the sails become tat-tered and torn. Some churches will become further entrenched in their institutionalism. The breath of God passes them by while new forms emerge that are more able to adapt to an organism reality. When God's Spirit moves, we are presented with a choice of ulti-mate proportion—life or death.

Is this not the choice presented to the Grand Inquisitor in Fyo-dor Dostoyevsky's masterpiece *The Brothers Karamazov?* Dos-toyevsky paints the hideous picture of the church that has turned the body of Christ into a cruel ecclesiastical machine. The writer returns Jesus to the Spanish town of Seville in the sixteenth cen-tury. The faithful recognize the Christ immediately, for he performs the same signs of life-giving power that he did during his first visit to the earth.

At the foot of the cathedral steps, the tragic scene of a funeral procession unfolds. A seven-year-old girl is being carried in an open coffin. The emotional scene is compounded as the lifeless girl's mother pleads for Jesus to raise her daughter. Once again, Jesus compassionately responds, saying, "Talitha cum." The young girl is dramatically presented alive to her mother. Enter the Grand Inquisi-tor, a tall, severe man in his nineties. His presence alone dampens the joy of the occasion. This religious kingpin has Jesus arrested.

As night falls, the Grand Inquisitor visits Jesus in his cell. "It is you, you!" he says. The Grand Inquisitor lectures Jesus about the bargain the church has made with the people: the people agreed to surrender their freedom to the church, and in return the church was to give them happiness. Jesus, says the Inquisitor, has no right to come and restore freedom to these people. All along, Jesus sits in silence and offers no verbal response. Then suddenly he rises, comes to the old man, and kisses him "gently on his bloodless, aged cheeks." The old man remains unmoved. Then Dostoyevsky levels his indictment against the entrenched church: "The kiss glowed in his heart, but the old man sticks to his idea." May it not be so with us.

Four major shifts must be made in order to bring in the organism nature of the church. We can stick to our "idea" and quench the Spirit, or we can do what is necessary to wake the sleeping giant and see the ministry returned to the people of God.

ORGANISM MINISTRY, NOT ORDAINED MINISTRY

The Reformers and contemporary interpreters of the implications of the Reformation speak with one voice. They all agree that the doctrine of the priesthood of all believers obliterates the caste distinction between clergy and laity. There is no qualitative difference between the two. Yet the gulf between clergy and laity remains. Our stated theology is not informing our mind-set and practice for reasons that we will explore in the next chapter.

If, in fact, Robert Munger is correct that the clergy-laity bifurcation is the "greatest single bottleneck to the renewal and outreach of the church,"[1] then we must begin to take drastic steps. John Stott is more direct: "I do not hesitate to say that to interpret the church in terms of a privileged caste or a hierarchical structure is to destroy the New Testament doctrine of the church."[2]

What is required for us to move toward a one people/one ministry New Testament church? In a word, repentance.

Biblically, the word *repentance* means a change of mind or direction. To repent is to have a second thought that corrects a first thought. It means to come to our senses, or as Jesus says of the Prodigal Son, "he came to himself." We need to "see" what we have become and therefore change our manner of thinking. This will in turn change our way of acting. "We have met the enemy and they are us."

Since repentance has to do with changes in our thinking, it will lead to a fundamental change in our vocabulary. "How is a change of language going to solve any problems?" we might ask. One answer: "Language is not merely a means of communication; it is also an expression of shared assumptions. Language transmits implicit values and behavioral models to all the people who use it."[3]

I propose that we banish forever from our vocabulary the terms *clergy* and *laity*. These words have become so corrupted in their juxtaposition as to be irretrievable. We observed in the last chapter that "clergy" has become synonymous with "ministry" (and in fact is defined that way in the *Oxford English Dictionary*). When we think of clergy, we mean a professional religious person whose role it is to represent the institution of the church. The *American Heritage Dictionary* defines clergy as "a person authorized to perform religious functions in a church." By implication, then, laity are the unauthorized.

"Clergy" and "laity" have such an unhealthy association that it is impossible to use one term without its opposite coming to mind. As dignifying as is the biblical meaning of laity, just so our popular usage of laity is demeaning. Laity has a pejorative ring. It has come to mean either what you *are* not or what you *can* not. Even if we speak as we do today of "lay" ministry in our attempts to move beyond the exclusive domain of professional ministry, we are creating a "separate but unequal" order. "Lay" ministry is still an attempt to tap ministry onto the root of ordained ("real") ministry.

Although the following quote refers to the use of gender language, it sums up this dilemma:

> If you have a group half of whose number are *As* and half *Bs* . . . if you call the group *A*, there is no way that the *Bs* can be equal to the *As* within it. The *As* will always be the real and the *Bs* will always be the exception—the sub group, the sub species, the outsiders.[4]

In other words, clergy do (professional) ministry; laypersons do lay (amateur) ministry.

In the place of *clergy* and *laity*, I propose the use of functional language. Organism implies function, not titles and offices. The hierarchical, top-down orientation of the old, tattered sail of institutionalism will be torn by the new breeze. When our starting point is one people as the body of Christ, then functional language describes roles that people perform within that one body without discriminating according to value. When we use the term "pastor" rather than "minister" or "clergy," we have moved from positional language to a description of what one does. I am particularly taken by Elton Trueblood's prophetic suggestion that the best modern image for pastor is "player-coach." I like it because it suggests an equipping model of ministry and also describes the role of pastor as a member of a team. The image of player-coach indicates that there is one team with the pastor as an integral part of it. There are not two teams of differing value.

When we speak in organism terms, members of the team have particular roles to play according to their giftedness within the body. In my own Presbyterian tradition, we have functional language that keeps everyone on the same team. The ordained offices of the church are threefold: "ministers of the Word" (and sacraments), "elders," and "deacons." This is institutional language, but functional language is also available. We speak of pastors as "teaching elders" who share ministry with "ruling elders." We must jettison the corrupted language of clergy-laity and in its place put functional language that reflects our ministry.

A word that I believe is retrievable is "minister" or "ministry." Even though we have tended to equate ministry with the ordained or have spoken of going into "the ministry" as referring to those who go into a holy order, the word *minister* does not seem nearly so tainted. Evidence of the New Reformation has shown up on church bulletins in lists of church staff: "Ministers: all the members of [church's name]. Assistant to the ministers: the church staff." We are attempting to recapture this term from its institutional imprisonment.

I have told the members of the churches I have served that my goal is to redefine "minister" so completely that when they hear that word they will think of themselves and not the professionals. One day I was almost caught in my own trap. I was visiting a deputation site where our high school youth were serving. At dinner that evening I was asked by a youth with whom our team served, "How many ministers do you have at your church?" Eavesdropping on our conversation was one of the adult leaders serving as a counselor for the week. I was about to stumble into the traditional answer when Dave saved me: "Yes, Greg, how many ministers *do* we have?" Catching his tone and myself, I said, "We have close to six hundred." I came perilously close to reinforcing the old-wineskin perspective and thereby undermining the new vision that Dave and others had already adopted.

As long as we use "ministry" to mean what the Lord does through his entire body and not some limited portion of it, then the recaptured term can be an embodiment of the New Reformation. Modifiers before the term "ministry," such as "lay" or "ordained," get us right back into the "separate and unequal" mentality.

MULTIGIFTED PEOPLE, NOT MULTIGIFTED PASTOR

Churches have a penchant for wanting to find the leader who can "do it all." As a clergy-dominated institution, the church seeks its "salvation" in the multitalented pastor. John Stott labels this "the desire for omnicompetence." Howard Snyder drips with sarcasm when he writes, "We seek a pastor who handles Sunday morning better than a quiz master on weekday TV. He is better with words than most political candidates. As a scholar he surpasses many seminary professors. No church social function would be complete without him."[5]

We want pastors who *can* do it all, so that they *will* do it all. The desire for "perfect" pastors creates a passivity in the congregation. People live out their Christian lives vicariously through "Mr. or Ms. Wonderful" as if his or her faith and abilities were theirs. The church members' role is to pay their dues so that the doors can be kept open and create a context for pastors to do their work. Howard Snyder characterizes this approach in these words: "If the pastor is a superstar, the church is an audience, not a body."[6]

Without denigrating the absolute necessity of leadership and its catalytic nature, the biblical emphasis is not on the "multigifted" pastor, but on a "multigifted" body. Jesus Christ was the only fully gifted human; and when he ascended to his Father, he chose to create an interdependent, multifaceted, corporate body as the only entity that could contain his gifts. No individual was ever meant to demonstrate the fullness of Christ to the world. We are meant to do that through redeemed communities. "We don't have it all together, but together we have it all." The Holy Spirit is mentioned fifty-six times in Paul's letters, each instance referring to his indwelling the community, not simply an individual. If we want to see Jesus manifest on earth, it will be corporately, through a community of people who lay down their lives for each other and build each other up through the gifts variously distributed throughout the body.

So the emphasis in our churches must be on the gifted community. The New Reformation seeks to discover experientially what the Bible teaches and demonstrates. We are all channels through whom the Holy Spirit works to bring strengthening grace to others . in the body so that we grow together into Christlikeness.

The church is fundamentally a charismatic community, for the *charismata* (grace-gifts) have been distributed and assigned to all in Christ (1 Cor. 12:11, 18). This makes each person an initiating center for ministry. All are directly connected to Jesus, the head of the body. The signals for ministry are sent directly from the head to the parts. Initiative for ministry can be taken by any responsible person, whether or not they hold an official position.

The bottom-up church is a bubble-up ministry. The body is not passively waiting for or resisting the pastor's next move. Nor is the congregation reduced to an audience who applauds the solo performance of a multigifted pastor. On the contrary, the pastor in the bottom-up church must hustle to keep up with and encourage the ministry that spontaneously erupts out of the organism.

Bubble-up ministries are grown out of a permission-giving atmosphere. This means there must be a release of control of ministry from the hands of paid staff and office holders so that ministry can originate at any point in the body. If we believe that if every part of the body is directly connected to the head of the body, then the head can communicate to the parts without going through the pastors and governing body. "The head does not tell the hand to tell the foot what to do." I know that statement terrifies those who are afraid of losing control. There are two key questions that every church must answer: (1) Where and how do ministries originate? and (2) Which ministries does our church support? My answer is the same in both questions. Ministry originates in the hearts and passions of any believer who can find a few others who share the same passion. The church then supports or makes room for those ministries that are grown and sustained in the hearts of its members.

This approach differs drastically from the institutional model. In the top-down approach the professional staff and the leadership board brainstorm the ministry needs to be addressed, set up the structure to meet them, and then recruit people from the congregation to fill the appropriate slots. People are then being asked to join predefined ministries that someone else has determined should be carried out. It is not the work of the pastors and leaders to say we should have a ministry to the seniors, junior high youth, or unwed mothers, for example, and then go out and recruit people to staff these ministries. They can point out the need, but the Holy Spirit must grow it in the hearts of his people.

The organism approach is based on the belief that the church is a multigifted body and that Jesus is quite capable of orchestrating the ministry of his church. The role of the pastors and core leadership team is to cultivate an environment that encourages the people of God to be stewards of the gifts God has given them and to discern the shape of the call of God on their lives.

The qualifier is that people are not just encouraged to run off on their own in our highly autonomous, keep-your-own-counsel society. Careful boundaries around explicit criteria do need to be developed by the leadership board to form teams around particular ministries. For example, in my previous church we had three basic criteria to establish a ministry. (1) A new ministry had to have a champion, or one with a heart call to bring it into existence. (2) Individuals from at least two other households must sense a call to be a part of this ministry. If the timing was right for this ministry, then the Lord was forming that same call in the hearts of others. Ministry was to be carried out in teams and not reliant on the sustained efforts of one individual. Also a multiplicity of gifts could be brought to bear to accomplish the ministry. (3) The ministry team needed to be accountable to and connected to our leadership structure.

What I am arguing for is a balance between top-down and bottom-up ministry. There is always a need for order within the organism. Yet the purpose of the leadership structure is not to control ministry but to create structures and a climate where ministry is fostered throughout the life of the church community. Paul Stevens says that the highest calling on church leaders is to point people to find their life and ministry in Jesus, and not become dependent on its leaders.[7]

A SACRAMENTAL PEOPLE, NOT A SACRAMENTAL PASTOR

There is a common assumption among God's people that as a result of their calling, pastors have conferred on them the sacramental presence of Christ. The ordained are seen as having a holy aura not attainable by ordinary believers. This myth has created a priesthood within a priesthood. Unwittingly the pastor assumes a mediatorial role, representing God's people before the Lord in a way they could never do for themselves. In other words, we have created a fiction that people of the cloth carry with them the mantle of Christ because of the holy order that they enter.

Even children are indoctrinated with a sense of separateness of pastors. I was talking to a young mother in the hallway of the church building just before a worship service was to begin. Since I was to assist in leading worship, I was appropriately attired in my black robe. As I stood talking to this woman, her shy, three-year-old daughter was playing peek-a-boo with me, using her mother's skirt as a curtain. After she had poked her head out a few times in discomfort, she pointed to me while looking up at her mother and said, "Is that God?" I suppose in her three-year-old mind she thought I resided in the bowels of the church building and only emerged for holy moments. As I like to say, "Being God is a tough role to give up!"

Associating the saintly, priestly role exclusively with those in a clergy caste is a hindrance to the full ministry of the body. As long as this myth is nurtured, "real" ministry will be performed by the ordained, and the "real" presence of Christ will be seen as coming through the duly authorized.

Jerry Cook, a pastor in British Columbia, tells the story of hearing through the church grapevine of a woman in the congregation he served who was upset with him because she had been in the hospital seven days and he had not found time to visit her. After she returned to her home from the hospital, he decided to give her a phone call. But before the call was made, he did some investigation and found out that she had been visited by an average of four people a day for the seven days she was in the hospital. The phone conversation went something like this:

Pastor Cook: "Well, Mrs. White, how are you feeling?"

Mrs. White replied curtly, "Well, I'm fine *now*."

Ignoring the sharp tone, Pastor Cook said, "I understand you have been in the hospital."

"Well, it's a little late."

Playing dumb, Pastor Cook responded, "A little late for what?"

"I was there for seven days and nobody came."

Pastor Cook informed her that he was aware that she had many visitors during that time. Then she revealed her true convictions: "Yes, people from the church came, but *you* did not come."[8]

What is the tragedy of this story? Was it that the pastor had failed to do his job? Hardly. He and others had created a ministry context wherein Mrs. White was well taken care of. People were mobilized for ministry. The tragedy is that she missed the real presence of Christ in them and failed to receive authentic ministry because for her, only the pastor could deliver "real" ministry. All those other people could not measure up to the pastor, for the pastor was viewed as someone special who bears the presence of Christ. The authentic ministry of the people of God could not be affirmed as of equal value because the pastor held an elevated position.

Unless we shift the priestly function from an elite core to the entire body of believers, the ministry cannot be returned to the people of God. Nowhere does the New Testament identify a group of gifted people who have a greater capacity to mediate the presence of Christ. The focus is on a sacramental people, not a sacramental pastor.

To illustrate this biblically, let us walk through an Old and New Testament survey of the dwelling place of God. Where does the holiness of God reside? By tracing the imagery of tabernacle and temple through the Scriptures, we will see that the temple in whom God dwells is the whole people of God.

Coincidental with the Mosaic covenant, God instructed Moses to build a tabernacle in the wilderness. What was the primary purpose of this movable worship center? It was a visible, sacramental symbol that God was abiding with his people: "And have them make me a sanctuary, so that I may dwell among them" (Ex. 25:8). Howard Snyder demonstrates in *The Problem of Wineskins* that this portable worship center, transported during the wilderness wanderings, was meant to be a permanent image: God's people are a pilgrim people. We are always to consider ourselves aliens and strangers in a foreign land. As the hymn says, "This world is not my home, I'm just a-passin' through."

The movable tabernacle was replaced by the permanent, immovable temple in Jerusalem. The request to build a temple first came from King David, though God had never sought an ornate permanent dwelling place (2 Sam. 7:5–7). The Lord agreed to the request much as he did to Israel's pleas to have a king. He assured David that his throne would be established forever, though David's son Solomon would be the one to build the temple. As this magnificent edifice was being constructed, the Lord promised Solomon that the temple would also represent his dwelling place among his people: "I will dwell among the children of Israel, and will not forsake my people Israel" (1 Kings 6:13). At the dedication ceremony of the temple, the Lord took up occupancy: "And when the priests came out of the holy place, a cloud filled the house of the LORD, so that the priests could not stand to minister because of the cloud; for the glory of the LORD filled the house of the LORD" (1 Kings 8:10–11). Under the old covenant, God was represented as dwelling among his people in the tabernacle and the temple.

The completion of the old covenant occurs in the coming of the One whom the old covenant anticipated. It is no wonder that Jesus is portrayed as the temple in whom God now dwells. The cult of Israel is the foreshadowing of the One who was to come. So the apostle John, referring to Jesus, writes, "And the Word became flesh and lived among us, and we have seen his glory, the glory as of a father's only son" (John 1:14).

Lest we miss John's intent, the word "lived" could be translated as "tabernacled" or "pitched his tent." In John's day this word had come to mean "settling down permanently in a place." That John meant us to understand Jesus as the fulfillment and embodiment of the Old Testament dwelling place of God is evidenced by his associating Jesus with the "glory" of the Father. The *shekinah* (glory) in whose presence neither Moses (Ex. 40:34–35) nor the priests (1 Kings 8:10–11) could abide is now resting on and dwelling in the only Son of the Father. Where does God now dwell among his people? In none other than the incarnate God—Jesus Christ.

Jesus underscores this truth in referring to his body as the temple that would be destroyed and in three days raised up (John 2:19–21). The place of the dwelling of the glory of God is the flesh of Jesus. The transitory tabernacle and temple are now fulfilled and superseded in the Word-made-flesh.

But where does Jesus dwell now? Where should we seek the presence of the Incarnate One who reigns at the right hand of God? Where does his sacramental presence reside? Jesus informed us that he would come to us in the form of the Holy Spirit: "And I will ask the Father, and he will give you another Advocate, to be with you forever. . . . You know him, because he abides with you, and he *will be in you*" (John 14:16–17). The Holy Spirit, the Spirit of Christ, will be the replacement for Christ and the one whose sole desire is to point to and give glory to Christ (John 16:14). Where does God now reside? Paul answers: "Do you not know that you are God's temple and that God's Spirit dwells in you?" (1 Cor. 3:16). God resides in his sacramental people, the church.

In chapter 1, I noted that Paul's favorite image for the church is the body of Christ. His second favorite image is a building. But Paul cannot think of a building simply in terms of an inanimate structure. He often fuses his understanding of the church as that life-animated body in whom Christ dwells with his image of building and comes up with the mixed metaphor of a "living building." Observe this mixture in Paul's pronouncement on the church as a new humanity: "So then you [Gentiles] are no longer strangers and aliens, but you are citizens with the saints and also members of the *household* of God, *built* upon the *foundation* of the apostles and prophets, with Christ Jesus himself as the *cornerstone*. In him the whole *structure* is *joined* together and *grows* into a holy [sacramental] *temple* in the Lord; in whom you also are *built* together spiritually into a *dwelling place* for God" (Eph. 2:19–22).

We have robbed the church of its power by identifying sacramental presence with a few! Nowhere in the Bible can a priesthood within a priesthood be defended. The holy presence of Christ is in his whole body. Each one in whom Christ dwells is a channel through whom he mediates his presence. To lift up a few is to denigrate the whole. Each person bears a charism of God's action, and all together make up the dwelling place of God.

COMMUNITY MEAL, NOT CLERGY MEAL

The last element in the one people/one ministry motif strikes at the most sacred stronghold of pastoral self-interest. Who has the right to preside at the Lord's Supper? It is my contention that the single greatest reinforcer of the pastor as priest is the exclusive right of the ordained to preside over the distribution of the elements of Communion. There is nothing that solidifies more in the minds of the people of God the priestly quality of the pastor than the sole right of the ordained to officiate at the table.

The visual image impressed on the consciousness of God's people gathered for worship is the pastor as priest, similar to the role that the priest played in offering sacrifice on behalf of the people under the old covenant. The communion table standing between the pastor and people represents the altar of sacrifice. The elements of bread and wine are the gifts of sacrifice broken and poured out upon the sacred table. The minister plays the role of the consecrated priest who alone has been set apart to this sacred role.

Thomas Torrance links ordination with the act of self-consecration, of presiding at the communion table:

> Those ordained are to be regarded as drawn in a special way within the sphere of Christ's self-consecration so that they can minister the word to others in His name. It is in this connection then that we have to see the relation of ordination to participation in the Lord's Supper, and see the Lord's Supper as the New Testament counterpart in which Aaron and his son participated at their consecration, a meal of thanksgiving and praise.[9]

The rites of ordination are not complete, according to Torrance, until the one who is ordained handles and dispenses the elements for the first time: "For it was when the gifts of bread and wine were put into his hands that the Lord Himself fulfilled this act of consecrating His servants to His ministry, as He consecrated the apostle-disciples at the Last Supper."[10] Torrance is influenced more by the Old Testament understanding of priesthood than by the New Testament conception of pastor. I would assert that any tradition that reserves the serving of Communion to the ordained is more akin to Aaronic priesthood than to the priesthood of all believers.

In many traditions, especially Reformed, the elements of Communion cannot be served unless an ordained pastor is present. We speak of ordination to the "Ministry of the Word *and* Sacraments." It is assumed that the sacred trust of ordination is to protect the mystery of the Word made visible in the sacraments. Part of the stewardship of a pastor's call is to protect this sacred meal from abuse and to make sure it is rightly administered. The fear that Communion can be taken casually without proper reverence, or abused by subgroups in the church that may operate as a church unto themselves, has historical warrant. There is a legitimate concern that there be proper order to protect this means of grace.

Restricting the serving of Communion to the ordained is an unfortunate way to solve a problem of order. Though John Stott believes the administration of the Word and sacraments should be reserved to the clergy, he makes it clear that this is a matter of church order, not doctrine.[11] In other words, there is nothing inherent in the call of pastors that gives them exclusive right to serve Communion. Giving pastors this right is a matter of expediency, not call.

It is noteworthy that nowhere in the New Testament is a special group set apart to protect and administer the sacraments. Leadership is not given an exclusive role in liturgy or worship. This is especially surprising since Paul had to correct the Corinthian church's abuse of Communion. The Corinthians had not discerned the mystery of the unity of the body of Christ implicit in the elements of bread and wine. When they came together to observe this meal, they displayed a horrendous party spirit, the rich lording it over the poor. In some of the harshest language in the New Testament, Paul warns the Corinthians that abuse of the sacred meal brings judgment on themselves (1 Cor. 11:29).

How does Paul propose to solve this problem? Does he offer an institutional remedy? Does he lay down laws or rules to be followed? Does he establish a group in the church to supervise the meal? That he does none of these is curious, since the discussion of the Lord's Table (chap. 11) is immediately followed by an exposition of spiritual gifts (chap. 12). Nowhere does Paul mention a charism given to persons having a special call to serve this meal.

The Lord's Supper is a community meal, and Paul expects the community to act consistent with the sacrificial death of Jesus displayed in these elements as the purchase price of the new community. To put the meal into the hands of a few would destroy the community sense that all participate in the sacrifice of Christ. James Dunn writes,

> If we accept that presiding at the Eucharist is not a charism (gift) distinct from the rest, that God's Spirit brings grace to expression through all believers, then we should insist as a fundamental theological expression of the body of Christ that *conduct of holy communion must not be confined to a particular group within the diverse ministries of the community of faith.* . . . [T]his single step of allowing the sacrament of the Lord's Supper once again to be the natural expression of fellowship wherever groups of believers come together, even when "the minister" is not present, could be one of the liberating steps in renewal and growth.[12]

The sails that will catch the wind of the Spirit will be fashioned from the cloth of organism ministry, gifted and sacramental people, and a community meal. While issuing the challenge of one people/one ministry, we have called into question the priestly overtones connected to pastors. If you are a pastor, you might well be asking, "What is left for me? What am I to do? You have taken it all away." In the next section we will examine the changes needed in the role for pastors if the ministry is to be returned to the people of God.

NOTES

1. Robert Munger, "Training the Laity for Ministry," *Theology News and Notes* (June 1973): 3.

2. John R. W. Stott, *One People* (Downers Grove, Ill.: InterVarsity Press, 1968), 19.

3. Casey Miller and Kate Swift, *Words and Women: New Language for New Times* (New York: Anchor, 1976), iii.

4. Alma Graham in Miller and Swift, *Words and Women,* 32. (A = Clergy = ministry; B = Laity = lay ministry)

5. Howard Snyder, *The Problem of Wineskins* (Downers Grove, Ill.: InterVarsity Press, 1975), 81.

6. Ibid., 83.

7. R. Paul Stevens, *Liberating the Laity: Equipping All the Saints for Ministry* (Downers Grove, Ill.: InterVarsity Press, 1985), 37.

8. Jerry Cook, *Love, Acceptance, and Forgiveness* (Glendale, Calif.: Regal Books, 1979), 102.

9. Thomas Torrance, in *Theological Foundations for Ministry,* ed. Ray S. Anderson (Grand Rapids: Eerdmans, 1979), 426, 419.

10. Ibid., 420.

11. Stott, *One People,* 42.

12. James D. G. Dunn, "Ministry and the Ministry: The Charismatic Renewal's Challenge to Traditional Ecclesiology" (Unpublished paper), 26.

Part 2

THE PASTOR IN THE NEW REFORMATION

Chapter 5

Dependency: A Counterproductive Model of Ministry

N THE PREVIOUS CHAPTER I identified four shifts that are necessary if the ministry is to be returned to the people of God. All of these shifts can be summarized in one sentence: *We need to move from a pastor-centered to a people-centered ministry.*

In Part I, our theological reflections were rooted in the juxtaposition of the church as organism versus the church as institution. In Part II we will examine the critical role of pastor in an every-member ministry. In this section our discussion will be centered in the contrast between a dependency versus an equipping model of pastoral leadership. An institutional understanding of the church leads directly to a dependency model of ministry, whereas an organism understanding of the church leads directly to an equipping model of ministry.

The paradigm of the dependency model is best viewed through the lens of interlocking expectations. Three questions are before us: (1) What are a pastor's self-expectations in the dependency model? (2) What are the people's expectations of the pastor in the dependency model? (3) What are the people's expectations of themselves in a dependency model? Paradigms are rooted in unspoken yet mutually assumed expectations. Expectations are the unquestioned and often unseen assumptions.

Joel Barker, in his book *Future Edge: Discovering the New Para-digms of Success,* has the best working definition of a paradigm that I have seen: "A paradigm is a set of rules and regulations (written or unwritten) that does two things: (1) It establishes or defines bound-aries; and (2) it tells you how to behave inside the boundaries in order to be successful."[1] The word *paradigm* comes from the Greek *paradeigma,* meaning "pattern." The dictionary defines a paradigm as rules, models, or patterns, which in fact interpret or set our view of reality. It is the set of glasses through which we view things. Par-adigms give structure, meaning, and predictability to our actions. The concept of paradigm turns the scientific dictum "seeing is believing" on its head. It is equally true that "believing is seeing." Our belief structure determines the parameters of what we see. Par-adigms are like blinders on a horse. Your field of vision is estab-lished by the limitations of your paradigm.

The problem with paradigms is that they are so second nature that we don't see our own. Paradigms are like water to fish. Fish can't imagine existing in any other medium. Water is just there. A paradigm is the basic way of perceiving, thinking, valuing, and doing associated with a particular vision of reality. It is so second nature that it is rarely questioned; and if it is questioned, the ques-tioner is considered a maverick or a "paradigm buster."

The burden of this chapter is to bring to consciousness the unexamined elements of the dependency model paradigm that have been firmly rooted in the institutional church. Only as we see what has been and how counterproductive it is to an every-member min-istry, can we set about to intentionally shift the paradigm. Working with Barker's definition of a paradigm, a paradigm *shift* establishes a new set of rules and regulations, which will reestablish the bound-aries and tell how to be successful within those boundaries.

Let's use worship as a way to understand paradigm. As I briefly mentioned in the introduction, when I arrived at the last church I served as pastor, unbeknownst to me there were at least three wor-ship rules and regulations in place that defined the boundaries and whether I would be successful in leading worship. The three rules were (1) never go over an hour; (2) keep the Doxology, Lord's Prayer, and Gloria Patri in exactly the same place every Sunday; (3) and never do anything in the worship service that you can't control. These rules were "known" to the value holders of the congregation, but unknown to me. The response was predictable when I violated the "unwritten" rules. The worship services I designed lasted 70 minutes instead of 60; the three elements mentioned were moved around and sometimes not even included; and the capper was the morning I took the microphone into the congregation for some "spontaneous" sharing of praises. Of course, that particular morning one of the least healthy members of the congregation grabbed the microphone from my hand and went off on an unintelligible rant. I got letters and reprimands from those who knew the rules. I had unwittingly introduced a paradigm shift.

As a case study for the dependency model, I will use Jethro's advice to Moses to change his leadership posture (Exodus 18) as the biblical frame to explore the questions identified above. Let's set the scene. Moses has been leading the people of Israel on an excursion through the wilderness after their dramatic escape following four hundred years of captivity in Egypt. The events that followed the Israelites' mass exodus were unrelenting in intensity. In Exodus 14 Pharaoh and his army bore down upon the Hebrews, who were backed up to the Red Sea with seemingly no route to escape. As the people cowered in fear, Moses stood to declare their salvation. The waters parted, and the people fled to the other side, while the same waters closed in upon the pursuing enemy. In Exodus 16 the people rose against their leaders because they were convinced that Moses had simply brought them to this barren land to die. God provided manna and quail daily (except on the Sabbath) to satisfy their hunger. In Exodus 17 they were convinced that thirst would be their undoing. This time the Lord brought forth water from a rock. As if this were not enough of a trial, the Amalekites mounted an offensive against this apparently defenseless band. Joshua lead the Lord's army while Moses oversaw the victorious battle from a nearby hill.

Finally, at Exodus 18 there is respite from the unrelenting intensity of bad news. Jethro, Moses' father-in-law, arrives with Moses' wife and two sons. Moses greets Jethro with the respect due to an elder in Oriental style. After bowing in obeisance before Jethro, Moses recounts all that the Lord has done for the people of Israel. This brings a response of delight from Jethro, who is now convinced that the God of the Israelites is greater than all the gods.

The next day Moses assumes the position of judge over the people (Ex. 18:13). One gets the impression that there have been accumulated disputes among the people that are unresolved. Any time this number of people is on an extended nomadic camping trip, one could expect that some complaints against each other would arise. When Moses hangs out his shingle in front of his tent, declaring court to be in session, a line immediately forms as far as the eye can see. Moses is positioned to hear each complaint and render a decision. All along, Jethro is observing the role that Moses has positioned himself to play. His questions and observations will serve as the means for helping us explore the interlocking expectations between pastor and people in the dependency model of ministry.

WHAT ARE A PASTOR'S SELF-EXPECTATIONS IN THE DEPENDENCY MODEL?

Jethro is not impressed with the way Moses chooses to exercise his leadership. "When Moses' father-in-law saw all that he was doing for the people, he said, 'What is this that you are doing for the people? Why do you sit alone, while all these people stand around you from morning till evening?'" (Ex. 18:14). Jethro veils his criticism in the form of questions: Moses, who do you think you are? Are you the only one who can perform the function of judge? Moses' self-expectation was that he was the only one qualified to act as judge over the people. He was the focal point and bottleneck. Everyone had to wait in line, so that case after case was presented for his resolution.

This vignette serves as a window into the dependency model of ministry that is firmly in place in the minds of most pastors and congregations. What is this model? *Pastors do the ministry, while the people are the grateful (or not so grateful) recipients of their professional care.* Pastors are viewed as experts in all things spiritual, while God's people see themselves on the receiving end of the pastor's ministry.

Three images or metaphors explain and reinforce the dependency model: the caretaker model, the medical model, and the unhealthy family system.

Caretaker Model

The pastor gives care and the people receive care. The experts take care of the unqualified. Caregiver has been a major part of the definition of the role of pastor under the institutional model of church. The unspoken emotional contract between pastor and people is that when something goes wrong in a parishioner's life, it is the job of the pastor to be there to bring the appropriate comfort in time of need. This was reinforced for me when I was speaking at a Methodist pastor's conference on the very topic of this book. Almost to a person, every pastor was linked to either a cell phone or beeper, ready to respond to the beck and call of a member of his or her congregation when a need was known. These pastors defined themselves as caretakers. To be a good shepherd of the flock was equated with reacting to quality-of-life-threatening interruptions in people's lives.

Medical Model

Just as we go to a doctor to get the diagnosis and prescription for the care of our physical health, so we go to a pastor for the diagnosis and prescription for spiritual matters. Pastors are considered the doctors of the spiritual realm.

Unhealthy Family System

But it is even more accurate and prophetic to compare the dependency model of ministry to an unhealthy family system. In the healthy family, the goal of parents is to grow children into responsible, self-initiating, caring, and serving adults. The church, on the other hand, has more often than not viewed the role of pastor as parent and the people of God as dependent children who need to be constantly cared for. As a result, the children remain perpetually children.

What would we think of parents who kept their children at home under their thumb well into their twenties and beyond? A number of years ago my wife and I led a summer mission team to a poor, rural southern community. Among the six of us on the team was a delightful woman I will call Jean. Jean made an immediate impression because of her enormous size. By any standard she was grossly overweight. During our eight weeks together we shared rather close quarters, which afforded opportunities for intimate conversation.

As we got to know Jean, she began to trust us with the story that revealed the roots of her enormous size. In her late elementary and early junior high years, Jean's mother packed her lunch. The daily fare consisted of seven or eight sandwiches among other things. Our team's reaction to her mother's "generosity" was the same as what is going through your head right now. Why? What would motivate a parent to so overfeed her child? Now in her early twenties, Jean was starting to get a handle on the emotional sickness that was controlling her mother's behavior. Jean's take on the situation was that her mother was so abused by her father that she transferred the meeting of her emotional needs to Jean. Her mother's greatest fear was that Jean would one day grow up and leave home. This would mean she would be left alone with Jean's father. In order to ensure that Jean would remain at home, her mother conspired against any eventual suitors. If Jean was so overweight and unattractive, who would be interested in her?

The pathology of this dysfunctional relationship is sadly obvious and repulsive. What may not be so obvious is this story's connection to a dysfunctional model of ministry. I believe Jean's painful struggle to grow out from under the crushing influence of her mother is a parable of the church. It is my conviction that the church of Jesus Christ has suffered under an equally sick model of ministry that has resulted in God's people becoming perpetual children, not able to grow up to their full stature as ministers of Jesus Christ. We have been trapped in the shackles of an interlocking set of expectations between pastor and people. There has been a conspiracy of dependency that has been entered into by pastor and people alike, and this has been equally unhealthy for both.

Moses saw himself at the center of all things. All roads led to his tent. All decisions ran through his office. He was the only one qualified. Just so, pastors have self-expectations that reinforce this dependency model of ministry. Pastors are locked into a role that fosters dependency because there are personal expectations for the role that have become integral to their identity. What are some of the self-expectations that buttress a dependency model of ministry?

Omnicompetence: "I must be good at everything."

John Stott uses the word "omnicompetence" to describe the pressure many pastors place on themselves. The variety of roles at which pastors are to be equally good can be overwhelming. Within a matter of moments in a typical day, a pastor may be called to exercise vastly different skills with expert ease.

A pastor is in her study attempting in scholarly fashion to call forth the nuances of the biblical text in preparation for a sermon. Her secretary buzzes on the intercom: "Pastor, there is a man here with his son. They look deeply disturbed, and are in tears. Can you see them?" From the introspective task of study, the pastor attempts to come out of herself in order to make sense of a critical moment in these two lives. After the counseling session is concluded, the secretary reminds her that a decision still needs to be made as to which bulletin cover to order for the special Sundays of the year.

At noon it is time for the pastor's weekly discipling time with two businessmen who are key leaders in the church. She shifts gears to get her mind into their world and onto the relevant biblical subject matter for the day. When she returns from lunch, the women's association asks her to stop by and see the items being created for the fund-raising bazaar. Into the rest of the afternoon she must fit in a trip to the hospital to console a dear member before major surgery before she keeps a premarital counseling appointment.

After a brief time at home with her family at dinner, the pastor will attend a special finance committee meeting, called because the current receipts are lagging behind the budget projections. In the space of one day the pastor has been called to be scholar, reconciler, organizational decision maker, discipler, pastoral showpiece, comforter, counselor, and expert fund-raiser.

The problem is compounded for average two-talent pastors when they compare themselves with the five-talent superstars in "megachurches" who seem to operate well-oiled machines. These "megachurch" pastors appear to be equally comfortable as the master of ceremonies in public worship and as the chief executive officer during the week. Ordinary pastors feel the pressure to be as gifted in the multiple demands of their position. In an attempt to become "omnicompetent," pastors become "seminar junkies," pursuing the latest "how to," such as being a multistaff leader, church planter, time manager, premarital counselor, visionary, and so on. Since the pastors do the ministry, the many facets of ministry must be a part of their portfolio so their church can "count itself fortunate."

Distrust/Control: "I am the paid professional."

I previously quoted Robert Munger as saying that perhaps the greatest single bottleneck to renewal is "the hesitancy of clergy to trust the laity with significant responsibility." "Significant responsibility" usually refers to those duties that have been traditionally connected with the priestly functions of pastors. In other words, pastors are reluctant to entrust the laity with the spiritual welfare of people's lives. As the trained professionals, pastors are the only ones qualified to counsel, teach (adults, not children), visit in the hospitals, or even lead someone to Christ. Though we are seeing many good signs that the New Reformation is taking hold in various places, this complaint from a parishioner is still true: "Too often our pastors seem to treat us only as fund-raisers (pastors don't want to be too closely associated with filthy lucre) or cooks or office equipment operators . . . when our hearts are crying out for a meaningful ministry."[2]

The flip side of distrust is control. At recent speaking events, I have had several conversations that center around a common complaint. Each of these people had been hired to fill an increasingly popular staff position as directors of lay ministry. Once they assumed their role, they realized that the senior pastors had control problems. They tended to see the purpose of this new position as simply for volunteer recruitment. The directors of lay ministry viewed themselves as fostering a permission-giving atmosphere rooted in an understanding of the church as a ministering body of Christ. They were frustrated because the pastors feared losing their pinnacles role if the ministry of the body were decentralized.

Control is about holding onto power and making sure you get your way. How does control manifest itself? One pastor told me he could have only two home Bible studies in his congregation. When I asked why, he said, "Because that's all I have time to lead." I knew a pastor who would not allow a committee to meet in the church without his presence. Another pastor had an uncanny ability to know what was going on in the life of the community, even though it was a fairly large congregation.

We all have our control mechanisms that can undermine our stated desire to trust people with ministry. The way I tend to get what I want is to come to meetings better prepared than anyone else. If I come with my plans complete and my arguments lined up, then I have a better chance of controlling the outcome. The trouble with that approach is that I get no broad ownership, and most of the responsibility for implementation lands in my lap. What is your control mechanism?

This lack of entrusting to God's people both responsibility and authority for authentic ministry betrays the priestly view of the pastoral role. Pastors—perhaps unconsciously—have accepted the view that God's presence is borne by them to a higher degree, so by implication others cannot be full channels of God's activity. Pastors' distrust and control becomes an obstacle to equipping those who may be more gifted than they are to carry out certain aspects of ministry. For how can the professional trust the untrained with people's lives? If you want it done right, you must do it yourself.

Need to Be Needed: "Someone needs me."

Pastors generally go into professional ministry because of their love for people. They are warm, relational beings who are attracted to the role of caring for the flock. One of the psychological profiles suggested for those who become pastors is they have a "need to help people." There is nothing wrong with that unless this becomes an inordinate need to please people. There is a very fine line between helping and being hooked on pleasing. Before you know it, you are addicted to comments like "Thanks for being there, Pastor. I don't think I could have gotten through that [name the situation] without your being there." Or "Pastor, that was the best message I have ever heard on that subject." Before one is even aware, our spirits are fed by being the "savior" in people's lives.

I received the following note after visiting a seventy-five-year-old man in the hospital following his surgery. With tears Joe spoke deeply of the emotional and spiritual encounter with the Lord in preparation for his surgery and the peace he had received. This was truly an epiphany for which the congregation was willing to give me considerable credit.

Dear Greg,

Busy as you were, you came to visit Joe. We consider this a great blessing. Yes, many saints visited too, but still your visit meant the most!

Prayers were answered through the nurses, doctors, and you. Joe is doing well.

Enjoy your well-earned vacation.

> With our love,
> Joe and Evelyn
> (not their real names)

Wow, what an emotional hook! "Busy as you were." I brought a blessing. I am more important than the rest of the saints. Emphatically God answered my prayers. "Enjoy your well-earned vacation." Unbeknownst to them, these sincere and wonderful people were reinforcing my need to be needed and were feeding my emotional reward system. The emotional reward and identity of being a pastor is being the vehicle of Christ's presence in their lives.

Pastors begin to live off of the ego-satisfaction that comes with being "special" to the church community. To be fussed over and paid deference to at a church social function can be extremely ego-gratifying. How many times as a pastor have I made my way through the potluck line? With my plate in hand I go in search of my spot at a table. As I am ready to sit down, those already gathered look up, and invariably someone says, "Aren't we privileged? Please come join us." As a result, pastors get to the point where they believe in their own self-importance. When this occurs, a psychological corner has been turned toward a sick pursuit of affirmation. It is intoxicating to be perched on the pinnacle; to be the person atop the church pyramid.

A chief reason why the dependency model of ministry is still dominant is that many pastors' sense of worth and value is derived from being a benevolent lord reigning over the little fiefdom. From a psychological view, we would be appalled at parents who assert their authority by keeping their children dependent on them even though they are adults. Yet we do not evidence the same disgust at anemic churches made up of perennial spiritual children who are not allowed by their parent pastors to grow up. Underlying the dependency model of ministry is a distorted and unhealthy means of seeking value. Pastor and people are co-conspirators, denying the addiction and fostering the sickness.

To shift to an equipping model, pastors must change their emotional reward system. Instead of finding their fulfillment in their own doing of ministry, the satisfaction must come in assisting others to blossom to their ministry potential.

Motivated by Guilt: "What if people think I am lazy?"

It has been observed that pastors have as many bosses as there are members in the congregation. The unwritten job description in the minds of most pastors is the composite of the myriad voices of the people they serve, who freely express their expectation of pastors' responsibilities. As pastors we can begin with a sincere desire to serve people's needs but end up being slaves to people's varied expectations. The voices are rarely still. In sermon preparation we try to satisfy the person who states, "You are too scholarly," at the same time someone else is telling us, "I need more stories or application to life." We know the voices. A parishioner calls at 9:00 A.M., saying, "I hope I didn't wake you." Implicit in that comment is the idea that the pastor's life is not as strenuous as others.' It also indicates that the lifestyle of pastors is invisible to the people we serve, and therefore we must continuously be proving we are not lazy by attempting to cover all the bases.

Dependency model pastors, manipulated by guilt, tend to be reactors rather than initiators. Pastors are expected to respond to the urgent or needy. Being responders means allowing others' needs to set the agenda. As you examine your date book, do you find the names on your appointment calendar are people who have requested time, or are they ones you have sought out because of your agenda to develop ministry? I suspect that most pastors allow their agenda to be set for them, which means spending considerable time with those who are problem-focused and therefore inherently draining. An inordinate amount of time is spent with emotionally dependent people, and minimal attention is given to stronger, more mature believers who could be motivated and trained to minister to the care needs that take so much of a pastor's time. As long as pastors are available to all comers rather than strategically using their time to build up and deploy people in ministry, the body will remain dependent.

The dependency model remains the dominant pattern because pastoral self-expectations foster it. I have attempted to peer into the mind-set and perhaps unconscious assumptions that control pastors' stance vis-à-vis congregations. This is where the battle is fought. Paul admonishes us to be "transformed by the renewing of your minds" (Rom. 12:2) because our minds contain our perception of reality, the worldview through which we see things. The New Reformation is a spiritual battle bent on replacing our old thinking patterns, which have crippled the church, with a new set of pastoral expectations that can empower God's people for ministry.

WHAT ARE THE PEOPLE'S EXPECTATIONS OF THE PASTOR IN THE DEPENDENCY MODEL?

As we continue our exploration of the interlocking expectation between pastor and people that reinforce the dependency model paradigm, let's rejoin the dialogue between Jethro and Moses. Jethro has questioned the leadership role that his son-in-law has chosen for himself. "Why do you sit alone?" he questions Moses (Ex. 18:14). Moses offers his justification: "Because the people come to me to inquire of God. When they have a dispute, they come to me and I decide between one person and another, and I make known to them the statutes and instructions of God" (Ex. 18:15). In essence, Moses' rationalization was that he was just meeting the people's expectations: This is the role they see me playing, and I don't want to disappoint them. Moses had become a larger-than-life figure. He had become a giant in his own time—and perhaps a legend in his own mind.

This leads naturally to the question, what are the peoples' expectations of their pastors that reinforce the dependency model ministry? What does a traditional congregation want from its pastor?

The Multi-talented Pastor: "We count ourselves fortunate. Our pastor can do everything."

Churches want pastors they can be proud of and brag about. We want pastors who can do it all so that they *will* do it all. Many churches are in turmoil today because they have hired mere mortals to lead them.

This is exacerbated by our times. We live at a historical moment when the once-friendly and supportive church culture has given way to, at best, an ambiguous and, at worst, a hostile church environment. Relativism reigns in society. The church of Jesus Christ, which dares to declare that there is an immovable truth that God has revealed in the person of his Son, will increasingly face the wrath of the god of Maximum Choice. The roles for pastor that were formed and honed under the Christendom model no longer work in our day. The church in friendly culture was essentially a maintenance institution that passed on the faith intact from one generation to another. Today we must turn the church paradigm inside out and move from maintenance to mission. This means that the roles of pastors must change to lead this charge. Any time there is shift in ministry model, there will be a commensurate shift in role expectations, which will lead to role confusion as the paradigms of church are changing.

This desire for a pastor who can do it all especially surfaces at the time when a church is searching for a new pastor. It has been often observed that Jesus himself could not fulfill the expectations that come with the composite of the ideal pastoral candidate. As a way of debunking these unrealistic expectations, I propose that we simplify the pastoral search process and substitute this anonymous chain letter instead.

Dear Church Member,

This chain letter is meant to bring happiness to you. Unlike other chain letters, it does not cost money. Simply send a copy of this letter to six other churches who are tired of their pastors. Then bundle up your pastor and send him to the church at the bottom of the list. In one week you will receive 16,436 pastors and one of them should be a dandy! Have faith in this letter. One church broke the chain and got their old pastor back.

As outrageous as this sounds, this is a way of making light of our search for the pastor who can do it all. Why are we in a constant search for the pastor who can be the magic bullet? When a winsome, charismatic figure is our leader, we can live off his or her energy. There is a transference of value. We feel good about ourselves because we are attracted to a representative and figurehead who embodies a corporate personality. This in turn places little personal responsibility on the body, and therefore a minimum of personal initiative is required. The leader covers the bases for us. The role of the congregational member is to be an enthusiastic supporter through verbal adulation and financial contributions. Though a crowd may have been attracted, still relatively few have been transformed into full ministers of Christ. The do-it-all pastor will never yield an every-member ministry.

The Christ Bearer: "Only the Pastor can deliver real ministry"

If pastors bear the presence of Christ in a way that an ordinary believer cannot, then the ministry of the members of the body will be disparaged and not fully received. In the last chapter I told the story of Mrs. White who was upset because Pastor Cook had failed to visit her while she was in the hospital. She failed to see the visit of fellow members of the congregation as ministry because her paradigm only allowed the pastor to deliver real ministry.

Any time we expect the pastor to be a priest in the Old Testament sense of one set apart to be the chosen vehicle through whom God especially works, then we have fallen back into the pastor-as-Christ-bearer motif. To the extent that the pastors' prayers are more efficacious, or the pastor is the only one through whom the word can be truly proclaimed, or the pastor is singularly qualified in the people's minds to hold the elements of Communion, or the pastor is the one whose presence sanctifies an occasion, then we believe that the pastor is a Christ bearer beyond the ordinary "saints."

I encounter this attitude frequently. Integral to my implementation of equipping ministry is a discipling network that is meant to multiply from one generation to another as it spreads organically throughout the congregation. But since I have had the vision and more experience than others, I am viewed by many as the chief discipler. I am the resident expert. To be invited into a discipling relationship by me is seen by others as an honor because I know how to do it "right." I have yet to be turned down. But as the intergenerational discipling chain moves away from me into the second and third generations, the luster fades; it is not considered to be as high an honor to be discipled by an average church member. Some who have been invited by others have even intimated that they are waiting for an available slot in my discipling schedule.

To the extent that we view the pastor as a bearer of the presence of Christ to a greater extent than can ever be true of the people of God, the dependency model is firmly in place.

The Inspirational Bandage: "Give me something inspirational to get through another week."

Donald Smith suggests that the people of God and the pastor often have differing perspectives about the aim of worship.[3] God's people come to worship as a way to escape from the troubles of everyday life. Worship is a moment of quiet, an island of tranquillity in the tumultuous and demanding sea of life. By contrast, an equipping pastor with a sense of mission views worship as the time to confront the hard realities of a broken world; he or she sees God's people as agents of reconciliation. The sermon is the means of outfitting the saints with substantive biblical content so that there is enough ammunition to wage war against a world under the domination of the Evil One.

Frequently what the *laos* want is an inspirational Band-Aid that can be applied to the bumps and bruises of life. A spine-tingling message that will get people through another week is sufficient. Worship is one time when some ray of hope can break through the gloom of sagging spirits. At heart, people want to leave worship with a good feeling. Therefore the pastor should embody optimism and an upbeat attitude.

The Church as Possession: "I go to Pastor Ogden's church."

So accepted is the dependency model in the consciousness of most people that we do not think it strange to speak of the church in the possessive. The language of God's people is peppered with "that's Pastor So-and-So's church." Pastors are also heard to say "my church" instead of "the church I serve." That is a small thing, you say. But I assert again that our language is evidence of how thoroughly debilitating the identification of the church with its leadership can be. The pastor is not the possessor of the church, but one called to give his life away so that the ministry of God's people may thrive.

There is an interesting reverse twist on the pastor as the possessor of the church: there is also a sense in which people like to possess the pastor. People speak of "having a pastor" in the same way they "have a family doctor or an attorney." The pastor is part of the package connected to life insurance. The pastor will be available in time of need and will provide comfort and make all the proper arrangements when death occurs. To have a pastor we can call our own is all a part of making sure things are set in order. Frances called the church to inquire if her husband's name could be added to the membership roles without attending the membership classes. Frances was now well into her seventies and had recently remarried after the death of her first husband. She rarely attended the church, though she had served significantly, perhaps three decades ago. Her request to add her husband to the church rolls was simply a way of making sure that they were covered, if they needed to call on the church for services. She was getting her late-in-life ducks in order.

Even if pastors wanted to break out of this unhealthy system, many revert to the dependency model because there is too great a price to be paid for becoming an equipping pastor. The expectations of the people make pastors feel trapped. The last thing they want to have implied is that they are failing to live up to the in-place expectations. The path of least resistance is to succumb to the pressures of congregational wants rather than to go through the painful process of reeducation.

Moses did not want to disappoint the people. His stature had grown. The pressure to render wise decisions in the contingencies of life mounted. He had an image to preserve. Pastors feel the same pressure. They know that there is a standard in the minds of the people that they violate at great peril.

WHAT ARE THE PEOPLE'S EXPECTATIONS OF THEMSELVES IN THE DEPENDENCY MODEL?

Returning to the story of Jethro's advice to Moses, we see that Moses has just given his reason for acting alone as judge over the people: The people have come to see me as the answer man; I am just fulfilling their perceptions. Jethro sees disaster here not only for Moses but also for the people. His initial question hinted at the problem for the people: "Why do you sit alone, while all the people stand around you from morning until evening?" (Ex. 18:14). Jethro is unimpressed with Moses' justification, "What you are doing is not good. You will surely wear yourself out, both you and these people with you" (Ex. 18:17–18). What roles do the people have in this scenario? They stand in line. They passively wait until it is their turn to make their case before Moses and receive his wisdom.

What are the people's expectations of themselves in the dependency model? Not much. What roles do people play?

Critics or Spectators: "Evaluators of the Pastor's ministry"

The analogy has often been drawn between the way we play church and a football game. Bud Wilkinson, legendary former head coach at the University of Oklahoma, was asked, when he became head of the President's Council on Physical Fitness, "What contribution does professional football make to the fitness of Americans?" He answered, "A professional football game is a happening when 50,000 people desperately needing exercise sit in the stands watching 22 people desperately needing rest."

Sunday morning worship is like this. The sanctuary is filled with spectator critics who come with a reviewer's attitude. After preaching on a Sunday, I have often wondered if I should turn to the choir to get an instant rating on my sermon. I expect them to raise cards from their laps like we used to see judges hold up at an ice-skating competition. This morning's sermon is a 5.8 out of a possible 6. Worship is viewed as an event that we evaluate. As we greet the pastor at the door upon leaving the sanctuary, we must say something about the performance of the day: "Good sermon, Pastor." "That service really touched me." This indicates that we tend to see ourselves more as spectators than as active worshipers.

When people don't like what they see happening in a church, one of the means of protest is to withhold their giving. Why might this be the method of choice? My guess is that people feel powerless to influence the direction of the church toward their wishes, so one of the only avenues to express their power is through their money. Money talks. This indicates that people do not truly feel integrally a part of the church family and that its ministry has not become theirs. The dependency model creates a vast number of spectators who watch others do ministry and then pass judgment on how well they perceive they are doing it.

Resistant to Pastoral Approaches: "The Pastor always wants something"

Dr. Roberta Hestenes tells the story of a lunch appointment she had with one of the elders of the church when she was on its staff. She had invited him to lunch with the sole agenda of getting more fully acquainted. About forty-five minutes into an enjoyable conversation, the elder paused and said, "OK, what is it that you want?" Dr. Hestenes, somewhat taken aback, said, "What do you mean, what do I want?" The elder skeptically said, "I have never been taken to lunch by a pastor who did not want something. What is it that you want?" Dr. Hestenes assured him that the only thing on her mind was the desire to have a deeper connection with someone she did not know.

But this points out a potential mind-set that grows out of the dependency model. It is the pastor's job to recruit, and the people's job to resist. Ministry is what we pay the pastor's to do. People don't expect it of themselves.

Adjuncts to the Pastors: "Only because the pastors are too busy"

God's people often serve in ministries because the pastor is too busy to do it. Pastors need help. The underlying assumption is that if the pastor had bionic bodies and unlimited time, then they could do it all. Since they can't, they need help. The people of God don't have ministries or calls in their own right, but they minister under the *imprimatur* of the pastor. Pastors extend their authority to the one representing them.

Georgia Harkness cites a study of 12,000 Methodist laypersons in order to see what their view of a layperson was in the church.[4] Those surveyed were given four options:

Laity are. . .

- ◆ members of the people of God called to total ministry of witness and service in the world
- ◆ those who are ministered to by the clergy, who are the true church
- ◆ people in part-time Christian service
- ◆ nonordained Christians whose function is to help the clergy do the work of the church.

Of those surveyed, 59.9 percent chose the fourth option. Laity, according to this self-perception, are simply extensions of the pastor's ministry. The people of God do not see themselves as ministers in their own right, nor is doing ministry an expression of Christian discipleship in all spheres of life.

CONCLUSION

Admittedly, the characterizations in the dependency model just described may be somewhat extreme—even caricatures. Yet I believe the overall picture of a church as a dependent child with a sickly attachment to parental pastors is a sad but fair one. The church in general remains stunted, with only a small percentage of God's people having grown up with a view of themselves as authentic ministers. The dependency model fosters emotionally sick pastors who need a reliant church because there is a need to be needed. God's people are starved for responsible ministry but are unable to break free from the hierarchical model.

The dependency model is a ministry paradigm that has shaped our perception of reality. The roles of pastor and people have been in place for so long that we just assume that what is, is the way it is supposed to be.

A far healthier model views the pastor, not as the caretaker of those who can't fend for themselves, but as the equipper who encourages and provides a context to train all God's people for ministry. In the next chapter we will explore the biblical image of equipper as the fundamental posture of the pastor in relationship to God's people. Then in chapter 7, as a way of implementing a new equipping paradigm, we will return to the story of Jethro's advice to Moses to change his leadership role.

NOTES

1. Joel Barker, *Future Edge: Discovering the New Paradigms of Success* (New York: William Morrow, 1992), 32.

2. John R. W. Stott, *One People* (Downers Grove, Ill.: InterVarsity Press, 1968), 31.

3. Donald Smith, *Clergy in the Cross Fire* (Philadelphia: Westminster Press, 1974), 35.

4. Quoted in Paul Stevens, *The Other Six Days* (Grand Rapids: Eerdmans, 1999), 15, 16.

Chapter 6

A Biblical Vision of an Equipping Ministry

OVER THE LAST GENERATION AS the priesthood of all believers—the ministry of the whole people of God—has made a resurgence, it is quite common for pastors to quote Ephesians 4:11 and 12 in their résumés when describing the view of their role. Yet there appears to be a broad interpretation of what it means to "equip the saints for the work of ministry." Admittedly, there is no detailed description of the role of pastor in the New Testament. Because of this, expositors have chosen various biblical images to serve as their interpretative picture for how best to understand the role.

Some would say that an equipping pastor is primarily a *shepherd*. This can mean various things. To "shepherd" can mean anything from exercising spiritual oversight over a body of believers, to providing crisis care to bleating sheep, to acting as a spiritual parent over a church family. Others would stress that equippers are primarily *teachers* of the Word. It appears that the only role or task that Paul clearly identifies for those holding the position of pastor, elder, or bishop (seeing these as synonymous) is the ability to teach the Word and confound or refute false teaching (1 Tim. 3:2: "an apt teacher"; Titus 1:9: "He must have a firm grasp of the word that is trustworthy in accordance with the teaching"). Those who equate equipping with teaching often hold a reductionist position that says that all people need for growth to maturity in Christ is Scripture, truth, and doctrine. Fill people with biblical principles and all will take care of itself. Still others might view the role of the equipping pastor as *spiritual sage*. The pastor is a contemplative who communes with God and walks close to him so that he or she can act as a spiritual director to the congregation and speak from a wellspring of wisdom that comes from a life of communion with God.

Certainly all of these roles have something to contribute to an overall equipping ministry. Yet my concern is not so much the functions that pastors play as the end to which they are to exercise their ministry. For example, let's explore the following statement about the role of "Minister of the Word and Sacrament" from the *Book of Order* for the Presbyterian Church USA. Notice that the role of pastor is defined by the many things that a pastor is called upon to do. You might want to circle the verbs as you read this statement:

> The pastor is responsible for studying, teaching, and preaching the word, for administering Baptism and the Lord's Supper, for praying with and for the congregation. With the elders, the pastor is to encourage the people in their worship and service; to equip and enable them for their tasks within the Church and their mission to the world; to exercise pastoral care, devoting special attention to the poor, the sick, the troubled, and the dying; to participate in governing responsibilities, including leadership of the congregation in implementing the principles of participation and inclusiveness in the decision making of the church, and its task in reaching out in concern and service to the life of the human community as a whole."[1]

The question that screams for an answer in a statement like this is: To what end is all of this activity directed? What is it to accomplish? We do see that one of the activities is to "equip and enable them for their tasks within the Church and their mission to the world." This would indicate that equipping is one of the many things that a pastor is supposed to do.

I believe the closest thing to a job description that is given for the pastoral role is Ephesians 4:11–14 and that it defines the fundamental posture and purpose for pastoral ministry: "The gifts he gave were that some would be apostles, some prophets, some evangelists, and some pastors and teachers, *to equip the saints for the work of ministry,* for the building up of the body of Christ, until all of us come to the unity of the faith and of the knowledge of the Son of God, to maturity, to the measure of the full stature of Christ. We must no longer be children, tossed to and fro and blown about by every wind of doctrine, by people's trickery, by their craftiness in deceitful scheming." Paul appears to define equipping, not in terms of pastoral images or functions (as above), but in terms of results. In other words, equipping is a means to a greater end. Paul is concerned that an equipping ministry produce a certain product. We know that equipping is occurring if the saints are doing the work of ministry, the body of Christ is being built up, the whole body is attaining a unity of faith, and the community together is expressing the full stature of Christ. Or to put it negatively, equipping is happening if people are no longer children in the faith who are so impressionable that the latest "wind of doctrine" leads them astray.

Ray Stedman's pictorial diagram of Ephesians 4:11–12 (Figure 6.1) sets the purpose of the pastoral function incisively:[2]

Figure 6.1

The Goal of Equipping:
The Priesthood of All Believers
Ephesians 4:11–12

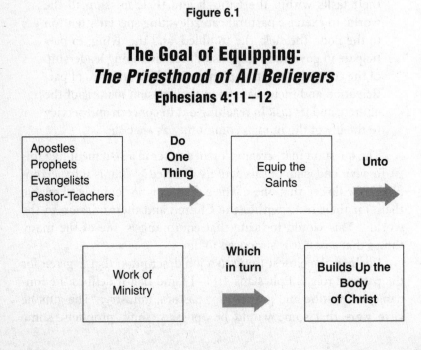

As figure 6.1 indicates, the "support" gifts (apostles, prophets, evangelists, pastor-teachers) do one thing: *equip the saints*. The Greek word for equip (*katartismos*) has drawn much interest and is a good place to begin our biblical survey. *Katartismos* is variously translated as "equip" (RSV), "perfect" (KJV), or "prepare" (NIV). An examination of how *katartismos* and its related family of words are used in Scripture will help us grasp the scope of equipping ministry and therefore the environment that equipping pastors are to cultivate in a local church.

The best summary of the role of equipping pastor I have seen was articulated a generation ago by a "layman," Elton Trueblood: "The ministry is for all who are called to share in Christ's life, *the pastorate is for those who possess the peculiar gift of being able to help other men and women to practice any ministry to which they are called.*"[3] The equipping pastor initiates the maturing of the body by assisting the people of God to practice the ministries to which they are called. In other words, equipping pastors deploy their gifts in such a way that the members of the body discover and are developed in accord with their God-ordained function in the church and world.

In this chapter I want to delve into the Greek word *katartismos* and its related family of words that has been at the center of equipping ministry. By doing some biblical reconnaissance in both the Old and New Testament, we will see the full-orbed nature of what an equipping ministry entails. This will move us beyond the limitations of seeing the role of pastor as simply shepherd, teacher, spiritual sage, and so forth. Before us will be a vision of a functional equipping environment and the many dimensions that must be addressed if the whole people of God are to become a ministering and maturing community in Christ. The secondary benefit for those of you "who possess the peculiar gift of being able to help other men and women practice any ministry to which they are called" is that you will be able to see where your heart and gifts tend to fall in the spectrum of equipping ministry. The New Testament vision of leadership is always plural, never singular. No one individual has all the gifts or heart to cover the whole territory of equipping ministry. Biblically, the title "solo pastor" is an oxymoron. We need a team of equippers who cover the totality of equipping if a balanced ministry is to emerge.

BIBLICAL OVERVIEW OF EQUIPPING

Biblical Terminology

1. *Artios*—The root of *katartismos* (Eph. 4:12), *artios,* can be translated as a predicate adjective ("he is *complete*"). *Artios* conveys the goal of equipping, either for an individual disciple or for the whole body of Christ. It covers a range of meanings: suitable, complete, filled out, operating appropriately, or meeting requirements. In 2 Timothy 3:17 Paul states that the intent of the God-breathed word is to present the person of God as *artios*—"complete" (RSV).

2. *Katartizō*—The various forms of the verb *katartizo* are by far the most common appearance of this word in the Septuagint and the New Testament. It is found nineteen times in the Greek translation of Old Testament and is the preferred word to translate no less than seven different Hebrew verbs. In the New Testament it is used thirteen times in a variety of contexts, as we shall see.

3. *Katartismos*—This well-known participle is used only in Ephesians 4:12.

4. *Katartisis*—In 2 Corinthians 13:9, Paul prays for the church's "improvement" (RSV), which can also be translated "restoration, completion," or "being put in proper order."

5. *Exartizō*—Used only once, in conjunction with the singular use of *artios* in 2 Timothy 3:17, this verb means that the Word of God is able to fill out, finish, complete, or equip.

A quick survey of the Old and New Testament will help us get a sense of the breadth of usage of *equip.*

Selected Old Testament Passages

As we explore the Old Testament terrain, we will note the wide variety of translations of *equip* and the images they invoke. During the celebration of Yahweh's triumph over the Egyptian army at the Red Sea, God's people are assured that the Lord will plant them on the holy mountain as their sure abode and *establish* a sanctuary by the Lord's hand at the same place (Ex. 15:17). Upon return from exile, Nehemiah found the walls of Jerusalem in disrepair; he received permission to *finish* the walls and repair the foundations (Ezra 4:12, 16; 5:3, 9, 11; 6:14). The Lord's glory is written into the wonders of the heavens and chanted by the mouths of babes. For those who don't acknowledge this glory, the Lord "has *founded* a bulwark" against his foes (Ps. 8:2). During a time of testing by his enemies, David claimed "my steps have *held fast* to your paths" (Ps. 17:5). The psalmist reviews the faithfulness of God from the Exodus on, and he describes the Lord as *restoring* the heritage of Israel by providing water in the wilderness (Ps. 68:9). Finally, the unshakable tone of the word *equip* is captured as God is said to have *established* the fixed courses of the moon, sun, and stars (Pss. 74:16; 89:37).

Selected New Testament Passages

The same breadth of meanings for *equip* can be found in the New Testament. When Jesus calls James and John to be disciples, they are *mending* their nets (Matt. 4:21; Mark 1:19). A disciple will be fully *taught* until he is like his teacher (Luke 6:40). God has *prepared beforehand* vessels that are the objects of his mercy (Rom. 9:23). Addressing the division at Corinth, Paul urges the congregation to "be *united* in the same mind" (1 Cor. 1:10). He prays for the *improvement* of the Corinthians and exhorts them to *mend* their ways (2 Cor. 13:9, 11). Christians are to intervene in the lives of those who have stumbled by *restoring* them in a spirit of gentleness (Gal. 6:1). Paul hopes to come to the Thessalonians to *supply* what is lacking in their faith (1 Thess. 3:10). Of Christ's incarnation, Hebrews 10:5 states that a body was *prepared* for him. By the word of God the world was *created* (Heb. 11:3). Christ is sufficient to *equip* us for every good work (Heb. 13:21) and to *establish* us in our faith after a trial (1 Peter 5:10).

How can we make sense of this variety? It appears that all the various ways that "equip" is used can be classified under three categories:

Mend/Restore
   Ezra 4:12, 16; 5:3, 9, 11; 6:14
   Psalm 68:9
   Matthew 4:21; Mark 1:19
   1 Corinthians 1:10; 13:9, 11
   Galatians 6:1
   1 Thessalonians 3:10

Establish/Lay Foundations
    Exodus 15:17
    Psalms 8:2; 17:5; 74:16; 89:37
    Luke 6:40
    Hebrews 11:3; 13:21
    1 Peter 5:10
Prepare/Train
    Romans 9:23
    Ephesians 4:12
    Hebrews 10:5

After surveying the contexts of the various forms of the word associated with "equipping," a complete picture of a full-orbed, well-balanced ministry of the body emerges. "Equip" conveys both a style of ministry and the content of that ministry.

To simplify what appears to be complex, we can depict the images of equipping as clustered around these three foci and all with the ultimate purpose of deploying the entire body for ministry.

Figure 6.2
An Equipping Ministry

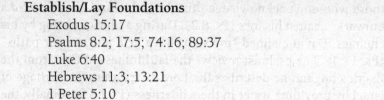

MEND/RESTORE

Figure 6.3

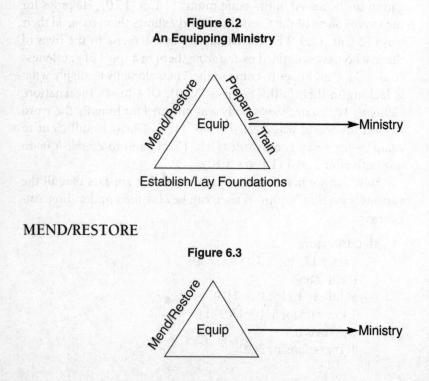

The image of mend/restore was part of common usage in the Greek society in the biblical era. It was used in a medical context. When a limb was broken or pulled out of joint, doctors *equipped* their ailing patients by putting it back into proper alignment. Thus, the secular meaning entails restoring what was broken and correcting what was out of place so that it can return to its original, intended function. Three different nuances relate to the mend/restore aspect of equipping: to fix what is broken, to bring back into proper alignment, and to supply what is lacking.

1. *To fix what is broken.* R. Paul Stevens says in his book *Liberating the Laity* that the equipper in the church is like a "stone mason." Six times in the book of Ezra (4:12, 16; 5:3, 9, 11; 6:14) the Septuagint uses the verb *katartizō* to mean "finish." Upon return from the Babylonian exile, Ezra and Nehemiah found their beloved city of Jerusalem in a state of ruin and disrepair. The walls that enclosed the city were marred by gaping holes. In some places stones were heaped in piles where the enemy had broken them down and left them to gather moss. Erected to provide protection against warring tribes and a sense of security for those who took refuge behind them, the walls were now dysfunctional. They needed to be repaired and "finished" in order to fulfill their purpose. So the fallen stones had to be laid back in place and new stones cut in order to fill in where there were no replacements. Before the walls could perform their intended function they needed to be equipped by someone *mending* and *restoring* them.

The New Testament captures the same nuance with a different image. Early in his public ministry, Jesus walked beside the Sea of Galilee and met future disciples hard at work as fishermen. The Scripture says that Jesus came upon James and John, the sons of Zebedee, "who were in their boat *mending* the nets" (Mark 1:19; see also Matt. 4:21). A fishing net is not much good with a hole in it. So before the net could be useful, it must be *equipped.* James and John were getting the net ready to return to action, to be restored to service. But they had to undo the damage before its utility could return.

2. *To bring back into proper alignment.* Psalm 68:9 states, "Rain in abundance, O God, you showered abroad; you *restored* your heritage when it languished." Referring to the Exodus experience of wandering in the wilderness, the covenant people were restored to

their heritage under the direct, protective care of Yahweh. For four hundred years they cried out under their Egyptian oppressors, feeling cut off and abandoned by the God of their fathers. As the Lord through Moses led them through the wilderness to the Promised Land, there was a sense that they had been realigned with their legacy. They were once more in the stream and flow of God's activity. He was working out his plan through a chosen people.

In Galatians 6:1 Paul uses the word *equip* in the sense of *bring back into proper alignment*: "Brethren, if anyone is overtaken in any trespass, you who are spiritual should *restore* him in a spirit of gentleness. Look to yourself lest you too be tempted" (RSV). Paul addresses our responsibility to those "overtaken" by trespass. The word "overtaken" suggests members of the body of Christ who have unknowingly and unwittingly violated a law of God and therefore put themselves out of proper alignment with both God and his church. What is our responsibility? "You who are spiritual are to *restore* him in a spirit of gentleness," writes Paul. The secular, medical image serves here as the appropriate backdrop for "restore." As a doctor would gently realign a broken bone or a limb that is out of joint, so we are to sensitively help a brother or sister be realigned with God and restored to fellowship in the body.

In 1 Corinthians 1:10 Paul confronts the party spirit that has torn apart the Corinthian fellowship. The people are polarized to the point where subgroups are defending their own views of the truth based on a cult of personality—"I am of Paul, I am of Apollos." Paul exhorts these factions, "I appeal to you, brethren, in the name of our Lord Jesus Christ, that all of you agree, . . . that you be *united* in the same mind and the same judgment." Instead of being disjointed and disconnected, be *united*. Line up with the same mind and purpose. Fix your broken and flawed thinking and become whole through agreement.

3. *To supply what is lacking.* Paul tenderly relays to the Thessalonians that he and his colleagues, Silvanus and Timothy, are "praying earnestly night and day that we may see you face to face and *supply what is lacking in your faith*" (1 Thess. 3:10 RSV). The Revised Standard Version uses the verb *supply* to translate *katartizō*. The meaning of *supply* here is to complete what is incomplete, make up for what is deficient, and add what is missing. There is a deficit that must be made up if the Thessalonians are to minister at full capacity.

This same sense is conveyed to the Corinthians when Paul writes, "What we pray for is your *improvement*" (2 Cor. 13:9 RSV). Here *improvement* translates *katartisis,* which in this context focuses on improvement in one's understanding and experience of the faith. Paul is fighting a battle for the Corinthians' affection. They have been attracted to "super apostles," who don't seem to accept the weakness shown in a crucified Savior. When Paul modeled the way of the cross, it looked to the Corinthians like weakness because he had "decided to know nothing among you except Jesus Christ, and him crucified" (1 Cor. 2:2). What was lacking in the Corinthians' faith was the knowledge that the power of God is released when we realize we have nothing in ourselves to commend. So Paul concludes with the exhortation, "Mend [*katartizesthe*] your ways" (2 Cor. 13:11 RSV). He wants them to understand that at the heart of our faith is the weakness of the cross, which is the power of God. He calls them to be people of the cross because such people are by nature humble and therefore can "agree with one another" (2 Cor. 13:11).

The Equipping Ministry of Mending/Restoring

What might the mending/restoring phase of equipping ministry look like in the local church? The church is to be a therapeutic community. It is a place where broken, struggling people can become well and whole. The atmosphere of a therapeutic community immersed in grace says to those who enter, "We take you as you are." Bruce Larson years ago chided the Christian community when he said that the local bar often communicates a more accepting atmosphere than the church. The bar is a place where people can say, "I'm sunk. I've had it. I can't go on." In the midst of a casualty-creating world, the church needs to be a place where we come with wounds exposed and hear, loud and clear, "Grace dispensed here."

Any equipping ministry begins with the assumption that we are all broken people because of our own self-destructive sin or because of having been victimized by the sin of others. We should enter into the sanctuary for worship like those who attend twelve-step addiction recovery meetings. As we cross the threshold, we each would introduce ourselves, "Hi. I'm Greg, a sinner saved by grace." Paul writes, "We have this treasure [the gospel] in earthen vessels" (2 Cor. 4:7 RSV). In other words, we are all "cracked pots."

As broken people we "leak" the presence of the Holy Spirit. The mending/restoring ministry pays attention to our cracks so that we may better contain the presence of Christ in us. Therefore, an equipping ministry makes provision for restoring all who bear the damage of physical, spiritual, and emotional brokenness. Our ministry will be only as effective as we are whole in Christ.

1. *Fixing what is broken.* To fix what is broken means to be committed to healing ministry. I use *healing* in the broad sense of wholeness in Christ in body, mind, and spirit. Healing covers a wide spectrum, from prayer for the restoration of physical health to the mending of damaged emotions or spirit. This means that the healing ministry of the church will assume many forms. There will be opportunity for public healing in the context of the prayerful and expectant faith of the gathered community. There will also be opportunities for long-term care by trained counselors who can apply the healing salve of the Holy Spirit. The tender care of non-judgmental listening will allow fearful and traumatized people to expose hurts and pain long buried from conscious recognition. Memories are healed and the guilt of past sins released through the forgiveness of Jesus Christ as he is embodied in healing agents.

The breadth of healing is illustrated by a remarkable Saturday I once experienced. My day began with one-on-one time with a man in our new member's class. He had been attending the church for about six weeks, having heard about the church via the Yellow Pages. Though full of shame, he was eager to tell the journey into his dark side. His life had collapsed because of a moral failure. Not only had he brought disgrace upon his wife and two daughters, but he also faced an uncertain future with pending court action. He told me that he had been raised without any religious training and therefore, in his words, he had "no moral core." As if he had been reading a script from the book of Romans he said, "I will not repeat my behavior because I am afraid of the legal consequences. But the law cannot change my heart. Do you know how I can get a new heart?" I felt like a home run hitter crouched across home plate. This pitch looked the size of a beach ball, ready to be hit out of the park. What a joy it was to be able to tell him that Jesus offered him a new heart!

Later that same Saturday, I was asked to be a mediator between a young mother of two small children and her father, who had abused her sexually as a teenager. The young woman had grown enough in Christ that she knew further growth toward wholeness meant she had to face the one who had perpetrated these hideous acts of betrayal. Wisely, she did not want to confront him alone. It was one of the most remarkable two hours I have ever spent. This courageous young woman was able to articulate the pain of this treachery, while the father amazingly allowed the pain to enter his spirit. Nothing of this nature is healed in a day, but the first steps toward release from the prison of hatred were taken by the young mother even as the father wondered if he could ever forgive himself. Over time the young mother was able to draw from the depths of Jesus' love on the cross to set her father free to embrace forgiveness and new life for himself as well.

The churches in which I have served have offered several insights into how the various dimensions of a healing ministry function. Public worship is an appropriate context for healing and intercessory prayer. Through celebrative worship and biblical teaching, the Spirit speaks to the heart and prepares people to deal with the brokenness in their lives. Prayer stations in the form of kneeling benches are staffed by trained teams of two. Those who have been identified with gifts of healing and sensitivity to the Holy Spirit's leading, enhanced by careful training, are stationed along the front of the sanctuary. People are invited to bring their personal needs before the Lord. These may involve some spiritual blockage, broken relationship, besetting sin, or need for physical healing. On one particular Sunday I was overwhelmed with the depth of need. A middle-aged man asked for release from crushing lust; he was followed by a senior couple trying to know how to lovingly relate to an openly gay son; then a young woman shared that the effects of a rape a couple years previous was severely affecting her ability to be close to her husband. Public worship creates an air of expectancy as the congregation enters into the faith-enhancing prayer.

Most healing is not instantaneous, but long-term. Traumas from the past are deeply buried and have multiple ramifications. Often the public setting is simply an impetus to the long-term process of fixing what is broken. Gifted Christian counselors can be instruments of the healing salve of God's grace that must be applied over time. Longer term care has taken different forms in the congregations I have served. First, those gifted in inner-healing prayer make a commitment to take a person through the levels of pain to get at the roots of troubling behavior that is evidenced as sin. This kind of prayer is often described as "healing of the memories." Addictions are often best dealt with in support groups based on the Alcoholics Anonymous twelve-step process. The air of mutual confession and the accountability of a sponsor are the lifelines to deal with habits that are leading to destruction. Christian twelve-step groups have ranged from Adult Children of Alcoholics, to sexual addiction, to chemical dependency, and so on. Unfortunately, many Christian communities are so superficial and inauthentic that those who have had to be brutally honest with themselves cannot handle the phoniness of Christians "looking good" before each other. Thankfully, in this day when authenticity is being demanded by the younger generation, the Christian church has a chance again of being a "fellowship of sinners."

All of us have something broken that needs to be fixed if we are to be whole people.

2. *Bringing back into proper alignment.* The second aspect of mending/restoring implies that a relationship that was once solid is now in a state of disrepair. The disciple has done something to put himself out of alignment with Christ. Therefore, a mending/restoring ministry exercises discipline. Grace is balanced by truth. A therapeutic community accepts people as they are but loves them enough not to allow them to remain that way. Love without teeth is sentimentality. We do no favors by allowing people to hurt themselves in their sin. Paul writes, "You who are spiritual should *restore* him in a spirit of gentleness" (Gal. 6:1 RSV). This means that the spiritual leaders who share oversight with pastors must be equipped in their role to protect the spiritual health of the body. This will require intervention into lives where people, knowingly or unknowingly, live self-destructively. The body of believers will need to be structured (as by small groups) and the community equipped to call people back to Christ when they are living contrary to the Lord's will.

The third appointment I had on that fateful Saturday described above had to do with an act of discipline. Our staff had discovered inadvertently that one of our new members shared the same address with a woman in our congregation. He had stated a desire to be involved in our children's ministry. I drew the short straw at our staff meeting. It was my responsibility to confirm that this couple was living together and if this was the case to call the man to obedience in Christ. I shared with him that a concern had come, since he had become a member. It appeared that he was living with his "lover" out of wedlock. Was that right? He shared that it was. Though he wished it could be different, for financial reasons and other complications, marriage was just not possible at this time. I told him that it would not be possible to serve in our children's ministry under the circumstances. Then as compassionately and firmly as I could, and looking him straight in the eye, I said, "Joe, as a brother in Christ and as your pastor, I call you in the name of Jesus Christ to a life of holiness and obedience as a follower of Jesus. Make this right before God and the one you claim to love." He left with no promise as to what he would do, only that he would take seriously the word of discipline that was issued. This story has a happy ending. He did make it right; they are happily married today.

Discipline generally requires a context of intimacy and accountability. I have deliberately included these two ingredients in discipling relationships. I encourage a triad, in which one person invites two others into an intense journey together toward maturity. A covenant is mutually negotiated that establishes the disciplines to which the parties will be mutually accountable. Explicit permission is given to each member to raise concerns whenever we see something in another's life that is a blind spot to his faithfulness in Christ. In one discipling triad we spent considerable time on one person's inability to manage his employees in a tone that was consistent with the way Christ would treat people. This person was consciously aware that his volatile outbursts were not honoring to the Lord. He needed a means to be called on it and to be encouraged to see transformation.

A more critical form of intervention is needed when someone is out of alignment with Christ as a result of demonic activity. Some people in the body have gifts of discerning spirits, intercessory prayer, and wisdom. These gifted people can form prayer teams for a deliverance ministry when it is clear that every other attempt to break the bondage of sin has pointed to a force of darkness that is not the result of damaged emotions or willful sin but is the foothold of the Evil One. An equipping ministry recognizes the need for deliverance from the powers of darkness.

We cannot be fit for ministry unless we are released and realigned with the One who calls us to ministry.

3. *Supplying what is lacking.* When the circumstances of life collapse around us, we need our faith to be built up through the encouragement of others. This building up takes many forms. Ministries traditionally associated with pastoral care—hospital visitation, bereavement counseling, and crisis intervention—are all focused on supplying what is lacking.

An anxious member is riddled with fear while awaiting surgery. The equipper—faith builder and hope creator—supplies faith by pointing him to the loving God who is present and who gave his life for him. People who have lost a loved one need to know they are not alone and have not been abandoned by God. The equipper is the sacramental presence of Christ conveying that they will never be left or forsaken. For example, the person whose world has been torn apart by divorce needs the stabilizing hope that says there is life beyond this pain. Hope is incarnated when we say, "I'll stay with you and see you through this."

The ministries associated with mending and restoring have traditionally been the province of ordained pastors. Professionalizing care, as I have asserted, has had a very debilitating impact on the ability of the body of Christ to give and receive care ministry from one another. When I moved to my previous pastorate, we had an opportunity to shift the model of care ministry from a pastor-focused to a people-focused ministry. We banished the phrase "pastoral care" from our vocabulary. The preamble to our reconceived "Ministry of Care" began like this: "We find the phrase 'ministry of care' preferable to that of 'pastoral care.' Strong habits of thought link the latter phrase exclusively with ordained clergy; while the former phrase allows unencumbered interpretation." When I arrived, the expectation was that the senior pastor was the primary caregiver. We set about to intentionally change expectations and expand what we meant by care and who could deliver it. A ministry of care grew under our "care deacons," led by an equipper pastor who multiplied the ministries and the people who shared in their staffing and delivery. Within a couple of years, we had gone from the care focused on a pastor, to ministry involving well over a hundred people with teams of grief ministers, hospital visitors, those ministering to the unemployed and underemployed, recovery ministries, and support groups for those with cancer and chronic pain. All of these ministries were led by the people of God called to address the pain in people's lives.

The focus of *mending and restoring* should be on wholeness so that people can become effective ministers. People are put back together again so that they can be useful channels in God's service. We are not trying simply to create *happy* people who feel better about themselves, but *whole* people who build up the body of Christ and bring the message of salvation and the witness of compassion to a broken world.

ESTABLISH/LAY FOUNDATIONS

Fig. 6.4

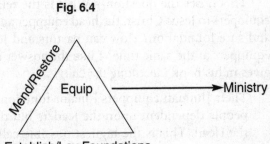

The second major focus of equipping concerns laying solid foundations in Christ. The biblical images related to laying foundations evoke strength: fixed, immovable, established, unshakable, solid, not tossed to and fro, unwavering, and firmly planted.

1. *Jesus Christ, the True Foundation.* It should not surprise us that when we come to lay firm foundations, Jesus Christ himself is described as the head equipper. In the benediction to the book of Hebrews, Jesus is presented as the One who directly equips and provides the resources necessary to do his will: "Now may the God of peace, who brought again from the dead our Lord Jesus . . . *equip* you with everything good that you may do his will, working in you that which is pleasing in his sight, through Jesus Christ" (Heb. 13:20–21 RSV). Christ himself, who dwells in us and mediates his life through us, prepares and makes us suitable to accomplish the particular will he has for us. This invokes the widespread New Testament theme that there is only *one foundation* that can be laid in

our lives, "which is Jesus Christ" (1 Cor. 3:11 RSV). So Christ is both our foundation and our equipper.

Peter makes a related point when he writes to Christians suffering terrible persecution. They are living under a reign of terror to the point where the devil is described as a "roaring lion ready to devour." When the ground shakes, our feet can easily slip. So Peter encourages the believers with these words: "And after you have suffered for a little while, the God of all grace, who has called you to his eternal glory in Christ, will himself *restore,* support, strengthen, and establish you" (1 Peter 5:10). It is God himself through Christ who will set his people on their feet and strengthen them for service.

This raises the question—What is the relationship of human equippers to Jesus Christ, the head equipper and the only sufficient and sure foundation? How can pastors and Jesus Christ both be equippers at the same time? I like the answer that R. Paul Stevens gives in his book *Liberating the Laity:*

> Their [human equippers'] major function is not to make people dependent upon the leaders but dependent upon the Head. This is the highest possible calling. It requires the strongest possible leadership in the church to lead people in such a way that they do not become dependent on the human leaders. . . . Equipping, directing people to find their life and future in Christ Himself, makes the highest claim on leadership.[4]

The equippers God gives to the body must constantly be pointing to the all-sufficient Christ, to whom each member of the body is directly connected. Here it is appropriate to review one aspect of the church as organism. "Christ is the head of the church" is not a theological platitude; it is the only way the church can be the church. Each member of the body is directly connected to the head and therefore receives orders directly from the head. Stevens notes, "The head does not tell the hand to tell the foot what to do. The head is directly connected to the foot."[5] So every part needs to stay connected to Christ. Every part must take full responsibility for its proper functioning. The role of human equippers is to promote that connectedness with the head and consequently with the rest of the body, the church.

2. *The Word of God, Inherent Power.* Along with Jesus Christ as both our foundation and the builder on it, the written Word of God is fundamentally connected to establishing and laying foundations in a believer's life. Scripture, in fact, has an essential role in the equipping ministry generally, as we discover in the well-known New Testament passage on the inspiration and authority of Scripture: "All Scripture is inspired by God and profitable for teaching, for reproof, for correction, and for training in righteousness, that the person of God may be complete [*artios*], equipped [*exertismenos*] for every good work" (2 Tim. 3:16–17 RSV). As a pastor friend often says, "The Word of God not only informs, it performs." The Word of God plays a vital part in equipping in several ways:

  a. Teaching—Creating a new worldview rooted in the new reality of the death and resurrection of Jesus Christ. (Establishing/Laying foundations)
  b. Reproof—Confronting the sinfulness in our lives and setting us on the right course. (Mending/Restoring)
  c. Correction—Exposing false teaching and reestablishing the only foundation, Jesus Christ. (Mending/Restoring)
  d. Training in righteousness—Walking morally upright, with heart, mind, and spirit harnessed in devotion to God. (Establishing/Laying foundations)

The goal or outcome of this work of God's Word is to make us "complete" so that we are "equipped for every good work." "Complete" does not convey "perfection" (KJV), but merely the suitable requirement for the task, readiness for the job. "Complete" means that we are prepared or enabled to do the ministry (good works) God has for us. The use of the perfect passive tense (*exertismenos*) means that the Word of God acts upon us at a point in the past and continues to affect us in the present, empowering us for every good deed.

Just as we asked the question, What is the human equipper's relationship to the head equipper, Jesus Christ? so we need to ask, What is the human equipper's relationship to the inspired Word? When we examine the four gifted ones who are to equip the saints for ministry in Ephesians 4:11, we see that what they have in common is the different ways they wield the Word of God. The use of God's Word varies according to the particular equipper's function. Ray Stedman proposes that the role of these gifted individuals is analogous to a life support system of the human body:

a. The *apostles* are to the church what the *skeletal system* is to the human body. The human body needs a frame on which to hang all its parts; otherwise there is no structure, but only a mass of quivering organs. So the apostles spoke revelation that became the framework of truth and authoritative basis for the New Testament.

b. The *prophet's* message is meant to quicken and activate the body to action, just as electrical impulses are passed through the *nervous system* to stimulate each bodily part to act appropriately.

c. The *evangelist* can be compared to the *digestive system* since it is the responsibility of evangelism to take in new life (food) and change it into a form that renews the body. The evangelist's passion is to carry the word of the gospel to those who are perishing and to see lives redirected to Christ and incorporated into the body.

d. The *pastor-teacher* is likened to the *circulatory system*, since his call is to make sure food and oxygen get to all the cells of the body and waste is removed. The pastor-teacher helps feed and cleanse the body by accurately teaching God's Word and by providing such an atmosphere of love for God's Word that God's people feed themselves through their own study.[6]

3. *Modeling, the Incarnational Way.* Human beings are the filter through which the word of God comes to us. People are the ongoing embodiment of Christ and the written Word. God's approach is fundamentally incarnational. He showed himself in a person. He continues to show himself through the vehicle of people in whom he dwells.

We can say, therefore, that the Lord's basic teaching method is modeling. "A disciple is not above his teacher, but everyone when he is fully *taught* [equipped] will be like his teacher" (Luke 6:40 RSV). Christian maturity does not result from the accumulation of head knowledge. Reflecting the rabbinic educational model, Jesus believed that a teacher's role was to model, or be an example in his life of what the students were expected to learn. A rabbi was said to be "the living Torah." Students were to copy every aspect of a rabbi's life. Referring to the rabbinical approach, Gerhardsson writes, "To learn one must go to a Teacher. . . .But they also learn a great deal by simply observing: with attentive eyes they observe all that the teacher does and then proceed to imitate him. Torah is above all a holy, authoritative attitude towards life and way of life. Because this is true, much can be learned simply by watching and imitating those who are learned."[7]

The three aspects of establishing and laying solid foundations are (1) Jesus Christ, the true foundation, (2) the Word of God, inherent power, and (3) modeling, the incarnational way. Let's see how each of these translates into specific ministries of equipping.

Jesus Christ, the True Foundation

At the heart of an equipping church is worship. Worship defines the church's reason for being and is the constant reminder that every member is directly connected to the head. The depth of the people's sense of call to ministry will be in direct proportion to their encounter with the head of the church each time the church gathers. It is the responsibility of the worship leaders to uphold the living, reigning Christ. It is the responsibility of God's people to get themselves ready each Sunday to exalt Christ, place their lives at his disposal through confession, and be open to the Word proclaimed so that they are invigorated for ministry. The equipping congregation will place a high priority on a thoughtful, prayerfully planned, and focused worship experience where the Word of God is clearly and powerfully expounded and applied to the particular needs and challenges to discipleship facing the particular congregation and community.

Planning the order of worship has had a high priority on my weekly schedule. Each service is carefully crafted around a one-sentence theme and an attribute of God closely related to the theme. For example, the worship service one Sunday centered around the following theme: "The church is to reflect the oneness that exists already between the members of the Godhead." The attribute of God that served as our focal point was "the Triune God—the model of unity."

Each week a rough draft of the service is presented to a planning group made up of the pastoral staff and worship and music leaders. We then creatively shape the service through broad discussion and prayerfully recruit worship leaders based on our knowledge of what they particularly have to contribute to the unique experience of this worship event. Each worship experience has a distinctive flavor. This creates a sense of newness and anticipation in the worshipers. The worship content is also carefully integrated into the small-group ministry, complete with study guides that cover the same content taught in worship. This provides a context of community in which to process and apply the preached word. Worship is not pulled out of people, but it flows out because people have already put something in.

Corporate worship is a spiritual discipline as well as is private worship. Solid foundations are laid in Christ when believers make daily time for a private rendezvous with their Lord. The purpose of spiritual disciplines is to put us into a place and space where the Lord can form our hearts. By quiet attention to the Lord through prayer, meditation, and devotional Scripture study, we are expanding the space in our hearts that can contain the presence of the Lord. These rooted disciplines then serve as a foundation for our daily activities.

The Word of God, Inherent Power

The written Word of God that points to Jesus Christ is central to both formal and informal gatherings of God's people. Formally, it is right to make provision for people to "sit under" the teaching and proclamation of the Word. God has gifted and set apart prophets whose passion for truth energizes the body to faithfulness. Prophetic preachers keep a community of believers stirred up, having to confront truth in the context of the spirit of the times.

There must also be formal structures for teachers to explain and fill in the whys and wherefores of the breadth of the biblical message. In the image of an orchestra, prophets have been compared to the trumpeters who sound a clear note, whereas teachers are analogous to the violin section that fills out the sound. Teachers who can open the Word and make it live need a place to exercise their gift among hungry people. The teaching ministry of the equipping church is never satisfied with mere information but teaches for transformation in Christ. Larry Richards says, "We don't want a truth system, but a reality system approach."[8]

Informally, foundations are laid in God's Word as people "sit around" the Word of God. The Bible in Protestant tradition is the "book of the people." It is sufficiently clear for people to gather around it and seek to understand and discern its message individually and corporately. A basic structure for equipping is the small group, allowing face-to-face encounter before the Word of God. Often the method of study in these types of groups is inductive, meaning that people are guided through a mutual investigative process by a series of questions that unlock the meaning of the passage and then apply this meaning in specific ways to their lives.

Those who equip by establishing and laying foundations hold the person of Christ before the community. They have a facility and passion to feed people with God's Word. Paul's letter to the Galatians expresses the equipper's heart: "My dear children, for whom I am again in the pains of childbirth until Christ is formed in you, how I wish I could be with you now" (Gal. 4:19–20 NIV).

Modeling, the Incarnational Way

Another approach to laying foundations that I believe is fundamental to people's coming to full stature in Christ is *discipling*. I am using "discipling" in a narrow and technical sense. Elsewhere I have written, "Discipling is an intentional relationship in which we walk alongside other disciples in order to encourage, equip, and challenge one another in love to grow toward maturity in Christ. This includes equipping the disciple to teach others as well."[9]

One essential way to see solid foundations laid is through long-term investment of life into life. Ninety percent of believers have never had someone take them under their wing and make sure that the basic disciplines, doctrines, character qualities, or ministry issues have been inculcated in their lives. This occurs when someone invests himself in the life of another to guide him into the breadth of the new life in Christ.

In the next chapter, we will explore the implementation of a intergenerational multiplication of discipling relationships as one of the fundamental strategies for establishing/laying foundations.

PREPARE/TRAIN

Figure 6.5

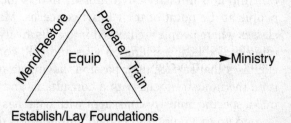

To examine the last leg of the triangle, it will be helpful for us to recall the secular use of the term *katartismos*, "equip." We have already seen that "equip" was used in a medical context to refer to the setting of a broken limb or realigning a limb wrenched out of joint. In relation to artistry and craftsmanship, "to equip" meant to work with the hands to produce something useful or beautiful. Ephesians 4:12 has a product in mind. Those with support gifts are to "equip the saints for the work of ministry." In other words, the people of God are to discover their aptitudes and abilities for ministry as the equippers exercise their gifts. This implies that particular training will be needed to prepare people to exercise ministry in the body and to the world. Refining skills and practicing tools will be essential for a prepared ministry.

1. *Being a steward of one's gifts and call.* An equipping ministry is one that assists each member of the body of Christ to function in accord with his or her God-given assigned function. This function is primarily determined by the gifts distributed by the Spirit and by the shape of the call on one's life. Much of the will of God for persons is written into them. It is not so much a matter of finding something outside to give ourselves to, but to be attuned to our inner design and then find the context in which we best flourish.

Spiritual gifts are analogous to tools in our toolbox that we are empowered by the Spirit to use; whereas call is the context or settings to which our heart is drawn in which we use our spiritual gifts. For example, just knowing that you have the gift of administration does not tell what you are to administer. The call, focused on a need you care about, guides you to the place to use your gift. Spiritual gifts are the means; the call is the end.

Equipping churches provide ample opportunities for people to discover their gifts and passions for ministry. This will involve multiple discovery opportunities, but even more important is a relationship and ministry environment that is focused on engaging people at the point of their heart concerns. Many churches have classes where people are invited into a discovery process by examining the biblical teaching on gifts and call, completing reflective exercises that surface their passion, having an opportunity to fine tune the ministry focus with a consultant, and then being placed into a specific ministry consistent with what has been learned. This is good up to a point. But equally important is the opportunity for people to be in a relational small-group environment, where in community, the members of the group have a chance to naturally affirm the gifts and heart they see in each other.

2. *Mobilizing for ministry in teams.* In my experience, gifts for ministry surface most clearly in the context of a ministry team. An equipping environment is a mission-oriented culture where ministry is accomplished in teams. This is my working definition of a ministry team: *a small group called together by God who covenant to care for each other while exercising their spiritual gifts to minister to a need for which they mutually care.* Spiritual gifts are communal. They are given, not for individual fulfillment, but for the common good. Ministry teams are formed around a common heartfelt need to which all the team members are drawn. As they strategize together to address the common need, the gifts naturally come to the fore. For example, the church I formerly served has a Romania Ministry Team. The common call is to provide a Christian "home" environment for thirty-five HIV positive children in an orphanage in Constanta, Romania. People only serve on this team if their heart is touched by the plight of these orphan children. Then the question becomes, What gifts and skills do members bring to the team that will contribute to the accomplishment of the mission? There is a need for an administrator, a visionary leader, a pastor with a heart for the needy, a communicator, and those with the gift of faith.

3. *Specialized training.* An equipping church is a training center. Just as small, untrained children will not be able to read without instruction, people should not just be told to do ministry without being given training in the particular skills for a particular ministry. If you are going to visit sick people in the hospital, it is helpful to have observed someone who has training and experience in this type of ministry. Effective small-group leaders have mastered the skills of leading an inductive Bible study, learned the techniques of how to foster a sharing atmosphere, and discovered methods that work well to cultivate group prayer. Small-group leaders are then given a coach who can help them grow in their role and be available to assist as problems arise. They are also part of a larger team of small-group leaders, where the vision for this ministry is kept before them, new skills are acquired, and support is provided by fellow small-group leaders. Apprentices are identified and trained at the small-group level and then added to the small-group teams.

What is true for small-group leaders can be true for any number of other ministries inside or outside of the church.

An Equipping Ministry

In summary, an equipping ministry recognizes that people are broken and therefore are in need of *mending and restoring* if they are to be useful channels through whom God can work. Such a ministry is built upon *establishing and laying foundations* by providing effective approaches to grounding people in Christ through public and private worship, rooting people in the truth and power of God's Word, and growing people to maturity through intentional discipling relationships. Finally, there is specific provision given for *preparing and training* people for particular ministries by assisting them to discover their unique ministry contribution in the context of ministry teams. There is also a regimen of training so that appropriate skills are mastered consistent with the role of ministry.

As I stated at the outset of this chapter, this three-fold scheme can be used for two purposes. The overview gives a church an opportunity to evaluate their strengths and weaknesses in the areas of equipping. As you look at the three phrases of mending/restoring, establishing/laying foundations, and preparing/training, what are your strengths to build on, and what are your identified gaps?

The same question can be asked of those individuals who *"possess the peculiar gift of being able to help other men and women to practice any ministry to which they are called."* In what arena do your equipping gifts primarily lie? When I was on the staff at St. John's Presbyterian Church in West Los Angeles, there were three of us on the professional ordained staff. In retrospect, but not by design, we were able to cover the waterfront of equipping fairly effectively. Joan's interests and heart were primarily in the *mend/restore* portion of the equipping triangle. She resourced our deacons ministry that cared for those in need within the congregation and pioneered a ministry to the homeless in West Los Angeles. Her gifts of inner healing and counseling made this area a natural habitat. Darrell, the primary preaching pastor, pointed people to Jesus while proclaiming the Word with power. As people fell in love with Christ, their energies were directed toward ministry. His equipping ministry was firmly in the *establishing/laying foundations* arena. My heart was drawn to discipling, and I carried a particular concern that people know their makeup and be given the particular skills to be effective small-group leaders. I straddle the establish/lay foundations and the prepare/train territories.

My conviction is that we can only replicate ourselves in the areas for which we have a passion and calling. We don't need to be, nor can we be effective along all the fronts of equipping ministry. The equipping triangle (Figure 6.2) can be used as a tool to build a balanced team.

What do we mean when we say that a pastor's fundamental role is to be an equipper? T. H. Thayer notes that equipping is "to make one what one ought to be."[10] In more contemporary terms, Ray Stedman says that equippers are to "shape up the saints."[11] In other words, equippers prepare, complete, put in order, and make ready for service the people of God. Equipping is not so much about the functions of a pastor, but it is about the results of deploying an increased number of God's people in ministry. It is really a question about *whose ministry it is*. Equippers for ministry find their fulfillment and joy in seeing the people of God come alive to their ministry potential.

John Stott sums up well the burden of this chapter. On the significance of Ephesians 4:11–12, he writes,

> The New Testament concept of the pastor is not of a person who jealously guards all ministry in his own hands, and successfully squashes all lay initiatives, but of one who helps and encourages all of God's people to discover, develop and exercise their gifts. His teaching and training are directed to this end, to enable the people of God to be a servant people, ministering actively but humbly according to their gifts in a world of alienation and pain. Thus, instead of monopolizing all ministry himself, he actually multiplies ministries.[12]

In the next chapter, as the basis for outlining the implementation of an equipping ministry, we return to Jethro's advice to Moses to change his leadership strategy.

NOTES

1. *The Book of Order*, Presbyterian Church USA, 2001-2002, Chapter VI.
2. Ray Stedman, *Body Life* (Glendale, Calif.: Regal Books, 1972), 81.

3. Elton Trueblood, *The Incendiary Fellowship* (New York: Harper and Row, 1967), 41, italics added.

4. R. Paul Stevens, *Liberating the Laity* (Downers Grove, Ill.: InterVarsity Press, 1985), 37.

5. Ibid., 36.

6. Stedman, *Body Life*, 70ff.

7. B. Gerhardsson, *The Origins of the Gospel Tradition* (London: SCM), 17.

8. Lawrence D. Richards, *Creative Bible Teaching* (Chicago: Moody Press, 1970), 51.

9. Greg Ogden, *Discipleship Essentials: A Guide to Building Your Life in Christ* (Downers Grove, Ill.: InterVarsity Press, 1998), 17.

10. T. H. Thayer, as quoted by Ray Stedman in *Body Life*, 82.

11. Stedman, *Body Life*, 82.

12. John R. W. Stott, *The Message of Ephesians* (Downers Grove, Ill.: InterVarsity Press, 1979), 167.

Chapter 7

Implementing the Equipping Model of Ministry

MY GOAL THROUGHOUT THIS BOOK, and especially in this chapter, is to offer an alternative paradigm to the dependency model that I would label an *equipping or interdependency model of ministry*. The equipping model gives expression to the church as organism. If biblically the starting point to define ministry is the whole people of God, then the question is, What role is the pastor to play in helping bring this to fruition? A paradigm shift is in order. To paraphrase Joel Barker (whom we met in chapter 5), we need a new set of rules and regulations that redefines the boundaries and therefore creates a new set of expectations of what it means to be successful within those boundaries.

When we left Jethro and Moses two chapters back, Jethro was observing a disaster in the making. Jethro watched as Moses perched himself on the judgment throne as the only one qualified to render decisions to the people's complaints against one another. His question to Moses was laced with sarcasm, "Why do you sit alone?" Who do you think you are, Moses? Moses justified his self-perception by saying that he was just living out the people's expectations of him.

Observing the long line of people waiting to present their cases before Moses, Jethro sees the ultimate end. Both Moses and the people will wear themselves out with this approach. Moses must not attempt to carry this load alone. Jethro offers the following advise, which contains within it the guidelines for the shift to an equipping model of ministry:

> "Now listen to me. I will give you counsel, and God be with you! You should represent the people before God, and you should bring their cases before God; teach them the statutes and instructions and make known to them the way they are to go and the things they are to do. You should also look for able men among all the people, men who fear God, are trustworthy, and hate dishonest gain; set such men over them as officers over thousands, hundreds, fifties and tens. Let them sit as judges for the people at all times; let them bring every important case to you, but decide every minor case themselves. So it will be easier for you, and they will bear the burden with you. If you do this, and God so commands you, then you will be able to endure, and all these people will go to their home in peace." (Ex. 18:19–23)

Embedded in this advice are three admonitions to Moses that have relevance for the equipping ministry. Jethro says to Moses:

♦ Change your role
♦ Share and develop leaders
♦ Decentralize your structure

CHANGE YOUR ROLE

Moses has become a bottleneck. All decisions have to go through his tent. Now Jethro is advising Moses to move primarily into a teaching role and be the backup person for difficult cases while the appointed leaders render most of the routine judgments. In other words, Moses is to be an instructor in the ways of the law, placing the responsibility on the people themselves to apply the law to their day-to-day affairs. Moses could easily reduce the legal case load by simply putting his energies into effective teaching. As people apply the law, the disputes will naturally decrease. Moses is to shift the burden from himself as the "answer man" to the people. Like Moses, pastors need to get themselves out of the position of being the spiritual bottleneck with everyone dependent upon them.

If the pastor under the dependency model is akin to an unhealthy parent who does not want the children to grow up, then what is the role of pastor in the *inter*dependency model that fosters an every-member ministry? In Chapter 6 I quoted Elton Trueblood as saying that the primary role of the pastor is "to help other men and women practice any ministry to which they are called." What is the contemporary image that captures the function or role that an equipping leader will have with a congregation?

Trueblood proposes and dismisses a number of images that might be used for an equipper. If we call a pastor *the minister,* then, as we have observed, it means that the ordinary people of God are *not* the ministers. We could use biblical language like *elder,* but that tells us nothing about their function and leaves the impression that you need to be older to be an equipper. *Preacher* is a relic from the frontier days, so that will not do. *Pastor* would actually be the ideal image because it does describe function rather than just position. Yet the image of *pastor* conjures up a wide variety of meanings, depending on one's association with the word. Trueblood moves beyond biblical imagery to a fresh one—one with which we have generally positive associations. He proposes the image of "coach" as the best modern equivalent of an equipper. He actually qualifies that with the addition of "player-coach." Coach by itself could sound as if pastors are shouting instructions from the sidelines, whereas the pastor as "player-coach" faces the heat of the game along with fellow teammates (parishioners).

One of the consequences of urging pastors to shift from the role of teacher/caregiver to equipping leader is a crisis of identity. If I am not the one on whom people must rely, then who am I? Upon what is my worth and value based? Trueblood addresses this by saying, "The idea of the pastor as the equipper is one which is full of promise, bringing back self-respect to people in *the ministry* who are sorely discouraged by the conventional pattern. . . . To watch for underdeveloped powers, to draw them out, to bring potency to actuality in human lives—this is a self validating task."[1]

Being a coach does in large measure describe what an equipping pastor is to be about. "The glory of the coach is that of being the discoverer, the developer, and the trainer of the powers of others. This is exactly what we mean when we use the Biblical terminology about the equipping ministry."[2] I have clear recollections of the impact of first using the term *coach* to describe my role. I was called to be an associate pastor with the working title of Pastor for

Leadership Development and Discipleship. Since equipping people for ministry in the areas of small groups, spiritual gifts, and discipling were integral to my job description, I was reaching for a way to define my equipping identity. When I somewhat inadvertently signed off my first newsletter article to the congregation with "Your coach, Greg," I was caught off guard by the reaction. First, it seemed to remove some of the distance from the pastoral role and make me more accessible. It was common for people to slap me on the back with comments like, "How's the coach?" But I recall one interchange especially that reinforced how much this image communicated. Shirley came up to me and said, "Let me see if I have this right. If you are a player-coach, then we are on the same team, right?" I assured her that there were not two teams—a clergy team and a laity team. She went on, "If you are the player-coach, then it is your job to help me discover my role on the team and assist my development in it, right?"

"You got it!" I said.

Let me anticipate some objections: Isn't equipping simply one function among many that a pastor performs? Some pastors are gifted in equipping, while others make a different contribution. It is true that there is a trend today to hire "directors of lay ministry." This could imply that equipping is a particular ministry of certain people with unusual skills. When I was called as the Pastor for Leadership Development and Discipleship, I was perceived as the one having the responsibility of handling equipping ministry. The other two ordained pastors covered the terrain traditionally connected with a pastor's role—preaching, pastoral care, and counseling. As mentioned above, my duties included devising a way for the members of the body to discover their spiritual gifts and be deployed accordingly: training small-group leaders as undershepherds, setting up a discipling network, and overseeing the adult education classes to deepen people's biblical knowledge. The impression I received from the other staff and from our elders was that "equipping has now been taken care of; that is Greg's job."

I became increasingly uncomfortable treating equipping as a specialty in pastoral ministry. Equipping is not the latest fad in ministry; it is not something just a few are called to do. It is a fundamental approach that needs to be integral to the identity of anyone who is a pastor. The role of a pastor is "to help men and women practice any ministry to which they are called." The New Reformation returns pastors to their proper role in relationship to God's people: equipping them for ministry. The raison d'être of pastors is to die to self so that members of the body can come alive to their ministry. So the rediscovered role of pastors in our day is not to do ministry for those who are passive recipients of their care, but to empower the body through the avenues of the pastors' individual gifts and to call forth every person's potential for ministry.

To move to an equipping ministry in many instances will require a redefinition of the pastoral role. How does one go about this process? Equipping pastors will need to work on four fronts simultaneously to change the expectations. Pastors must have clarity of *self-expectation* as an equipper, while building a shared philosophy of ministry with *staff* and the *official leadership*, at the same time casting vision to the entire *congregation*.

Pastor's Self-Expectations

My first advice to those wanting to become equipping pastors is to *define yourself*. Leaders have only two options when it comes to managing expectations. You can allow people to write their expectations on you as if you are tabula rasa, or you can articulate your expectations of yourself as a player-coach. Without clarity from the pastor, people will superimpose their understanding of what a pastor is to be. But if you teach that it is the pastor's role to "prepare the saints for the work of ministry," then over time a pastoral paradigm shift can and will occur.

When I became senior pastor at Saratoga Federated Church in 1988, I had an uphill battle ahead. I followed a much-beloved (rightly so) senior pastor who fit the prototype of a dependency leader. His strengths were effective and careful teaching of God's Word and being a caregiver to the relatively large congregation. Though others were involved in delivering care, the general impression was that our senior pastor takes care of us in times of need.

The big question on my mind was, would I survive attempts to bring about a transition to an equipping model of ministry? It was incumbent upon me to articulate to staff, to the council of elders, and to the congregation the role I saw myself playing as an equipping leader as well as to put in place a transition plan in the most sensitive area—the delivery of crisis care. I made my share of mistakes in making this transition. But one of the things I did well was to be clear about who I was as an equipping leader and what an equipping ministry looked like. It is a generally accepted leadership principle that people around a leader function best when the leader clearly defines him- or herself. On the other hand, confusion reigns when leaders sound a muted trumpet about their role and their vision. Leaders need to state who they are and where they want to lead people so that others can define themselves in relationship to the leader.

My clarity had immediate benefit to the staff. We began to redefine pastoral care in terms of a ministry of care. Since care and counseling were not my primary area of giftedness, it was natural to look to another on staff who might be a better fit for this ministry. As it turned out, there was an associate who was a perfect fit. He had been overshadowed by the senior pastor, and therefore his gifts and heart were not fully appreciated in this arena. Since it was my desire that all the staff have roles that matched their gifts and passion, it was appropriate to publicly shift the ministries of care and counseling to this associate. This allowed us at the same time to not only shift the responsibility for pastoral care from me to an associate, but also to reconceive the entire philosophy of the care ministry. It was at this time that we banished the phrase "pastoral care" from our vocabulary. We moved to a ministry of care model, which threw open the doors to the body at Saratoga Federated Church to expand their involvement in traditional areas like hospital visitation and grief ministry, and generated new frontiers heretofore untouched as well. The care ministry became multiplied teams of people addressing the needs to which people were drawn. Within two years we went from the perception that the senior pastor provides all the care to well over one hundred members of the congregation finding their voice and starting ministries to cancer survivors, people with chronic pain, those with various addictions, and the unemployed, among others.

This was not without its considerable pain. Changing expectations is difficult in the most pliable of circumstances. But when you assault the emotional bastion of who is allowed to care for you in time of need, you can expect not only resistance but claims that "the pastor doesn't love or care for us" or that "the pastor is not doing his job." This accusation is normal and inevitable. It is a price that must be endured on the way to a better ministry future. A leader must be convinced that an equipping model greatly enhances the breadth and depth of care in a way that never could happen if people simply pay for professional services. The temptation is to get sucked back into the "messianic" role of being people's savior in times of need. This is the emotional addiction. Withdrawal is painful. Only a commitment to the vision of equipped ministry that far exceeds the dependency model can sustain you. As someone has said, trying to make a shift of this magnitude is like trying to change a tire while the car is moving.

Defining myself as an equipping leader needed the specificity of articulated priorities. What does it look like to be an equipping leader, and how might that differ from the dependency model leader? Working with staff, the elders, and the personnel committee, my ministry priorities were established and mutually agreed upon. A leader needs to have allies in the ministry structure who can "defend" a new model of pastoral leadership. The elders and staff, especially, become a buffer to the congregation who will always lag behind the core leadership. It takes them a longer time to catch up to the changes in expectations. In outline form, the following categories became the structure of my job description:

Equipping Priorities

1. **Worship Designer:** Approximately ten hours a week were given to drafting thematically focused worship experiences. This was all done in conjunction with staff and worship ministry teams of invested people who creatively contributed to elements and execution of worship.

2. **Preaching:** Approximately fifteen hours a week were given to worship teaching preparation. My messages were manuscripted, since the content of our small-group studies was tightly connected to the content of worship.

3. **Vision for SFC Leaders**
   Strategic Elders: I met almost weekly with four to five elders who formed a Strategic Elders Ministry Team. Together we were the keepers of our ministry values, and we prayerfully discerned the vision for the broad direction of the church to be processed with a leadership core.

A. *Staff:* I led staff meetings and gave myself weekly to three key staff members for mutual encouragement for fulfillment of goals in their areas of ministry advance. In particular, I was concerned to help them make the transition from being *doers* of ministry to becoming leadership developers and visionaries in the arenas of ministry.

B. *New Leader Development:* Though in retrospect these efforts were too focused on the needs of the church structure, I constantly focused on raising up apprentices who could become strategic leaders in the church.

4. **Equipping within Saratoga Federated Church**
   Small Group: Since our ministry was built on the foundation of small groups, my wife and I led a group and regularly focused on the development of apprentice leadership. As an aside, one of the ancillary benefits to small-group involvement was the fueling of my teaching ministry. Our small group, as did many others, studied the passage of Scripture that was to be the basis for the teaching the following weekend. Regular insights from the group interaction become part of the teaching in worship.

   A. *Staff:* I saw myself as a coach of the staff corporately and for key players individually. For example, when we were transitioning from committees to ministry teams, in-service training was a necessity so that we could all have the same vision and skills in making this change.

   B. *Gifts and Call Ministry:* I came to the church with an every-member ministry vision and some experience in the arena of gifts mobilization. I built a team to support this ministry and equipped co-teachers to deliver its content.

   C. *Discipling Triads:* In my weekly schedule there were always two men who formed a discipleship threesome for mutual mentoring and intensive growth toward maturity in Christ. I will share more about this later in the chapter.

   D. *Elective Training:* I would periodically provide training input for small-group leaders and others.

5. **General Pastoral Duties:** Though the activities outlined above formed the core of my equipping commitments, there were still the responsibilities of premarital counseling, funerals, and the attendant care that goes with them, oversight of the larger office staff and personnel via an administrative assistant, and so forth.

In addition to shaping one's job description around equipping priorities, the leader is further assisted in managing expectations by having a clear list of core ministry/theological convictions. These convictions form the theological vision for an equipping ministry. They are the basis for what we refer to today as "core ministry values" and a "philosophy of ministry." They are the culture-shaping principles. A leader teaches these to the staff, ministry board, and congregation on a repeated basis. At one of my first meetings with the Council of Elders on arriving at Saratoga Federated Church, I conducted an inductive study of Exodus 18:13–23. We discovered together how Moses' leadership style inhibited empowering the people and how his change in style would bring greater shalom. In this way, the leaders were guided into their own discoveries.

On a personal level, the equipping leader will benefit from having partners of the heart who share a passion for equipping ministry. Almost from the first day of my ministry at my first pastorate, at St. John's Presbyterian in Los Angeles, I began to share with Grant, a member of the board of elders, my heartfelt conviction that all God's people are called to ministry. Weekly meetings cemented a bond between us. I watched Grant catch a vision for an equipped and released people. Out of the hours we invested in each other came a number of opportunities to be partners in ministry. One moment that I will never forget was the Sunday we shared the pulpit around the theme, "Called to the Ministry." As I strode to the pulpit that morning, Grant uttered, "Greg, preach the New Reformation!" A jolt of energy surged through my body. It truly felt as if the Holy Spirit was ushering in a new day and we were simply tools in his life-giving work.

An equipping leader is fundamentally a player-coach. A coach has a game plan, a vision of how the game can be played. He or she also is vitally concerned that all the players on the team are valued for their contribution and growing in their giftedness so that they can make the maximum contribution to the whole team. With this understanding, our church motto at Saratoga Federated Church was "On this team everyone plays."

Jethro advised Moses to change his role. In broad strokes that meant Moses was to be a teacher of the law, putting before the people the heart of a Holy God. Instead of attempting to apply the law to every individual case, he was to shift the responsibility to the people to know and apply the law themselves. Since this would reduce but not resolve all the disputes, Moses was advised to create a decentralized system of shared leadership. This leads us to even more clarity about the nature of an equipping leader.

SHARE AND DEVELOP THE LEADERSHIP

Not only was Moses to teach, but he was also to identify, train, and deploy leaders. "You should also look for able men among all the people, men who fear God, are trustworthy, and hate dishonest gain; set such men over them as officers over thousands, hundreds, fifties and tens" (Ex. 18:21). Moses needed partners in this ministry who could share the load with him. Second to teaching, Moses was to be a developer of leaders.

How should "player-coaches" spend their time? Training up leaders. Coaches coach. They spend their time developing people who want to be engaged in ministry. Here is my rule of thumb: 80 percent of a pastor's time is spent with the 20 percent of the congregation with the greatest ministry or leadership potential. It is an inviolable truth that our ministries can only extend as wide as there are self-initiating, Christ-honoring leaders.

The dependency model, on the other hand, encourages pastors to spend 80 percent of their time with the 20 percent who are the most needy. I often ask pastors, "How do people get on your schedule?" Most dependency-model pastors spend the majority of their time on care needs or institutional oversight matters. Dependency pastors are essentially responders, while equipping leaders are creators, identifying and investing in growing fully devoted followers of Jesus.

In the future, paid staff will be measured, not on their ability to do ministry or put together a program, but first and foremost by their ability to develop leaders. Carl George has written, "The work and ministry of the professional staff is to create volunteer ministers who are capable of being leaders of groups and teams."[3] Equipping leaders are ministry multipliers who leverage their investments by growing leaders who become initiating centers.

There is both a *manner* and *style* to being an equipping leader that is consistent with fostering an every-member ministry. Fundamentally, what we are working toward is a partnership between pastor and people that aims to deploy as many people as possible in the mission of Christ to the world.

The Manner of an Equipping Leader

If a pastor is going to be in partnership and share the leadership, this will require a deportment that "comes alongside" rather than "lords it over."

1. Be a real person. Equipping leaders are on a journey of discipleship together with those they serve. This means that just as God's people have chinks in their armor, so does the pastor. If we are on the same team, the coach struggles with the same temptations and brokenness as do the other members of the team. Pastors must come off the pedestal and come alongside. A generation ago there was a school of thought that said that for pastors to retain authority they must keep their distance. Too much familiarity would diminish the pastoral mystique and therefore the perception of holiness. Keeping up the pretence of false perfection was the basis for maintaining authority.

I believe the people of God need to know that those in pastoral leadership have the same struggles to be whole as everyone else. For example, anyone who is around me for any length of time will know that I have been crippled at times with undefined fear and anxiety. Because of some emotional disconnect in my growing up years, I have had a deficit that has manifested itself as an inner tension or uneasiness in public contexts. Often I have felt threatened in the presence of authority figures whose validation I highly valued. As one who desired to be whole in Christ, I finally had to seek help in addressing these feelings that served as a barrier to the joy I sought in Christ. Substantial healing has come through the assistance of those with spiritual gifts of inner healing. Does sharing that diminish my authority? Not at all. It sends two messages. First, I want to be all that Christ has made me to be. I am willing to do what it takes to apply the salve of Christ's grace to the wounds of my spirit. Authority, in part, is a by-product of people seeing the passion to follow Christ in a life. Secondly, people say, "He deals with the same stuff that I do. If he can face it, so can I."

2. Accept limitation of giftedness as a blessing from God. Equipping pastors are good to themselves. They have given themselves permission not to have to be able to "do it all." One of the most freeing things pastors can do for themselves is to accept their limitations.

Equipping pastors allow themselves to be finite. I have had to accept the fact that counseling and its related dimensions of healing ministry are simply not a part of my gift profile. Much of the ministry associated with *mending and restoring* does not match what motivates me. Moreover, I have not been given the commensurate gifts to carry out these activities. I could waste a lot of energy going to seminars and workshops to make myself passable in these dimensions. Or I can simply admit to our leadership board that God passed me by as he was distributing these aspects of ministry to others.

One of the responsibilities of a church's leadership board and personnel committee is to know the spiritual gift profile and passions of the heart of an equipping pastor so that they become good stewards of their pastor's time and energy. This will involve writing a job description that sets pastors free to pursue their "calling." I certainly cannot equip people in every area of a church's ministry. For me to train paraprofessional counselors would be about as appropriate as my teaching someone to skydive. But I can help people discover their spiritual gifts and be deployed accordingly, I can be an instrument to see that solid foundations are laid in discipling relationships and communicate a vision for a transgenerational discipling network, and I can teach and preach from Scripture effectively so that the Word stretches people to take the next steps of growth in discipleship.

It is also important to state what the pastor will not do. By delineating the areas of ministry that are outside the pastor's call, the leadership has a clear agenda for the ministry of the whole body of believers. Jerry Cook writes, "The pastor should be working all the time toward giving away everything that is peripheral to his/her own personal calling."[4] A pastor's articulation of need becomes an invitation to people of God to engage in a ministry partnership. Your need is another's opportunity. What God has not given to you, he has given to others.

3. *Trust God's people as full partners in ministry.* Trust is an attitude. To trust means to believe in. To trust people with full participation in the ministry means to believe that God's people are worthy of the trust. Trust is rooted in one's theology. I convey to the people with whom I share ministry that I have full confidence in them because I am convinced that they have full access to the

Holy Spirit just as I do. One function of an equipping pastor is to help people believe in and seek the Holy Spirit's empowerment for their ministry. People will rise to the level of expectations and begin to view themselves through the eyes of the person who believes in them.

Hud and I became partners of the heart first in the context of a discipleship foursome. As I was praying about leading a mission team to Romania, Hud was clearly placed on my heart. He received my invitation with a bit of fear and trepidation, because he was not at all sure that he wanted to be exposed to the needs of orphaned children. What would be the impact if our hearts are broken by what breaks the heart of God? However, Hud allowed the plight and severe needs of spindle-legged and love-starved kids to get under his skin. We wept together over what we saw.

When we returned from Romania, Hud could not shake off the condition of these children. My role was to continue to fan the flames of the passion that was growing in his spirit. What is the Lord saying to you? Nothing is too big for God. What do you believe that the Lord might want you to do about this situation? From that first visit in 1992, a ministry has been established under a nonprofit corporation in the United States with partners in Romania that continues today. This Christian ministry took over a state-operated orphanage and is now caring for thirty-five HIV-positive children in a family atmosphere. The head of the Romanian hospital in the community has called the House of New Life "a light in the darkness." The quality of care for these precious discarded children of God has dramatically improved because a pastor believed in one of the people with whom he shared ministry and this person was courageous enough to listen to the call of God upon his life.

A corollary to believing in God's people is sharing ministry with them. Dennis and Joanie became teaching partners with me in our Gifts and Call workshop. Many an hour was spent around my kitchen table writing and revising the curriculum together. The time came for each to take part in delivering the content in our workshop. They started teaching the material closest to their heart and life experience. We evaluated together the content, delivery, and format. We then decided to shift the workshop into the Sunday morning slot concurrent with worship. As the preaching pastor, that meant I could no longer be a part of the teaching team. It was now theirs. There is nothing more fun in ministry than seeing people find what God has created them to do and watching them blossom.

The ministries only become stronger, I have found, with a partnership approach. First, I am modeling what I am teaching about shared ministry, which speaks to the congregation as much as my words. Second, those with whom I share ministry sharpen me. Another's perspective opens up fresh insight when I am blinded by my own routine. Third, the vision grows with the input of others who have a passion for the same ministry.

4. *Share the Spotlight.* A fourth characteristic of the manner of an equipping leader is delight in highlighting the ministries of others. On the negative side, a leader's weak ego can get in the way of allowing others to flourish. Bill Walsh, former head coach of the San Francisco Forty-Niners football team, put it like this: "There is another side that can wreck a team or an organization. That is being distracted by your own importance. It can come from your insecurity in working with others. It can be the need to draw attention to yourself in the public arena. It can be a feeling that others are a threat to your own territory."[5]

I have long felt that personal security may be the most important quality of an empowering leader. Without personal security there will be little room for other competing egos to shine. If another's success is perceived as a threat to one's value, then the initiatives of others will not be welcome. But if leaders have a sense of their value and are secure in their strengths and weaknesses, then they can trumpet the ministry contribution others are making without feeling diminished. An equipping ministry rises or falls on this quality. Many who espouse the ministry of the whole people of God undermine it because they are not able to fully rejoice in the blossoming of others.

This is a major juncture between a dependency model and an equipping model of ministry. The question is: Where do pastors get their emotional fulfillment? In the dependency model, being needed is the emotional hook. Feeling like one is a "savior" in the lives of others is an underlying drive. If a pastor wants to make the shift to being an equipping leader, the emotional reward structure is different. Equipping pastors find their deepest satisfaction in seeing ministry emerge in the lives of those around them. An equipping pastor's value is enhanced by assisting others to discover their value.

The Style of an Equipping Leader

Equipping pastors not only have a *manner* that shares ministry, but they must exercise a leadership style that is consistent with an every-member ministry. There are leadership styles that inhibit the ministry of the whole people of God, and there are those that enhance it.

Inhibiting Leadership Styles

In my experience, three leadership styles are counterproductive to an equipping model.

1. *The Do-It-All Pastor:* In my capacity as director of the Doctor of Ministry Program, I received the following letter:

> In 1998 I submitted my proposal (for the Final Project) and it was approved. You pointed out that I needed to add your book to my bibliography. In my excitement I went out and purchased your book the same day. However, after I understood where you were coming from, my excitement turned to disappointment. I wanted to write my thesis on the "omnicompetent" pastor, and your book with its radical idea stood in the way of that.
>
> I was working 80 hours a week at the time, doing absolutely everything within my abilities in order to be a successful pastor. Yet my church wasn't growing, as a matter of fact, it was losing membership and finances.
>
> In December of '99 I was on my knees asking the Lord to transfer me to another church, but He did not. After my prayer that night I went to my basement to light up the furnace, and there on the top of the furnace was your book. That night I read the whole thing, anger burning within me because you were tearing down everything I believed was biblical about pastoral ministry. During the next six days I read it four times, and each time I felt better about your message.
>
> For a year and half now I have been applying your book to my ministry. People in the church are more relaxed. At this time we have twenty-six church members directly doing ministry that only a year ago would have been strictly my domain. Our attendance went from seventy to

one hundred and eighty. This year alone during the first six months we have had twenty-one baptisms. It took me a long time to internalize your message, but it has definitely been life changing.[6]

What a joy to see someone move from being the stifling do-it-all pastor to throwing open the window to a fresh breeze and allowing the Spirit to engage partners in ministry!

2. *Authoritarian:* There certainly are times when a leader needs to take charge and bark orders. When a house is on fire, this is not the time for consensus decision making. But in more normal times, authoritarian, top-down leadership is generally counter to an empowering model. This style often times masquerades as "team" ministry. I hear some senior pastors say they believe in team ministry. When you scratch a little deeper, what they mean is that they serve as the quarterback who calls the plays and assigns the players their part on the team. This type of team is simply an extension of the ego of the team leader. The players on the team are there to make the leader look good.

Authoritarian leaders see themselves like Moses did under the dependency model. Moses went up on the mount to consult with God and came down to the waiting crowd to deliver the message. In the authoritarian model all vision originates in the person at the pinnacle of the pyramid. People wait passively for the leader to get the next step in the vision.

This model, or a version of it, has been central to the profile of the next pastor churches are looking for. Search committees seem to be constantly looking for pastoral superstars who will be able, by their gifts of preaching and personal charisma, to excite the church community and attract a crowd. Congregations seem to be hooked on the one who can "save" them. Instead, how about someone who might come alongside and believe in the church as the whole people of God? Perhaps they should look for a team builder rather than an empire builder. A team builder gets emotional satisfaction from seeing the ministry of others come alive rather than from the body gathering so that the pastors can exercise their gifts.

3. *Laissez-faire:* A laissez-faire leader is one who occupies a position of leadership but does not lead. This can be an intentional leadership style. The reasoning goes like this: If I as pastor do not lead, this will force the lay leaders to assume responsibility. Laissez-faire

leaders create a leadership vacuum that others will be forced to assume. Again, this might be exactly the right leadership style under certain circumstances, especially when the leader is attempting to draw out and help others find their own leadership voice. But as a consistent style, laissez-faire leadership will either leave an organization without direction or foster a leadership power struggle as competing personalities step in to fill the leadership void. The end result is that confusion reigns.

Empowering Leadership Styles

As I have already acknowledged, leadership styles can vary based on the circumstances. Any of the above styles might be appropriate for a prescribed period and setting. But exercised as a general approach, these styles will work against an empowered ministry. There is a style that in general, I believe, encourages the body to fulfill its ministry. This is a style based on a partnership between pastor and people that I call "participative." It has the following characteristics:

1. *First among equals:* This statement affirms that leaders must lead. Anyone in a leadership position must influence the group in the direction of accomplishing its goals. Yet it must be done in such a way that there is not a distinction of value between the leader and those he or she is coming alongside. It is a leadership from the side, rather than a leadership from above. There is a very fine line that a participative leader must walk. Leaders either draw others to or share their vision with others, while inviting the team members to contribute or reshape the vision. This is based on the belief that Christ as head of the body is directly connected to every part of the body. Ministry and vision can come through the official structure or the fringes. I have found that often the true visionaries are not necessarily the ones who feel comfortable holding an office in the church. They are not organizational people. Yet they may be the very ones through whom God is speaking. These people must be given voice as well.

2. *Mutual visioning:* One of the simple ways I have attempted to lead while inviting others to join is the simple formula: "This is what I see . . . What do you see?" As leader, I can see by sharing my vision. As a team builder, I lead by inviting others to share what they see or to contribute ways they would refine the vision that I am sharing.

3. *Democratic:* Another way to look at an empowering leadership style is that it is democratic. This is perhaps most useful at staff and leadership board level, when the pastor is assured that those who hold these positions are mature, godly leaders. Democratic decision making with those who occupy positions but are not prepared spiritually is tantamount to turning over the church to the ungodly. By democratic, I mean that persons on the team assume responsibility for their own conviction, vision, and concerns. I have often had staff or elders come to me on the side and say, "I am concerned that we deal with such and such. Would you make sure that is a part of the agenda?" This usually means: Would you take care of that? You are the person in charge. My standard response when I sense deflection of responsibility is, "That sounds like an item close to your heart. Why don't you voice that the next time we are together?"

4. *Team Building:* Ultimately, an empowering leader is trying to grow teams of people who are applying their gifts to a mutually shared need. Staff teams function best when all are valued for their gifts, are in roles that match their motivated abilities, are united by a common vision and philosophy of mission, and are receiving recognition for their ministry. It is the joy of the empowering leader to be the catalyst to bring about that sense of teamwork at all levels of the church community or even in those teams that are launched from the church as a base community.

Moses was advised by Jethro to make the shift from doing all the leadership himself to sharing and developing the leaders around him. The people needed more leaders than just the one charismatic authority. Moses was to pour his life into growing "able men among all the people, men who fear God, are trustworthy, and hate dishonest gain" (Ex. 18:21). This leads to the third bit of advice that Jethro gave to Moses.

DECENTRALIZE THE STRUCTURE

Jethro advised Moses to decentralize the legal structure. He conceived a system where there would be multiple levels of leadership over groups of "thousands, hundreds, fifties and tens." This seems to be the appellate court process, with the initial decisions over matters of dispute handled at the group of ten. Everyone would be in a group of ten to whom they could go immediately to get resolution. Not only was Moses to share the leadership, but he was given a specific structure that defined the roles leaders were to play.

Our point of application is that an equipping ministry is a decentralized, permission-giving ministry. In my experience, there are three decentralized strategies that will transform a church culture into an every-member ministry:

◆ Build community and accomplish ministry through small groups.
◆ Multiply reproducing disciples by investing in a few.
◆ Mobilize for ministry around people's gifts and call.

Build Community and Accomplish Ministry Through Small Groups

There is no better tool to mobilize people for ministry than a group of eight to ten people meeting in face-to-face relationship. The best generic definition of small group I have found is this one by Roberta Hestenes: "A Christian covenant group is an intentional face-to-face gathering of 3–12 people who meet on a regular time schedule with the common purpose of discovering and growing together in the abundant life in Christ."[7]

The critical strategic question that must be answered by any church regarding small groups is, Will ours be a church *with* small groups or *of* small groups? A church *with* small groups views small groups as one option among many as to how people gather. A church *of* small groups is committed to small groups as a lifestyle; it is the way people live together in community. Just as a group of ten was in Jethro's mind the foundational group in Israel, so I believe they should be to the church.

The best argument for small groups as the living units of the new society is their multiple benefits. Small groups provide:

1. A sense of belonging: When does a person know that he or she belongs and is an integral part of the church? One significant mark of belonging is that a person has a place to honestly share the ups and downs of their spiritual journey in a nonjudgmental, caring environment. A second indication is that when you don't show up people come looking for you. This happens best in a small group.

2. A place of caring: The call came right after I walked through my front door on returning from Sunday worship. I was informed that Jim had had a heart attack on the church campus: "You'd better get right back here." By the time I arrived, Jim had been pronounced dead by the paramedics. Hester and Jim had become deep and cherished friends by this time. I knelt with Hester next to Jim's body, so that we could share our thoughts and offer Jim to the Lord. I accompanied Hester back to her home so she had someone with her as she informed her son and daughter of their father's passing. As Hester was on the phone, the members of Jim and Hester's small group began to arrive until the entire group filled their living room. We joined them. Hester and the group began to reminisce and even laugh a little. As I looked at the group, I realized that Hester's care system was in place. They would walk with her through the grief process in the months ahead better than any "pastoral care" could provide.

3. A context to discover and exercise gifts: What better place to exercise and be affirmed in the expression of one's spiritual gifts than in the relational community of a small group. Gifts are social. In a small group, one may see in operation the gifts of teaching, exhortation, mercy, pastoring, prophecy, evangelism, and so on as God's people naturally interact over the study of the Word, share vulnerably their personal walk toward faithfulness in Christ, and intercede for each other to grow into full stature in the Lord.

4. Leadership development: The best leadership development laboratory in the church is the small group. Small groups are not pastor reliant but lay led. Small-group leaders identify apprentices who are leaders in training. As apprentices are prepared, they can take over the group leadership or be sent out like missionaries to give birth to a new group. Leaders have a chance to learn the skills of leading a Bible study, developing a caring and sharing atmosphere, cultivating group prayer, and structuring for mission and service. The farm system for other leadership roles inside or outside the church is through the front-line ministry of a small group.

5. Evangelism: If it is true that "they will know we are Christians by our love," then as unbelievers can see Christians loving each other, they will be drawn to the source of that love. Small groups generally should be open communities where the members are free to invite and include those in their network of relationship.

Carl George recommended keeping an "empty chair" in the group circle to remind the group to be praying by name for those in the group's sphere of influence who have not come to Christ yet.

6. Maturity through community: I don't believe maturity occurs until we open ourselves honestly to God and each other. Then the Holy Spirit has a chance to make us different. In places of trust we can be transparent and confessional, see that we are not alone in our struggles, and allow ourselves to say to the Lord, "Change me."

An equipping ministry makes room for multiple types of small groups. The basic small group comes with many names and forms: nurture, koinonia, or kinship groups, and home fellowships among others. Generally they focus on four areas: Bible study, sharing, prayer, and service. Other types of small groups are evangelism (a core of Christians inviting unbelieving friends); discovery (self-motivated seekers are invited to examine the message of Christ); recovery (overcoming some form of addiction); and support (gathering around a common need that threatens one's quality of life).

A specific type of small group designed to carry out ministry is a ministry team. A ministry team is a small group called together by God who covenant to care for each other while exercising their spiritual gifts to minister to a specific need for which they mutually care. When we focus on the call in the New Reformation in chapter 10, we will look at how call is best expressed in the context of a ministry team.

Multiply Reproducing Disciples by Investing in a Few

The closing chapter in Howard Snyder's book *Liberating the Church* is entitled "Pastors: Free to Disciple." Snyder states that discipling is the primary focus of a pastor's ministry:

> Essentially, the pastor's first priority is to so invest himself or herself in a few other persons that they also become disciplers and ministers of Jesus Christ. It is to so give oneself to others and to the work of discipling that the New Testament norm of plural leadership or eldership becomes a reality in the local congregation. In other words, it is to bring the ministry of *all* God's people to functioning practical reality.[8]

Our Lord's approach to ministry serves as the model for the way we are to do ministry. Integral to Jesus' strategy was to select twelve with whom he would be in close association (Matt. 10:1–4; Mark 3:13–18; Luke 6:12–16). What was Jesus trying to accomplish by selecting a few from the larger entourage that was following him at this time in his ministry? It is estimated that Jesus had been about his public ministry for approximately a year before he clearly identified his inner core. What did Jesus think was going to be so fruitful about this approach that he was willing to risk arousing jealousy from the masses? Why not simply continue to enlarge the crowds and turn his initial popularity into a mass movement? I believe Jesus accomplished at least two things by this strategy: internalization and multiplication.

Internalization. Jesus was skeptical about the depth of devotion of the crowd that followed him. The populace was enamored by the miracle-working power of this authoritative teacher. But Jesus read the motives of their hearts. John records the thoughts of Jesus about the crowds: "When he was in Jerusalem during the Passover festival, many believed in his name because they saw the signs that he was doing. But Jesus on his part would not entrust himself to them, because he knew all people and needed no one to testify about anyone; for he himself knew what was in everyone" (John 2:23–25). Jesus knew that people were fickle; they were with you one minute and your enemy the next. As soon as the cross became the focus of Jesus' gaze and he began to instruct them in the eventuality of his own sacrifice, the crowd began to lose their infatuation. It was a short five days from Palm Sunday's shouts of "Hosanna! Blessed is he who comes in the name of the Lord!" to Good Friday's "Crucify him! Crucify him!"

Jesus didn't stake his future influence and kingdom on the groundswell of mass support. If he had, he would be a footnote in history grouped with other revolutionary leaders squashed under the Roman boot. Instead, Jesus had a big enough vision to think small. A. B. Bruce has stated this well in his classic work, *The Training of the Twelve:* "The careful, painstaking education of the disciples secured that the teacher's influence in this world should be permanent; that the kingdom should be founded on the rock of deep and indestructible convictions in the minds of a few, not on the shifting sands of *superficial* impressions in the minds of many."[9]

Multiplication. Jesus' way to reach the multitudes was not to hold ever larger gatherings. His ministry would not have been any more successful if he had fed ten thousand or a hundred thousand instead of five thousand. Robert Coleman comments, "His concern was not with programs to reach the multitudes, but with men the multitudes would follow."[10] Eugene Peterson captures this truth humorously: "Jesus, it must be remembered, restricted nine-tenths of his ministry to twelve Jews because it was the only way to reach all Americans."[11]

Jesus' model teaches pastors that one essential way to carry out ministry is to invest in a few who in turn can be equipped to invest in others. It requires vision to think small and to anticipate the long-term impact. In discipling, we lay solid foundations in Christ in a systematic way. This model also entails a view of sanctification that eschews instantaneous maturity. Through discipling, people are empowered to see themselves as channels who can assist others in growing up in Jesus Christ.

In *Discipleship Essentials,* I define discipling as "an intentional relationship in which we walk alongside other disciples in order to encourage, equip, and challenge one another in love to grow toward maturity in Christ. This includes equipping the disciple to teach others as well."[12] Most people do not have the confidence to assist someone toward maturity because they themselves have not been discipled. When teaching about discipling, I have repeatedly asked, "How many of you can point to someone who has acted as an intentional model and guided you through the foundation-laying stages in Christ?" People can identify models from afar or people they have respected, but fewer than 10 percent can point to someone who painstakingly gave themselves, week in and week out, to make sure that Christ is "formed" in them (Gal. 4:19).

Anything worthy to be called "discipling" must be transferable from one generation of believers to the next. A major obstacle to moving from one generation to another is the dependency created in a one-to-one model of discipling. The dynamic itself creates a hierarchy of teacher over student. I have discovered in my discipling that *triads* are the most powerful context for transformation. One person invites two others into a relationship of mutual accountability for the purpose of exploring what it means to be fully faithful to Christ. This takes the discipler out of the spotlight and makes him a member of the group, free to bring the natural impact of life in Christ. An interdependency develops rather than the debilitating hierarchy common in a one-to-one context. In the triad, people enter the discipling process knowing *in advance* that they are being equipped to disciple others, and therefore they do not enter into an exclusive, unhealthy attachment.

A pastor needs a visionary view of three to five years down the road. As the discipling network multiplies, moving out from the pastor, people will mature into self-motivated, reproducing disciples of Christ. Who wouldn't want to be pastor of a church where the people of God are self-feeders (in the Word and prayer) and self-starters (in using their gifts for ministry)? Robert Coleman sharpens the focus: "One must decide where he wants his ministry to count—in the momentary applause of popular recognition or the reproduction of his life in a few chosen ones who will carry on his work after he is gone."[13]

Mobilize for Ministry Around People's Gifts and Call

Gordon Cosby, pastor of the Church of the Savior in Washington, D.C., believes the church is to be "a gift-evoking and a gift-bearing community."[14] The phrase "gift-evoking" suggests that a regular part of the church's ministry is calling forth gifts of the Spirit from the members of the body and challenging them to be stewards of those gifts on behalf of the body. The phrase "gift-bearing" implies that when gifts are recognized, the community must make room for them to operate.

Gift-evoking

Desire. One of the pastor's responsibilities is to motivate and fan the flames of desire for people to discover their gifts and be deployed accordingly. This desire can be stirred within people when they are given a glimpse of how God has fashioned them as creatures with a unique profile of giftedness. When people catch hold of the exhilarating fact of their God-given individuality, the juices of desire begin to flow. Each person, I believe, has been created by God with the inner motivation to make a contribution or have an impact. We want to know the value for which we have been created.

Elizabeth O'Connor tells an apocryphal story in her book *Eighth Day of Creation*. Michelangelo was pushing a large hunk of stone down the street toward his sculpting studio when a neighbor cried out, "Hey, Michel, what are you going to do with that old piece of stone?" Michelangelo replied, "There is an angel in there that wants to come out."[15]

Fanning the flames of desire can occur in a number of ways. Public worship provides the community setting. Creative annual preaching series allow opportunities to regularly return to this theme and related matters. One of my recent favorites was to trace the ministry of encouragement in Barnabas through Acts around the theme "Fearfully and Wonderfully Wired," inviting members of the congregation to share their stories of coming alive as they have discovered and used their gifts. Peers speak to peers. At Saratoga Federated, January became the month to annually reflect on one's call to ministry and recommit to one's present or another place of service. Ministry fairs are becoming a common way to "advertise" to the congregation the variety of ministries that may be hidden to the rest of the congregation. On a Sunday morning after worship the patio bustles with excitement. As people roam the patio, inquiring into the opportunities for ministry, they can discover which ones fire their ministry passion. People have the opportunity to browse, converse, and sense in what context their gifts might best be used.

Discover. If we are going to stir people up to find their gifts, there should be a strategy in place to funnel those people who are eager to explore the possibilities. The church, as a gift-evoking community, must provide the tools for the discovery process. There are many approaches and tools available to implement the discovery process. One intake strategy uses a workshop. The workshop covers the essential biblical teaching on gifts and includes practical exercises to help people discern their unique profile. The same content can be repackaged for a weekend retreat or put into a small group's curriculum. Each approach is followed by individual interviews that build on the group sessions and home in on a person's own gifts. This deductive approach is limited and will reach no more than 25 percent of the congregation. This is why a fully developed small-group system and ministry teams are important, because most people will discover their ministries by doing or experimentation rather than through the cerebral approach of a class.

Deploy. Spiritual gifts sometimes find expression in *formal* positions within the church structure, whereas others are expressed *informally* in the natural interchange fostered in the dynamics of service. A person who has the gift of teaching may become a teacher (formal) of a particular class of students. But other gifts are exercised in a natural (informal) process of interaction and therefore go almost unnoticed. For example, someone with the gift of exhortation may simply, in the course of a small-group discussion, exhort the group not to be so self-focused. The exhorter is exercising a gift, yet not occupying a formal position.

Some churches have computerized systems to assist deployment. Attempting to match people's stated profiles with identified needs can be a massive administrative task. Though some churches have been successful at this, my personal focus has been to target desire and discovery and not to attempt a formal job-placement program. This is consistent with my theology of the church, which says that our Lord, as its head, is perfectly capable of running his body. It is important that each person know his or her gifts and accept the responsibility of being a good steward of them. In other words, the initiative needs to be on the individual to try to plug into ministry in a satisfying way.

Gift-bearing

The church is to be an affirming community. Not only are individuals to be responsible for their gifts, but the community must be the stewards of the gifts of one another. I have mentioned that the church's leaders should have a clear understanding of the pastor's gift-mix so they can be stewards of their own gifts. The same consciousness must be among the worshiping community at large. An affirming environment allows God's people to develop and refine their gifts. Permission-giving marks a community moving from a professional-focused to a body-focused ministry. People with identified gifts in teaching will not start out in full command of their materials, teaching techniques, and class presence; a supportive environment encourages fledgling teachers as they stumble, stutter, and stammer into maturity. A spirit of graciousness must pervade a community so as to create an environment of experimentation and risk.

I first encountered Karl as a guarded, self-protected individual. His self-confidence and sense of usefulness to God were at a low ebb as the result of a recent hurtful situation in another church. Disappointed in himself, he was convinced that he had failed God. For a year we met weekly in a discipling relationship. I watched Karl appropriate the forgiveness of God and develop a heart for discipling others. As our commitment period was coming to a close, Karl expressed a growing desire to do college ministry. The only trouble was that such a ministry did not exist in our church.

As Karl's call grew into unwavering zeal, we made room for his gifts and call by validating his desire to start a college ministry. Karl and I prayed for others to come forward who might share the same vision. As a result, the Lord guided Karl to a couple who also sensed a call to college ministry. I clearly recall the excitement on a summer Sunday morning as this newly formed team read the names of the college students in our community and challenged them to be the foundation for this college ministry. Karl's call had been affirmed. To foster body ministry, the church needs to be a gift-evoking and gift-bearing community.

Paying the Price of Change

As we look back over this chapter, we will note that the vision for an equipping ministry will entail almost wholesale change from the dependency model. Pastors are being asked to shift from care-giver to coach, from responders to proactive leadership developers, from those who do it all to helping God's people to do it all. The equipping ministry shifts the church from its traditional program base to a small groups community, from a haphazard approach to growing people to intentional, reproducing disciple making, from fitting people into preconceived slots to building ministry around people's gifts and call. What will it take to get there?

A key commitment question must be answered: Are you convinced before God and for the sake of the long-term health of the church of Jesus Christ that you are called to pay the necessary price to see the equipping ministry become a reality? Fear of the price to be paid is often the reason we are long on talk and short on substance in implementing the equipping ministry. The changes I advocate in the pastoral role will move a pastor into behavior that is generally contrary to the congregation's expectations. Confronting these expectations will precipitate scrutiny of a pastor's motivation for ministry.

Since God's people find their place in relation to the projected role model of the pastor, it must be the pastor who leads the congregation into equipping ministry. Because people resist change, the pastor needs to be prepared to take the brunt of resistance. Criticism such as "Why doesn't the pastor do more home visitation?" or "Why didn't he attend our committee meeting?" must be seen up front as a price to be paid. Are we willing to experience short-term pain for long-term gain in ministry? The truth is, we cannot be dependency pastors and equipping pastors at the same time. We cannot simultaneously invest ourselves in developing the ministry of a few and keep all the plates spinning. We must decide what we believe: Are we convinced that for the sake of the long-term health of the church of Jesus Christ, interdependency is the right model?

If our answer is yes, then the word *no* will become an important part of our vocabulary. It will be a no said graciously and winsomely, but a no nonetheless. This no is said to requests to fulfill the expectations of the dependency model of ministry in order to say yes to efforts that multiply the ministry of the body. There is biblical precedence for this. In Acts 6:1–7 the apostles are drawn into a dispute between the Greek- and Hebrew-speaking widows. The Greek-speaking widows feel they are being slighted in the daily distribution of the food. Reading between the lines, one gets the sense that the apostles have almost allowed themselves to become distracted from their primary call. They say to the community, "It is not right that we should neglect the word . . . to wait on tables" (v. 2). I don't believe it would have been stated this way unless they had been asked to assume this responsibility and add it to their portfolio. They had to say a gracious no in order to fulfill their God-ordained role of preaching the word and prayer (v. 4). As it turned out, ministry was actually multiplied because new roles were created for those who were full of the Holy Spirit and wisdom. Their no became another's opportunity.

To what must you say no in order to say yes to your role of "helping other men and women practice any ministry to which they are called"?

SUMMARY

Over the first seven chapters of this book, I have compared the impact of the New Reformation to dominoes falling in very different directions than we are used to. The first domino concerns seeing the church as organism from the bottom up versus the church as institution from the top down. The second domino involves a radical shift from a dependency-fostering role for the pastor to an equipping one.

The third and final domino challenges fundamental assumptions about the way we have traditionally conceived leadership. In the next chapter I will propose a way to look at leadership that does not recreate a priesthood within a priesthood. I will also attempt to identify more objective criteria to measure those whom the body should set apart to be equippers. In chapter 9 I will challenge the generally accepted hierarchical leadership model and argue that servant leadership as modeled by Christ is the style necessary to see the body come alive to its ministry. Finally, our journey will end in chapter 10 with restyling "call" and "ordination" according to an organism view of the church.

NOTES

1. Elton Trueblood, *The Incendiary Fellowship* (New York: Harper & Row, 1967), 41, emphasis added.

2. Ibid., 43

3. Carl F. George, *The Coming Church Revolution: Empowering Leaders for the Future* (Grand Rapids: Revell, 1994), 117.

4. Jerry Cook, *Love, Acceptance, and Forgiveness* (Glendale, Calif.: Regal Books, 1979), 106.

5. Richard Rappaport, "To Build a Winning Team: An Interview with Head Coach Bill Walsh," *Harvard Business Review*, January-February 1993, 112.

6. Used by permission of the author.

7. Roberta Hestenes, "The Church in Community through Small Groups" (Course syllabus, Fuller Theological Seminary), 1983.

8. Howard Snyder, *Liberating the Church* (Downers Grove, Ill.: InterVarsity Press, 1983), 243.

9. A. B. Bruce, *The Training of the Twelve* (reprint, Grand Rapids: Kregel, 1971), 13.

10. Robert Coleman, *The Master Plan of Evangelism* (Old Tappan, N.J.: Revell, 1964), 21.

11. Eugene Peterson, *Traveling Light* (Downers Grove, Ill.: InterVarsity Press, 1982), 182.

12. Greg Ogden, *Discipleship Essentials: A Guide to Building Your Life in Christ* (Downers Grove, Ill.: InterVarsity Press, 1998), 17.

13. Coleman, *The Master Plan of Evangelism,* 37.

14. Elizabeth O'Connor, *Eighth Day of Creation* (Waco, Tex.: Word, 1971), 8.

15. Ibid., 13.

Part 3

LEADERSHIP IN THE NEW REFORMATION

Chapter 8

Who Are the Equippers?

SOME ARE CALLED BY GOD, in Elton Trueblood's words, "to help other men and women to practice any ministry to which they are called."[1] If this is the case, the body of Christ needs to be sensitized to identify the equipping leaders. This chapter addresses two concerns related to this need:

1. How do we conceptualize leadership in such a way that we do not slip back into a hierarchical, top-down, institutional approach that creates a two-tiered division? How can we avoid what the Protestant Reformation attempted in theory but was unable to avoid in practice—a priesthood within a priesthood?

2. What criteria will provide a measuring stick for individuals who are pondering a call from God? Since the church is to be the ratifying body, how do we raise the consciousness of the Christian community so they can identify, affirm, nurture, and deploy from within their ranks the equippers God is raising up?

A FUNCTIONAL CONCEPT OF LEADERSHIP

Let me return to the image that has served as the frame for this book. To keep from creating an upstairs/downstairs church, we must conceive of leadership fundamentally in terms of the church as organism. The New Testament stresses function over form, operation over organization. Paul repeatedly uses functional language to describe the living organism operating under divine endowment. People are graced with ministry gifts in order to edify the body. Ministry is not restricted to professional or official positions within the body. Paul focused on behaviors that motivated people instead of on authority structures and official job descriptions.

This is not to say that the New Testament is uninterested in offices and structure. Rather, the key principle is that *function precedes position.* In other words, the biblical pattern is that a person demonstrates leadership gifts in practice before officially holding a leadership office. Office does not create authority but is the result of authority in evidence. The following formula summarizes the New Testament teaching on the elements necessary for authority:

(1) Gifts/Call (Recognition) + (2) Character of Christ = Authority (Leadership)

The first criteria for identifying equipping leaders is the *recognition* by the body that the appropriate spiritual gifts (which we will define) are operating under the anointing of the Holy Spirit. The second component that is essential to Christian authority is a life that reflects the servant character of Christ.[2] When leadership gifts are exercised in a manner consistent with a Christlike character, spiritual authority is the result. Members of the body implicitly validate a person's authority by "making room" for that ministry.

In what practical ways do we identify those who are called into leadership? How are leaders to be discerned in the body, and how is authority given? There is a significant contrast between the function/organism and the form/institution views of leadership.

Authority Is Rooted in the Recognition of Gifts

The starting point for authority is not title, position, office, or rank but the endowment of the Spirit on one's life. Ideally, there should be no conflict between the position one holds and the authority one exercises. David Watson writes, "The church should give official recognition to those in whom the Spirit of God is manifestly at work."[3] Let's look again at the model for selecting leaders that is recorded in Acts 6:1–6.

The apostles turned the problem of food distribution into an opportunity to recognize other gifted leaders in the body besides themselves. But note who chose the leaders! The apostles gave responsibility to the body to decide who would best serve them: "Therefore, friends, select from among yourselves... and they chose ..." (vv. 3, 5). The church chose seven Greek men "full of the Spirit and of wisdom." Though I assume that the body selected people gifted with administrative skills to handle the relief program, they placed their imprimatur on men whom they had already recognized for their godly life and leadership qualities. In like manner, the church body at Antioch set apart Barnabas and Paul to heed God's call to communicate the gospel message to the Gentiles (Acts 13:1–3).

Conversely, simply occupying an office cannot make up for deficiencies in personal qualities or spiritual gifts. Saul's jealousy turned into an uncontrollable rage against David. Why? The people recognized God's anointing on the new king, David, long before Saul was willing to leave his office. The women sang David's praises, and Saul fumed: "They have ascribed to David ten thousands, and to me they have ascribed thousands; what more can he have but the kingdom?" (1 Sam. 18:8). Saul's obsession with David's prowess made him unworthy to hold the office of the Lord's anointed. Long before he was officially crowned king, David was anointed by God; whereas Saul, because of his personal deficiencies, was king in name only.

It is painful to watch the tragedy of a person who occupies the office of pastor but does not evoke the authority. Position cannot establish one's identity or provide one with authority. There must be a congruence between person and position. One person I know struggled from day one in his new position as pastor because there was confusion over what he had to bring to the church. Without a clear sense of the shape of his own call or guiding ministry convictions, he could not get clarity on the leadership steps to take. A number of the key members in the church body sensed this man's confusion and therefore had difficulty submitting to his authority, which to them appeared only positional. When there is an evident disjunction between person and position, chaos reigns in the body, as it did in Israel during Saul's latter days.

Authority is not derived from office but is bestowed from above. There could be no clearer model for this than our Lord himself. Julian Charley writes,

> The authority of Jesus during his public ministry was not
> an assumed role. It stemmed from the reality of who he was.
> When he spoke, it was recognized to have the ring of truth

and the authority of God. When he healed or performed miracles, it was recognized that this was the finger of God. When he prayed, it was clear that here was a uniquely intimate relationship with God. . . . Yet his ministry all along had been one of sacrificial service and humility. Now this should be the pattern of authority in the church, but the underlying principle has far too often been forgotten.[4]

Sadly, what we often observe in church structures is an inverse relationship between spiritual and institutional authority. When the new life of the Spirit is not being spontaneously generated from within the organism, there is a power vacuum. Anointed leaders are replaced by managers. Authority shifts from empowerment from on high to the centralization of institutional structures. There ensues the pitiful attempt to resurrect life from the dry bones of the institution through restructuring. The endless shuffling of committees and agencies should, it is thought, spontaneously release life. When dead institutionalism replaces the dynamics of organism authority, leaders with an institutional mind-set demand that their constituents pledge allegiance to the organization. A dead institution is a skeleton bound together by wires, not sinew and muscle, flesh and blood.

We cannot do without authority. When spiritual authority is absent, it is replaced by the dry bones of bureaucratic centralization. Authority needs to be rooted in the recognition of gifts.

Authority Is Tested in the Crucible of the Body

The body of believers out of which one is called is the gatekeeper for its leaders. The community of believers ratifies or gently refutes the sense of inner call. Edmund Clowney writes that "no Christian can determine his calling in isolation from the throbbing organism in which he is called."[5] We can give a person a battery of tests to determine whether the gifts are present for ministry, but the validity of the tests can only be confirmed in doing ministry. Siegfried Schatzmann, writing about the relationship between gifts and authority, quotes Ernst Käsemann: "As charisma is only manifested as genuine in the act of ministry, so only he who ministers can have authority and that only in the actual experience of his ministry."[6] In other words, authority is not given through office, but demonstrated through action.

Once I was caught up short by a respected colleague, the youth pastor, who pointed out that I was living inconsistent with my stated views. I shared ministry with this man who clearly has a passion for Scripture, a desire to live in conformity to it, and an ability to communicate its meaning in a winsome and disarming fashion. In a pointed letter to me, he said (paraphrased): "Of all the people on staff, you have trumpeted the cause that we don't need the official sanction of ordination to operate in the realm of our gifts and authority. Why then have you not gone to bat for me to provide preaching opportunities when I have demonstrated abilities that have been confirmed in the body?" I could only admit that it was an obvious inconsistency between my stated theology and my practice. His message to me was that for the church to be the gatekeepers, he had to have opportunities for his call to be tested in the crucible of ministry.

What some denominations have done is to bypass the local body as the place to confirm calling. Instead, they have divorced authority from the community and have placed it further up in the hierarchical structures of the church. The procedure in my denomination tragically minimizes the place of the origin of call in the confirmation process. It seems that all a person needs is the personal, inward call of God, what Calvin termed the "secret" call. (It is called "secret" because the heart of a person is not open to the witness of the church but is known only to that individual's conscience before God.) A person discloses this sense of "inner" call by making his desire to pursue vocational ministry known to the ruling body, which in turn sponsors him to the next highest level.

Thomas Gillespie, formerly a pastor and now president of Princeton Theological Seminary, has written about the ironic inconsistency between the way we in my denomination select elders and deacons in contrast to pastors. Church nominating committees survey a congregation, prayerfully considering elders and deacons on the basis of godly qualities as recognized by the body. By contrast, we wait for pastors to step forward with a sense of inner "call," and we assume they have heard correctly. Seldom do we survey the congregation for those who are called to equipping leadership, nor do we often provide opportunities to test gifts and cultivate ministry.[7]

Instead of assuming that the best place to test calling is in the nurturing body, the church, we send people off to seminary and expect the testing and refinement of a calling to happen there. In fact, seminaries are not the best place for this to occur, because the test shifts from a functionally demonstrated ministry in a church to academic criteria in a seminary. Passing the right courses and applying this knowledge to an academically oriented ordination exam is characteristic of the requirements of many denominations. It is as if we expect that during seminary the *charisma*—"the gift"—needed for ministry will be bestowed as a result of theological study. In fact, we have reversed the biblical process. The usual seminary model could be called "pre-service" training. A person is trained with a minimum of ministry experience to assume pastoral roles, the contour of which he or she can only imagine. In contrast, the biblical model appears to be "in-service" training in the context of the church community where the body has had the opportunity to affirm demonstrated gifts.

The irony in the "pre-service model" is that the final step in the confirmation of call is to receive "a call" (job offer) from a church that barely knows the candidate. The calling body hopes this unproven, fledgling pastor will bear fruit. How contrary this is to the New Testament model! Leadership was nurtured within the body of people served in order to serve the body from which they came. David Watson writes, "In the early church the leaders were nearly always appointed from the area in which they served. They had the advantage of knowing the local scene intimately, and were therefore naturally placed for fulfilling an effective pastoral and preaching ministry according to the gifts given to them by God."[8]

The calling of a pastor transplanted from one locale to another is analogous to a skin graft. Often the skin graft does not take and is rejected by the body. The reasons for a new pastor's failing to "take" are myriad. For some the cultural leap from one setting to another is greater than anticipated. Even within the United States there are enormous differences in the cultural milieu from the South to the Midwest to Southern California to New England. In the interview process both parties are putting on their best face. What you see may not be what you get. Gaining and giving accurate information in the highly competitive atmosphere of a beauty contest creates illusion, not reality. This process has led to a high failure rate in matches made between pastors and congregations.

We have established such enormous institutional constraints in my denomination that it is almost impossible for someone to become ordained to serve in the body in which their calling was given birth. Between the high rate of mobility and the institutionalizing of the church through layers of regulations (e.g., no associate can become senior pastor in the church in which he serves), homegrown leadership is extinct in the denomination. We need somehow to restore the local church as the place where leadership gifts are identified, nurtured, and deployed. Authority is tested in the crucible of the church.

Authority Is Given Official Recognition in Ordination

What then is the relationship between authority and ordination? Authority is not conferred by ordination. Ordination is the body's formal acknowledgment of authority already exercised and a setting apart of that person to serve *for* and *among* the people. Ordination serves the function of protecting the church against those who could wrongly exercise the office of leadership. More positively, it is an official stamp of approval stating that the church has confirmed the gifts and Christlike character that are functioning in the life of this individual. Yet this is not how we have seen ordination generally practiced in the mainline churches. If the institutional mind-set prevails, ordination is generally understood to set apart a person "from and above" the body of Christ into a distinct category. Ordination has become the great divide. In an organic understanding of the church, authority for ministry originates in the sovereign God who graces a person with gifts that are confirmed through ministry in and by the body. This view will influence our conception of ordination. It is *charisma* that leads to office. Office is a confirmation of *charisma*.

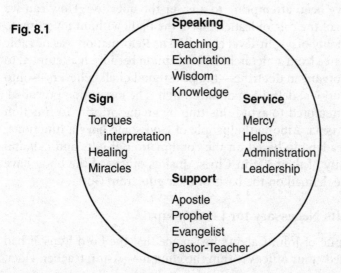

Fig. 8.1

Speaking
Teaching
Exhortation
Wisdom
Knowledge

Sign
Tongues
    interpretation
Healing
Miracles

Service
Mercy
Helps
Administration
Leadership

Support
Apostle
Prophet
Evangelist
Pastor-Teacher

The circle represents the one people (*laos*) of God. Among a set-apart people there are those who have the important functional distinction of helping the rest of the body reach their potential for ministry. Therefore, instead of being set apart *from* and *above,* the equippers are set apart *for* and *among* the people they serve. Ordination does not convey a sense of elevation but of being servants to the servants. Or as Rick Warren puts it, the staff are the "administers" and the people are the "ministers."

Michael Harper observes,

> The Church can only authorize those whom God has authorized, and can only recognize those whom God has gifted and empowered. No amount of theological training or human pressure can bestow *charisma* on a person. It is the sole gift of God, who gives it sovereignly to whom he wills, and when he wills. . . .The Church is utterly dependent on the Holy Spirit, and without *charisma,* however learned ministers may be, however dedicated and however many of the right hands have been laid on them, their work will be a failure. Much of the Church has yet to learn what this means, and its failure to honour the Holy Spirit is one of the main reasons why it has ceased to grow. The charismatic dimension is a crucial factor in the renewal of the ministry of the Church today.[9]

I have been attempting to answer the question, How can we conceive of the role of leadership in the body without reverting to the mentality of a split-level church? The Reformation was not able to break free from a hierarchical conception because it attempted to graft an organism doctrine—the priesthood of all believers—onto an institutional definition of the church. The institution prevailed. I have attempted to avoid this trap by giving priority to function and charisma. Among the people of God some have a functional call to leadership based on the combination of gifts and call and the quality of their life in Christ, just as others of the body have their role defined on the basis of their gifts from God.

Call/Gifts Necessary for Leadership

In spite of John Calvin's insistence that the Lord himself had "instituted" four offices within the church—pastor, teacher, elder, and deacon—many scholars contend that the New Testament does not portray a unified and uniform church order. The biblical picture resembles more a diversity of function and form at different stages of development in the church community. Form had great flexibility in order to accommodate the function of the body in particular localities. This truth points up the difficulty of moving from the organism nature of the church to one that invests order in church office. How do we translate charismata of the Spirit into official positions? We must return to the question I asked at the beginning of the chapter: If, in fact, the fundamental posture that pastors are to have vis-à-vis the people of God is "to help other men and women to practice any ministry to which they are called," what criteria can a searching person use to measure whether he or she is "called of God" to be an equipping leader? Equally as important, what standards of ratification can the church community exercise to test an individual's sense of call or to recognize someone operating under the Spirit's endowment?

If we hold a strictly organic view of the church, we might conclude that leadership offices are not needed. Is there a place for prescribed leadership? Absolutely!

As the early church expanded, it became necessary to identify leadership in some way. Paul and Barnabas retraced their steps through the towns of Galatia that they had visited on their first missionary tour, and they "appointed elders for them in each church, with prayer and fasting" (Acts 14:23). Paul instructed Titus to "appoint elders in every town" (Titus 1:5). By the time of the council in Jerusalem, the elders of that city had become so prominent that when the communiqué to the Gentile churches went forth, it came from the "apostles and elders" (Acts 15:23). Paul held a teary-eyed meeting with the elders of Ephesus in the town of Miletus (Acts 20:17). It is generally agreed that the fluid terms of "elder" (*presbuteros*), "bishop" (*episcopos*), and "pastor" (*poimen*) all refer to a same role in the church. This is all to say that there arose a need to formally identify those who would be recognized leaders in the church. Charisma was not enough; order demanded some structure.

The particular character of the leadership in the early church centered in two principal Greek verbs. The first is *proistēmi*. To the Thessalonians Paul writes, "We appeal to you, brothers and sisters, to respect those who labor among you and *have charge of you* [*proistamenos*] in the Lord and admonish you; esteem them very highly in love because of their work" (1 Thess. 5:12–13). Paul tells Timothy that those who *"rule well [proestōtes]"* are "worthy of double honor, especially those who labor in preaching and teaching" (1 Tim. 5:17). This is the same word used to describe a bishop who must manage [*prostenai*] his own household as a prerequisite for being able to care for the church of God (1 Tim. 3:5). It is noteworthy that this verb, which is descriptive of what leaders do, is considered by Paul to be a charisma of the Spirit (Rom. 12:8). The Arndt-Gingrich lexicon summarizes the intent of this word for leadership in two parts: (1) "be at the head of, rule, direct"; and (2) as if to capture the manner in which the leadership is to be exercised, "be concerned about, care for, give aid."

The second verb for leadership, *hēgeomai*, is found in Hebrews 13:7, 17, 24. This word creates a similar picture of the role of leadership and the expected response from the body as *proistēmi*. "Remember your *leaders* [literally, the "ones leading you," *hēgoumenon*], those who spoke the word of God to you; consider the outcome of their way of life, and imitate their faith" (v. 7). Stressing the proper response to leadership, the author of Hebrews writes, "Obey your *leaders* and submit to them, for they are keeping watch over your souls and will give account. Let them do this with joy and not with sighing—for that would be harmful to you" (v. 17).

From these two verbs and their rich contexts, we learn three things about biblical leadership:

1. *How leaders are to be treated.* Leaders are to receive "respect" (1 Thess. 5:12); we are to "esteem them very highly in love" (1 Thess. 5:13), consider them "worthy of double honor" (1 Tim. 5:17), "remember" (Heb. 13:7), and "obey . . . and submit," and "imitate their faith" (Heb. 13:17).

2. *What leaders are to do.* On behalf of God's people, leaders "have charge of you" (1 Thess. 5:12), "admonish" (1 Thess. 5:12), teach and preach the Word (1 Tim. 5:17; Heb. 13:7), and "keep watch over your souls" (Heb. 13:17).

3. *How leaders are to behave.* The leader's manner must be exercised as "those who labor among you" (1 Thess. 5:12; 1 Tim. 5:17), as those who must "give an account . . . with joy and not with sighing" (Heb. 13:17), as those who can be imitated (Heb. 13:7), and as those who exercise leadership in diligence (Rom. 12:8).

So from among the whole body of Christ, some are called particularly to provide oversight, rule, discipline, teaching, and care.

How do we identify those called to leadership as elders or pastors of the local church body? What distinguishes the equippers from the rest of the body? It would have been helpful if Paul and Barnabas had informed us of the basis for "appointing elders in all the towns." John Stott has written, "All God's people are priests, all are ministers or servants; but 'he gave *some* apostles, *some* prophets, *some* evangelists, *some* pastors and teachers.'"[10] The New Testament does not give us an infallible checklist. What follows is what I have deduced from Scripture and derived from experience as to the shape of the call and spiritual gifts that serve as the basis for equipping authority in the body. Remember the formula:

(1) Gifts/Call (Recognition) + (2) Character of Christ = Authority (Leadership)

Called to Be Equippers

When we speak of a "call" from God to ministry, the usual starting point is the secret or private call that resides as an inner compulsion in an individual spirit. In the *Institutes,* Calvin speaks of "that secret call, of which each minister is conscious before God, and which does not have the church as witness."[11] The experience of call is a sense of the weighty hand of God that will not leave us alone. Calvin calls this "the good witness of our heart." The burning drive and desire to serve God by building up his church is known only within the individual spirit.

Little can be said about the shape of the "inner" call, first, because it is subjective, and second, because it must be confirmed by the church. It is difficult to describe the mystical yet real and transcendent dimensions of call in human language. But we need to make the matter as clear as possible.

Ted Engstrom writes,

Leaders ... act in order to help others work in an environment within which each individual serving under him finds himself encouraged and stimulated to a point where he is helped to realize his fullest potential to contribute meaningfully.[12]

Building on the empowering nature of leadership, Michael Harper borrows an image from Juan Carlos Ortiz:

The work of the pastor is not that of a watchman who takes care that no one robs the bricks as they keep piling up, but a stonemason who builds them into the edifice.[13]

Finally, Gene Getz summarizes these definitions:

We are successful *only* as we are used of God "to equip the saints" to function in the body; we are successful only when the body grows and develops and ultimately manifests the "more excellent way"—the way of love and unity.[14]

The secret, or inner call moves beyond the mystical when we see what an equipping leader is to accomplish for the body. To pull the elements together from the definitions given, ask yourself: (1) Do you have a passion and demonstrated ability to see members of the body come alive to their ministry potential? (2) Have you demonstrated specific ways whereby you have helped people reach their potential for ministry? (3) Have you managed an environment where people are encouraged and motivated to find their place in accomplishing a ministry goal?

To carry this even further, an inner call becomes more than an undefined conviction or a shapeless tug of the Spirit when we use the specifics of an equipping ministry as a grid to identify our particular focus of equipping ministry. In my experience, a call to be an equipper has a particular concentration. Equippers can only reproduce ministry in the areas of their precise expertise and passion. The following chart reviews the equipping categories and the specific types of ministry that fall under each.

Mend/Restore	Establish/Lay Foundations	Prepare/Train

Healing:
  Emotional
  Physical
  Spiritual
Counseling
Discipline (correction)
Deliverance
Hospital/Shut-in
  visitation
Crisis intervention
Bereavement care
	Preaching
	  (proclamation)
	Teaching
	Worship planning
	Discipling
	Creating a nurturing
	  environment:
	  Small groups
	  Education
	Evangelism
		Help people find:
		  Spiritual gifts
		  "Call" to ministry
		Train for particular
		  ministry:
		  Tools
		  Skills
		Mission

Equippers will find themselves operating with an emphasis in one of these categories, though not exclusively so. Let me illustrate the process from my own call. The particular passion of my call is to make sure solid foundations in Christ are laid. My equipping focus straddles the *establish/lay foundations* and *prepare/train* categories.

Teaching is the gift that dominates my "gift-mix" and gives shape to my other gifts (establish/lay foundations).[15] I am motivated to help people see themselves as full ministers and as a result have a transformed self-perception of who they are in Christ. As a teaching pastor, I carry this out by systematically expounding portions of Scripture or through thematic studies of particular topics (e.g., prayer). Careful handling of the text of Scripture is critical for me. *Establishing/Laying foundations* is also expressed through weekly *discipling* appointments in a covenantal triad in order to see people deeply rooted in the spiritual disciplines, core doctrines, Christlike character qualities, and engagement in ministry. Those discipled are in turn equipped to do the same unto a third generation.

Central to helping create and manage an equipping environment is a commitment to small groups in multiple forms. This decentralized ministry shifts the focus of the church from a pastor to the body. At this point my call shifts to *prepare/train*. Small-group leaders are given the specific tools necessary to carry out their role. Multiple strategies are also employed to assist people in discovering and using their spiritual gifts in the context of ministry both inside and outside of church.

Finally, a gift of *visionary leadership* is exercised constantly to paint a picture of the church as a living organism or a ministering community. The church is like an athletic team with the pastoral staff serving as the "player-coaches," assisting the team members to find their place on the team and to develop in their contribution to the "victory" of the whole. The church is like an orchestra under the baton of the conductor Jesus Christ. Jesus blends the diverse sounds of the strings, wind, reed, brass, and percussion instruments together into a unity. The pastor is like the first violinist, who helps the orchestra stay in tune. Essentially, equipping leaders are the cultivators and managers of a ministry culture that is inclusive of the whole people who are given permission to be the initiators of ministry.

A colleague's profile in ministry serves as yet another illustration of the content of call. When I became the senior pastor at Saratoga Federated Church, Arvin had been an associate for ten years. Over those ten years he acted like a utility player on a baseball team. He was versatile and could play many positions. He had done everything from adult education, to starting a college ministry, to giving oversight to the children's ministry. Where there was a gap, he was asked to fill it. Yet he was not operating out of his sense of call. One of my first questions to him was, "If you could design a job description that gave expression to your heart passions, what would it look like?"

He said, "I would love to be the Pastor for Care, Counseling, and Family Ministry." Arvin's primary heart was in the *mend/restore* area. Providentially, I believe, this was a perfect complement to my emphasis and gifts. Arvin had a heart to enter into the traumas of people's lives in counseling and crisis intervention. Yet the challenge was to do this in such a way that this ministry was not just centered on him as the rescuer, furthering the dependency model, but that it also engaged those in the body who had a heart for the same ministry. This all became located under the care deacons, who multiplied these ministries through teams centered in the passions of God's people.

Over the years, under Arvin's leadership, a Barnabas ministry to the unemployed and underemployed was given birth, teams of grief ministers and hospital visitors were formed, ministries of various kinds to the addicted took shape; and cancer survivors and those with chronic pain had support groups. All of these ministries came about because a ministry multiplication environment was created that was connected to a staff person with a heart for this area and vision to see it grow beyond one person's ability to deliver this ministry. Thus, Arvin's ministry fleshed out the *mend/restore* arm of equipping.

I will define "call" in greater detail in chapter 10 as it relates to the whole body, but some descriptive elements are appropriate at this point. A call to be an equipper has the following characteristics:

1. A call comes in the form of an "inner oughtness" or burden that says, "This I must do." By "burden" I don't mean "weighted down," but an inner compulsion to see God's people come alive to their ministry potential.

2. Call can also be identified as that place of joy where energy flows and there is deep satisfaction in service to God. I come alive when I am sharing the vision of ministry spontaneously arising out of the body or the dream of an equipped ministry. When the geyser begins to erupt from within, I know I am operating at the heart of my call.

3. A genuine call takes more energy to stifle than it does to release. Jeremiah tried to repress his call to proclaim the prophetic word, but he became more weary putting the lid on the message than he did letting it flow: "If I say, 'I will not mention him, or speak any more in his name,' then within me there is something like a burning fire shut up in my bones; I am weary with holding it in, and I cannot" (Jer. 20:9). An equipper's passion will be, in one form or another, to help others be living stones that find their place in the edifice God is creating.

Gift-Mix for Equippers

In our quest to provide some objective criteria by which "call" can be tested, we have looked at (1) how to conceive equipping leadership, and (2) the focus of equipping ministry. The third criterion I propose is spiritual gifts. God's call to leadership in the body is directly related to the means or tools given leaders to carry out the call. Gifts and call are related to each other as means to ends.

Unfortunately, there is no direct correlation between sovereign organism gifts and institutional offices in the church. Discernment of God's will would be much simpler if there were a one-to-one relationship between equippers' leadership gifts and a particular role or office such as pastor, elder, or missionary. But I believe there is a cluster of gifts that could generally be subsumed under the category of leadership gifts for the body. In other words, there are gifts that would need to be present for someone to hold an office. Hans Küng holds this view: "The Pauline charisma cannot be subsumed in the clerical office, but the clerical offices can be subsumed under the charisma."[16] The Pauline perspective moves from charisma to recognition to commission. Organism always precedes institution.

Peter Wagner offers a helpful explanation of a spiritual gift-mix, which I draw upon here. Instead of seeing one gift as the dominant or primary way a person functions, I believe most leaders have a cluster of gifts that interact with each other to form the person's unique profile. For example, as I stated above, my profile includes the gifts of pastor-teacher, visionary leader, and exhorter. Within my gift-mix, teaching tends to give shape to the way I pastor, exercise leadership, and exhort. As a teacher, I want people to understand and see things as they have not seen them before.

The following descriptive list of equipping gifts serves as a self-test for personal examination:

Support Gifts	Others
Apostles	Leaders
Prophets	(a) Visionary
Evangelists	(b) Administrative
Pastors-Teachers	Exhorter
	Wise

What is your gift-mix as an equipping leader?

Support Gifts

The obvious place to begin is to define the gifts already specifically stated in Scripture as given to the body to prepare it for ministry. "The gifts he gave were that some would be *apostles,* some *prophets,* some *evangelists* and some *pastors* and *teachers*" (Eph. 4:11). These gifted members of the body bear in common the tool of God's Word. They wield the sword of the Word, but each with a different focus. Michael Harper has helpfully identified a key verb that captures the motivation of each of these gifted ones:[17]

1. *Apostles (Go).* The apostolic ministry is a constant reminder that each local church's parish extends to the ends of the earth. Although I do not believe there are apostles in the restricted sense of the original disciples called to be unique and authoritative witnesses and interpreters of the redemptive events of Christ, I do believe their spirit continues to be embodied in certain members of the church. In a general sense, the term *apostle* means "messenger" or "emissary," "one who represents another." The apostolic spirit is a missionary spirit. Paul expressed this spirit when he wrote that it was his "ambition to preach the gospel, not where Christ has already been named, lest I build on another man's foundation, but as it is written, 'They shall see who have never been told of him,

and they shall understand who have never heard of him'" (Rom. 15:20–21 RSV).

Those who embody an apostolic spirit have the passion to "go." There is a desire for adventure and living on the edge in order to take the gospel to new territories such as unreached people groups. Missionaries adapt well to another culture and can use their gift-mix in a cross-cultural setting. Apostles are filled with compassion for those who have never had the opportunity to be exposed to the living God. Our God is a seeking and sending God, and an apostle is captured by his spirit to go in his name.

Missionaries equip the church through the constant reminder that God's heart encompasses the whole world. We are being reminded today that missions is not just one aspect of what the church does, the *Missio Dei* is what the church *is*. In an era when the Christendom paradigm has collapsed and mission has returned to the doorstep of the church in the Western world, an apostolic spirit needs to be endemic to the church's identity. Missions is not about a hundred people amassing the resources to send one person across the globe, but about all of God's people engaged in mission next door. Jesus captured the apostolic spirit when he gave the church its mission statement that is true for all churches, "Go therefore and make disciples of all nations" (Matt. 28:19).

2. *Prophets (Hear)*. Listening to God's Word for a particular time and place marks the prophet's ministry. A prophet is literally one who speaks for another as Aaron spoke for Moses. The Greek word *prophētēs*, when broken down into component parts, conveys a prophet's role: *pro*, "before," and *phētēs*, "cause to shine." So a prophet is one who stands before the word of God and causes it to shine. A prophet's ministry can take various forms, such as a biblical exegete with a passion for truth or a person, spontaneously inspired by the Spirit, who has a word for a local body of believers.

Prophets hear a message from God and are inwardly compelled to deliver it. Truth is an obsession with prophets. They tend to see things in broad strokes with the instinctive sense of knowing what is right for a whole group of believers. Prophets paint in two colors, black and white, for they see things more incisively than the rest of us who muddle around in the shades of gray. A prophet intuitively understands the spirit of our times or the cultural drift so that his message cuts through those things that dull the spirit of Christian community, such as the comfort of wealth.

A prophet equips the body by inciting them to action or holding up the mirror so its members can see what they have become. Like the head sending the signals through the electrical impulses of the nervous system to stimulate it for action, the prophet passes on what he hears. Prophets help crystallize the vision of a local body and God's heart for these needs within the church.

3. *Evangelists (Grow)*. The fact that "evangelists" are rarely mentioned in Scripture may be indicative of the role they played to equip the saints. Paul exhorts Timothy, "Do the work of an evangelist" (2 Tim. 4:5). Philip embodied the gift of evangelism. When he encountered the Ethiopian eunuch on the road to Gaza and observed the eunuch's struggle with the scroll of Isaiah 53, "beginning with this scripture he told him the good news of Jesus" (Acts 8:35 RSV). An evangelist is a person with a particular passion and facility to tell of the overwhelming love of God individually or publicly so that people take the initial steps of Christian discipleship.

Perhaps the reason not many are identified with the gift of evangelism is that evangelism is a responsibility of the entire body of believers. Evangelists remind the body that it is natural for organisms to grow. Evangelists keep the body alive through a steady influx of new babes in Christ. It is then the responsibility of the church through a multigifted body to nurture them toward maturity in Christ. In a post-Christian environment, evangelism will come in the form of sacrificial service to the brokenness of people and the ability to listen to the needs of people's hearts that are just below the surface of everyday conversation.

4. *Pastor-Teachers (Care and Know)*. Though "pastor" and "teacher" are listed as two separate gifts in the Revised Standard Version, the Greek sentence structure indicates these are to be placed together as one gift. As evangelists are the obstetricians presiding at the birth, pastor-teachers are the pediatricians who provide the care and knowledge for growth toward maturity. Therefore, pastor-teachers function with a sense of protective care for the long-term spiritual welfare of the flock and teach the Word of God as the primary means to feed, nurture, and shepherd.

A pastor's heart is evidenced by a concern for the spiritual health of God's people. Positively, this is expressed by a desire to teach the Word of God so that there are proper nutrients for growth to occur. This suggests that those who enter pastoral ministry should have the characteristics of a teacher.

Teaching ministry comes into focus when we contrast this gift with preaching (Acts 5:42). Preachers announce and proclaim like trumpets in an orchestra, while teachers explain and expound like the violins that fill in the broader nuances. A preacher presses for a decision, appealing to the heart, but a teacher addresses the mind and desires understanding. Preachers stir up the troops to action; teachers are concerned with long-term change. You can be a teacher without being a pastor, but you cannot be a pastor without being a teacher.

The gift of pastor-teacher may have a direct correlation to the office of elder or bishop. When Paul refers to "elders who rule well . . . especially those who labor in preaching and teaching" (1 Tim. 5:17), it is difficult to see any difference between the office of elder and the gift of pastor-teacher. The only gift Paul seems to identify with those qualified to be elders is "an apt teacher" (1 Tim. 3:2); an elder "must have a firm grasp of the word that is trustworthy in accordance with the teaching, so that he may be able both to preach with sound doctrine and to refute those who contradict it" (Titus 1:9). Pastors are to be teachers.

As one having the ministry of oversight of the local body of believers, a pastor-teacher has perhaps the most relevant gift to an equipping ministry. Pastor-teachers manage an environment and set a tone for equipping.

Other Equipping Gifts

There are other equipping gifts that are important supplements to the essential support gifts:

1. Leadership. One word for leadership mentioned earlier is identified with Paul as a charisma (Rom. 12:8). *Proistēmi* can be translated to "stand before" or "be out in front." The gift of leadership thus has to do with helping the body to reach its potential and to arrive at its God-appointed destination. There are two types of leadership in the Bible. Some people are gifted with both these abilities, but most are not.

Visionary leadership. I link the gift of faith (1 Cor. 12:9) to leadership and come up with "visionary leadership." People with the gift of faith have the ability to apprehend the promises of God for a particular body of believers and become convinced that these dreams will be a reality. A visionary is someone who "sees before."

He has the ability to know what can be and then articulate those dreams in such a way that people come to see the possibilities they could not see on their own.

Visionary leaders are transforming leaders. They help people to see themselves differently and identify their roles in accomplishing the dream. Visionaries throb with a sense of urgency and intensity. Since the dream is from God, leaders will call God's people to account and cause them to examine the cost to accomplish a goal worthy of the sacrifice.

I view this entire book as an expression of my gift of visionary leadership. My hope is to lift our sights to the horizon of a biblical vision of the church as organism. If this vision has been sufficiently clear and is caught, then you have been lifted onto a higher plane accompanied by the energy that a vision unleashes.

The famous jurist Oliver Wendell Holmes once boarded a train but was unable to find his ticket. After watching Holmes fumble through his pocket in growing dismay, the conductor politely said, "That's all right, Mr. Holmes, I am sure you have your ticket somewhere." Looking the conductor straight in the eye, Holmes replied, "Young man, that is not my problem at all. I don't care about giving my ticket to the railroad, I just want to find out where in the blazes I'm going." Visionary leadership helps the church know "where in the blazes" it is going.

Administrative leadership. We discover the word *administration* in 1 Corinthians 12:28. Translated "governments" in the King James Version, the Greek word literally means "helmsman." This is the person who charts the course, steers the ship, and makes sure it arrives at the proper destination. Note that the administrator differs from the visionary, as the helmsman differs from the owner of the ship. The ship's owner determines its destination; the helmsman is responsible for getting it there. I repeat, the two gifts may exist in a single person, but this is rare. Often the administrator is a person who can accomplish someone else's vision. Thus, this gift could be defined as the ability to make decisions on behalf of others that result in the efficient operation and fulfillment of goals.

The gift of administration is integral to managing an equipping environment. Administrators have the ability to see the big picture as well as the necessary steps to reach the goal. They often have insight into the kinds of gifted people needed for the task. They will identify who has the gifts of pastoring, exhortation, or teaching long before others will, and they will urge them to play their God-given roles.

Administrators are the planners, strategists, and delegators of the body. They are good at decision making and are excellent problem solvers when the gift of wisdom is also present. Their leadership is best exercised when they help a group accomplish its goals by encouraging maximum participation so that the mind of Christ is corporately discerned. Administration is one of the most underrated gifts in the body because it does not sound supernatural. But when the gift is properly functioning, the other members of the body will be flourishing as well.

2. Exhortation. The word *exhort* is heard in our contemporary idiom as confrontation. It can conjure up images of ranting individuals with flailing arms. Exhortation reminds me of the cartoon of a pastor shaking his finger at his congregation from his lofty perch and saying, "Naughty, naughty, naughty!" But biblically the gift of exhortation (Rom. 12:8) is derived from Jesus' word for the Holy Spirit: *paraklētos* (John 14:16; 16:7). Far from having the sense of standing over another in judgment, the word literally means "to be called alongside to help" or "to speak to someone by being at his or her side." An exhorter is essentially a motivator.

Biblically there are three nuances of exhortation.

Encouragement. Barnabas was called a "son of encouragement" for doing such deeds as selling property in order to support those in need in the early church. His heart went out to those in the church who had little. The ministry of counseling in its various forms captures the spirit of Barnabas in today's church. Counselors tenderly "come alongside," providing an atmosphere of acceptance in which someone can learn to be safe. In an atmosphere of safety, people's hurts, wounds, and fears can be exposed and hope for wholeness can be instilled.

Cheerleaders. Exhorters are the cheerleaders of the body. They are able to stir up joy and enthusiasm for the Lord's work. They could be called spark plugs, inciters, and promoters. Like a coach at halftime igniting his team for action for the second half through a rousing pep talk, exhorters call people to be their best. They bring out the best in others because they fervently believe in the God-given potential of every person.

Challenge. Exhortation also comes in the form of challenge. Barnabas paved the way for the new convert, Saul, to be accepted among the apostles, who were justifiably suspicious (Acts 9:27). Barnabas saw the genuine change in Saul and challenged the apostles to see it also. Exhortation runs right up to the edge of command without crossing the line. Paul challenges the Romans by saying, "I appeal to you therefore, brothers and sisters, by the mercies of God, to present your bodies. . ." (Rom. 12:1). Based on the pattern of mercy God has demonstrated as described in the first eleven chapters of Romans, Paul draws some behavioral conclusions.

3. Wisdom. Another gift needed in a leader is the ability to apply Spirit-given insight to specific needs. The gift of wisdom is like the doctor who is a skilled diagnostician; he draws incisive conclusions from specific symptoms.

When Solomon became king, he was rewarded by God because he prayed for an "understanding mind. . .to discern between good and evil" (1 Kings 3:9). This "understanding mind" was immediately tested by the dilemma of the child claimed by two mothers. Solomon's command to divide the child in two revealed the compassionate heart of the true mother. So the story concludes, "All Israel heard of the judgment that the king had rendered; and they stood in awe of the king, because they perceived that the wisdom of God was in him, to execute justice" (1 Kings 3:28).

We have stood in awe when a striking solution is suddenly proposed to a complex and seemingly insoluble problem. People with wisdom seem to be able to penetrate to the heart of the matter. They are able to separate the wheat from the chaff. I have sat in meetings that have been hopelessly polarized until someone who has listened quietly offers a solution that both sides immediately see as a way out of the dilemma. Wisdom carries inherent authority and power. Truth knocks down dividing walls. Leaders with the gift of wisdom are perceived as fair and judicious without an axe to grind. Their word can be received.

Discerning Call

In summary, people who sense a call to professional leadership in the body should measure that call against their own and others' perception of their gifts. Leaders should have at least one dominant and one subordinate leadership gift in their gift-mix.

In this chapter we have interpreted leadership so as not to create de facto another clergy-laity split. By emphasizing the functional role of leadership within the one people of God, we have said that leaders are set apart from *within* and *for* the body. We have examined the shape of "call" and the gifts that might give some objective criteria whereby a person and the whole body of Christ can discern a call to leadership. In the next chapter we will examine the leadership style necessary to empower the body to its ministry. We will see how this applies to relationships among staff, between staff and the leadership core, and between the leadership core and the congregation.

NOTES

1. Elton Trueblood, *The Incendiary Fellowship* (New York: Harper & Row, 1967), 41.

2. The range of qualities a leader should exemplify is not within the purview of this book. These are examined elsewhere, notably in *Sharpening the Focus of the Church* by Gene Getz (Wheaton, Ill.: Victor, 1984).

3. David Watson, *I Believe in the Church* (Grand Rapids: Eerdmans, 1978), 262.

4. Quoted in Watson, *I Believe in the Church*, 262.

5. Edmund P. Clowney, *Called to the Ministry* (Chicago: InterVarsity Press, 1964), 34.

6. Quoted in Siegfried Schatzmann, *A Pauline Theology of Charismata* (Peabody, Mass.: Hendricksen, 1987), 97.

7. Thomas Gillespie, "The Call and Ordination in a Reformed Theology of the Ministry" (Unpublished paper), 10–11.

8. Watson, *I Believe in the Church*, 268.

9. Quoted in Watson, *I Believe in the Church*, 263–64.

10. John R. W. Stott, *One People* (Downers Grove, Ill.: InterVarsity Press, 1968), 45.

11. John Calvin, *Institutes of the Christian Religion* (Philadelphia: Westminster, 1960), 4.3.11.

12. Ted W. Engstrom, *The Making of a Christian Leader* (Grand Rapids: Zondervan, 1976), 20.

13. Michael Harper, *Let My People Grow* (Plainfield, N.J.: Logos International, 1977), 214.

14. Gene Getz, *Sharpening the Focus of the Church* (Chicago: Moody Press, 1974), 121.

15. "Gift-mix" is Peter Wagner's way of describing the unique and multiple combination of spiritual gifts working through an individual. See Peter Wagner, *Your Spiritual Gifts Can Help Your Church Grow* (Ventura, Calif.: Regal Books, 1994).

16. Quoted in Schatzmann, *A Pauline Theology of Charismata*, 86.

17. Harper, *Let My People Grow*, 44.

Chapter 9

Servant Leadership: Empowering the Body for Its Ministry

W E HAVE NOTED SOME SPECIFIC touchstones by which we might identify the people called to be equipping leaders in the church. We observed that biblically authority is not characterized by a position occupied but rather is the natural by-product of the anointing of God. This authority is recognized by the body when call and gifts are reflected in, and consistent with, godly character. Although there is one ultimate head of the body, Jesus Christ, gifted leaders play a necessary role within the organism of the church.

How is equipping or empowering leadership to be exercised? Are there leadership styles that enhance the ministry of the whole people of God? Are there leadership styles that inhibit the release of the giftedness of the body?[1] The following principle helps us to answer these questions: *The goal of leadership in an equipping ministry is for all believers to accept before God their responsibility to be stewards of their gifts and call in order to make a contribution to the health of the whole body of Christ and to the extension of its witness to all spheres of life throughout the whole world.*

In dealing with leadership styles I hope to move beyond the vague generalizations that often typify discussions of this subject. We will look at authority, accountability, and role expectations associated with senior pastors, staff members, leadership boards, and members of the congregation. Additional guiding questions are: How does ministry originate in the local church? Who has authority to initiate new ministries or determine when old ones no longer serve their purpose?

We will again contrast the institutional view of leadership with the organism view. Our starting point greatly affects our conception of the exercise of authority, accountability, and role definition.

THE INSTITUTIONAL MODEL

In the institutional or hierarchical model, authority is concentrated, if not by design then in practice, in the pastor, the head of staff. Pastors are the ones who "run things around here," people will say. If you want to get anything done, somewhere along the line it is assumed the pastors must at least give their blessing. All roads eventually lead to the pastor's office. Let's examine the pastor's role as head of staff in the hierarchical conception.

Senior Pastor

The following picture seems to be a generally accurate description of much of the entrepreneurial Western church. Admittedly, any generalization is a caricature, yet many of the new paradigm churches follow more of a corporate, institutional model than an organism model:

Chief executive officer. The ideal for the senior pastor in the Church Growth Movement has been described as "ensconced in managerial splendor, oozing charm and self assurance from a black leather swivel chair in his lavishly appointed executive suite."[2] Though this may refer to a small percentage of multigifted pastors of megachurches, the expectation is left that all senior pastors are perceived to be the administrative heads of the organization. They should have the skills to run an efficient operation. This usually means that all job descriptions are clearly delineated and all persons know precisely the tasks they are to perform for the organization. As CEO, the executive is the one who assigns responsibilities.

Team ministry. There is much talk today about "team" ministry, but the phrase is applied to two very different concepts. In the hierarchical structure the senior pastor's role is very much like the football coach who assigns the players to their position and calls the plays that are going to be run on the field. The staff knows clearly that their roles are defined for the efficient operation of the organization according to the senior pastor's perception of the needs of the congregation. Often the motivation behind team ministry is to make sure that the CEO looks good.

Initiation of ministry. The responsibility for initiating ministry ultimately resides in the senior pastor as the primary visionary. This is the trickle-down view of ministry. The vision for the church originates at the top and is carried out by the staff, who are called to fulfill that vision. The senior pastor is the primary goal setter, since he is the one who has access to the power position of the pulpit. Authority centers in preaching. A ministry that is not declared from the pulpit is not seen by the congregation as important or valid. The senior pastor is given the privilege and responsibility of articulating and supporting from the pulpit the full range of the church's vision for ministry. This leaves the validity of the ministries of other staff members subject to the senior pastor's stamp of approval.

Control. In a hierarchical model, control begins at the top and moves downward. Thus, the senior pastor will want to know and approve any initiative in ministry. For any ministry to begin, permission must be granted by "the boss." Control or the need to know is often a response to the fear that something might occur which will upset people. I once served with a pastor who would allow no committees to meet without his being present. In his mind, the pastor's role meant having his finger in every aspect of church life.

Accountability. Accountability flows only in one direction—from the top down. In a hierarchical structure a clear chain of command is intended. The senior pastor will review the work of subordinates and so on. Associates and assistants feel the same pressure to please their "bosses" and fulfill their expectations that is typical in any business hierarchy. To think that subordinates might also be able to hold their superiors accountable is inconceivable. A Christian attorney friend did the unthinkable when he told the partners of his law firm that he had asked those whom he supervised—paralegals and secretary—to review his work as a manager. Needless to say, the partners would never have considered allowing themselves to be in that position. Moreover, the subordinates who were asked to evaluate their boss were equally flabbergasted. This approach would very likely draw the same response in the church.

Hierarchical language. Perhaps our terminology is as clear an indicator of our institutional framework as anything. We confer titles to identify a person's rung on the authority ladder and to clarify his position relative to the pinnacle of power. From the top down it may look something like this: senior pastor, associate pastor, assistant pastor, assistant to the pastor, director, assistant director, executive secretary, secretary, and so on. The church has adopted language that communicates power via position, not via the call or function of persons. Therefore, we tend to make value judgments about the relative worth of individuals based on a pecking order.

Staff and Leadership Board

The role of the leadership board is usually an extension of the structure of the pastoral staff. If the staff is hierarchical and task focused, the leadership board will follow suit. The church is heavily influenced by a secular business model and tends to adopt the latest philosophy of management. Richard Hutcheson sees this managerial emphasis as one element that is stifling the life of the Spirit in the church:

> As useful as these tools (i.e., management by objective, etc.) may be for specific purposes, however (and they are), they have not proved to be the answer to the kind of decline exemplified by membership losses. Indeed the managerial revolution within the church, with widespread adoption of the assumptions as well as the technologies of management science and organizational sociology, may have been one of the reasons for the decline.[3]

As in the secular world, "management by objective" took the church by storm. This is what I would call a centralized, trickle-down approach to running the church. The central body establishes the specific objectives for the organization that are to be implemented by its various program entities, usually called committees. Flowing from the staff to the administrative board and out through its working groups will be the objectives that originate at the top. As a result, a church board will often have the following characteristics:

Rubber stamp or obstacle. In a staff-centered ministry, the church board often serves as a rubber stamp that unquestioningly approves the staff's dreams and goals. One pastor I know called the church board together only four times a year to receive new members and to fulfill other denominational requirements. In some denominations where board leadership is invested with considerable authority, the board sees its role as blocking the unnecessary, or it is so thoroughly entrenched in tradition that anything new is automatically suspect. Such a board is viewed by the staff as an obstacle to ministry, so the leadership style adopted by the senior pastor becomes one of persuader or salesman. An adversarial relationship exists between staff and board.

Administrators. Because the board's primary function is to handle the organizational business of the church, it oversees programs through committees. The board has an agenda and moves through it, making decisions that cover the entire gamut from starting new programs to replacing a cabinet in a particular room. This process can be particularly frustrating to those who find decision making and administration foreign to their gift-mix and contrary to the way they want to serve the church.

Committee focused. Committees are the administrative bodies used to carry out the program emphasis and oversight. Usually acting as conceptualizing and decision-making groups, they are not the ministry implementers. Frank Tillapaugh describes well the layered approach to administration represented by committees. He says sarcastically that a committee is a group of people who ask two questions: What should we do? and Who can we get to do it? The first thing a committee does is decide whether something should be done. This often involves considerable research and information gathering. One characteristic of Presbyterians (of which I am one) is that people are never ready to make a decision until all points of view are considered. This can consume considerable time and energy, which would not be so bad if that were the end of the process. But it isn't. Committees are not usually the direct implementers. So they must ask the second question, Who can we get to do it? Even if a committee finally decides to have a college ministry or church softball team, it must then recruit another level of structure to carry out what has been decided.[4] Thus, a committee functions as a think tank and an oversight body, not as doers of hands-on ministry. It expends great amounts of time and energy but is usually one step removed from the actual fulfillment of ministry.

Task focused. We tend to do the work of God without being the people of God. By that I mean we may serve on committees, task groups, or leadership boards without really knowing or ministering to the people with whom we serve. All eyes may be focused on the task to be accomplished as if it can be done without serving each other simultaneously. People may be experiencing a crisis of faith, turmoil in their work, disillusionment with their home life, loneliness, and so on, but this information is rarely known to the other committee members because with the hierarchical program orientation they value getting the job done rather than attending to each other while doing the job.

The Congregation as a Whole

How does the hierarchical, top-down, centralized approach to ministry affect the congregation as a whole?

Passivity. In general, concentrating power and initiative in the hands of a few creates passivity in those who are not a part of the leadership structure. The people wait for the vision of the church to be "delivered from on high." While Moses was meeting with God on the mountaintop, the people were deciding what to do in their leader's absence. People sense that they are the recipients of someone else's work and feel little ownership of the vision, for they receive it as fait accompli. Persons who are motivated in ministry but are not a part of the hierarchy may feel stifled; anything they propose must have the official approval of the church board. What significant role can a member have if he or she is not a part of the church hierarchy?

I believe the hierarchical structure creates a consumer mentality in the church. There is good reason why the "20–80 rule" is firmly rooted in many churches. It takes only about 10 to 15 percent of the membership to run the administrative machinery. Is it any wonder that the 20 percent provide for the 80 percent in most churches?

Value judgment. In a hierarchical structure those in the upper echelon are considered to be of greater value to the organization. If people decide that their value is determined by their position, they will hear the call to serve as leaders as a call to power, a call "to be somebody." This sets up an unhealthy dynamic in the church. Some may agree to serve for the wrong reasons, while others refuse to serve in order to avoid work.

Once an elder confessed to me that his motivation for accepting the call was to be seen as a part of the "in" group of movers and shakers. This was his way of addressing low self-esteem. Not having a genuine call or the necessary gifts, his zeal for being an elder flagged as the reality of the work required set in. Often people are willing to let someone else do the work and not accept their share of responsibility. For them the hierarchical approach creates a built-in excuse not to get involved.

The church in general has adopted a leadership style that is at odds with an organism view. The institutional, hierarchical approach to leadership stifles the ability of God's people to see themselves as initiating centers of ministry.

Much more consistent with body ministry is Jesus' model of servant leadership designed to empower others to reach their potential. Before I sketch an organism model of leadership, let us examine servant leadership as taught and modeled by our Lord. From him we can distill several principles from which an organism model of leadership can be derived.

THE PHARISEE MODEL: A STYLE TO AVOID

Jesus tells us, first, what servant leadership is *not*. Comparing the behavior he expected of his followers with the model of both Gentile and Jewish leadership, Jesus describes the prevailing concept of greatness and then calls his disciples to walk away from the only model they had known.

The Gentile leadership style is captured by the word *over.* "You know that the rulers of the Gentiles lord it *over* them, and their great ones are tyrants *over* them" (Matt. 20:25; also Mark 10:42; Luke 22:25). Gentile leaders gloried in their control over their realm. Their subjects felt the caprice and whim of a potentate's arbitrary desires. Rulers expected to be catered to because they were at the top of the pyramid with everyone else finding his place somewhere along the slippery slope.

The word translated "lord it over" (*kurieuom*), though it can refer to the authority of God (Rom. 14:9), is almost always used in the New Testament to mean "negative control." Paul uses it three times in Romans 6 to refer to the negative hold of death, sin, and law. Referring to Christ's resurrection and triumph over death, Paul concludes, "Death no longer *has dominion over* [lords it over] him" (v. 9). Since a believer in Christ is under grace and not law, "sin will have *no dominion over* [lord it over] you" (v. 14 RSV). Finally, Paul makes the point "that the law *is binding on* [lords it over] a person only during his life" (Rom. 7:1 RSV).

A different form of the word (*katakurieuom*) appears when Peter exhorts the elders to exercise their role with a servant spirit: "Do not lord it over those in your charge, but be examples to the flock" (1 Peter 5:3). J. B. Phillips captures the haughtiness of this phrase: "Don't act like little tin gods."

But Jesus reserves harsher condemnation for the Jewish leaders. They were supposed to be models the populace could follow. In Matthew 23:1–7 Jesus verbally dresses down the scribes and Pharisees and exposes their shame for all to see: "Then Jesus said to the crowd and to his disciples, 'The scribes and the Pharisees sit on Moses' seat'" (vv. 1–2). "Moses' seat" was a stone chair permanently placed in the synagogue on which a teacher would sit to expound the law. Jesus holds up the scribes and Pharisees before the disciples as the very model of leadership they were to avoid. By "sitting on Moses' seat," they positioned themselves as authoritatively carrying on the traditions of the law as given by Moses. The name Pharisee, meaning "the separated ones," tells us that they thought highly of themselves. Their holiness was to be observed. They expressed their holiness through *separation* from anyone or anything that could be considered unclean and by *purification* through ceremonial washing and keeping the laws that governed all aspects of life. They demonstrated their zeal for law keeping by fasting twice a week, although it was only required by law once a year, on the Day of Atonement.

What was the negative model the disciples were to avoid?

Hypocrisy: Disjunction Between Teaching and Doing

Jesus exhorts his listeners, "Do whatever they teach you and follow it, but do not do as they do, for they do not practice what they teach" (Matt. 23:3). The Pharisees embodied the old expression, "Do as I say, not as I do." Jesus says essentially that these leaders have good things to say, but their lives contradict their words.

They are not examples of their teaching. There is an incongruity between words and deed, and therefore these leaders cannot be trusted.

The result was that the populace was weighted down by the words of the scribes and Pharisees. "They tie up heavy burdens, hard to bear, and lay them on the shoulders of others, but they themselves are unwilling to lift a finger to move them" (Matt. 23:4). The Pharisees prided themselves on keeping the 613 laws that ordered every aspect of life from personal piety to social relationships. At the same time, they looked down their noses at the common person, especially those pejoratively called the *am ha aretz*—"the people of the land." The burden placed on the shoulders of the people was a legalism that says you are made right before God by law keeping. Their heavy backpack contained only condemnation, guilt, and fear.

Spiritual Pride

Underlying the behavior of "saying and not doing" is spiritual pride. "They do all their deeds to be seen by others" (Matt. 23:5). A characteristic of spiritual pride is that it is never content to remain secret in one's heart. What good is the knowledge that you are better than everyone else unless everyone else knows it as well? Pride cannot be kept under wraps; it must find expression.

Jesus exposes three forms this pride takes:

Religious piety. "They make their phylacteries broad and their fringes long" (Matt. 23:5). What are phylacteries and fringes? Taking literally the injunction of Deuteronomy 6:8 to bind the word of God on their wrists and foreheads, the Pharisees attached little leather boxes containing four portions of God's Word (phylacteries) to their wrists and foreheads by cords. Fringes, which reminded them of the many commandments, edged their prayer garments. In prayer a pious Jew rocks back and forth as a part of the ritual of piety, tossing the phylacteries and fringes rhythmically. This was how the scribes and Pharisees sought public recognition for their devotion to God and their favored status before him.

Honor. "They love to have the place of honor at banquets and the best seats in the synagogues" (Matt. 23:6). In the Pharisees' minds, special people deserved special perks. At a feast they wanted the positions of honor near their hosts. In the synagogue, which was carefully stratified on the basis of worth, the Pharisees placed themselves in the front for all to see, while women and children were safely hidden behind a screen in the back.

Titles. "[They love] to be greeted with respect in the market-places, and to have people call them rabbi" (Matt. 23:7). *Rabbi* literally means "O Great One" or "O Lord." The Pharisees and scribes loved this title of esteem. Like them, too often we seek titles as a measure of our greatness and spirituality.

What Servant Leadership Is Not

What principles can we derive from Jesus' teaching about what servant leadership is *not?*

- ◆ Leadership is not measured by how many people serve you.
- ◆ Leadership is not exercising control over a chain of command.
- ◆ Leadership is not using coercion to get what you want.
- ◆ Leadership is not receiving deference or being treated in a separate category of specialness.
- ◆ Leadership is not receiving honorary, positional titles.

I mourn for the church because we seem to display so many of the characteristics that Jesus said were "not so among you" (Mark 10:43). Shameful arrogance and haughtiness have reached epidemic proportions among church leaders. I attended a conference where five platform presenters shared their expertise as leaders of growing churches. Only one impressed me as winsome and self-effacing, with a contagious enthusiasm for our Lord. Typical of the other four was the pastor of a congregation of 2,400 members who exuded bravado and emitted a sense that he was God's gift to the church. He wanted us to know that his church had a net growth rate of two hundred a year and that he was the reason why. Another Christian leader was quoted as saying, "The board does not run these organizations. Legally it has the final say. If they said, 'You can't build a Bible college,' I couldn't build one. But you know what I'd do? I'd fire the board, because *I* am the spiritual head of this organization. It can't run without me."[5] Jesus says, "But it is not so among you."

We get the kind of leaders we deserve. It often seems that the world's view of greatness is the standard we use when we select our leaders. We have allowed arrogant, unaccountable, and self-professed channels of the Spirit to shoot off like loose cannons. We sometimes have a penchant in the Christian community for holding up the proud and arrogant as our ideal because "they get the job done." Using the world's view of power, we want leaders to exercise influence, work their way into positions of power, and throw their weight around. We therefore get what we ourselves honor—Christian leaders who act like potentates rather than self-sacrificing servants of Jesus Christ. In looking for the next "savior" to lead our church, we have actually reinforced a sick narcissism. The church exists as an audience for leaders to put their egos on display. Eventually leaders get to thinking, "It's all about me." Our actions show that we do not believe that real power is expressed through servanthood that leads to a cross.

The Church Growth Movement has identified strong pastoral leadership as a key ingredient in the growth of a congregation. I will grant that leaders must lead. But what gets passed off as leadership often has no resemblance to servant leadership as modeled and taught by our Lord. In the Church Growth Movement even autocrats may be considered servant leaders if they produce results, meaning bodies and bucks. Stating that we cannot prejudge leadership style because it must be an expression of the cultural milieu, Peter Wagner writes, "When a church is established within that culture, to a large degree the form which effective church leadership patterns will take is determined by that culture."[6]

Wagner tells of Pastor Kim of Kwang Kim Methodist Church in Seoul, Korea, the largest Methodist church in the world. Pastor Kim senses no tension between servanthood and leadership. He showed Wagner the conference room where he meets with the elders. At one end of this long table are two chairs. Standing behind the chair on the right side, Pastor Kim said, "This is my chair." Pointing to the one next to it, he said, "No human sits there—it is for Jesus Christ." The implication was that Jesus talks to the pastor, and the pastor tells everyone what Jesus has said. So even autocratic leadership is transformed into servant leadership.

Does this mean we simply accept whatever cultural expression is in vogue if it is expedient? Jesus apparently did not think so. What was Jesus doing if he was not upending the dominant cultural expression in both the Gentile and Jewish worlds? Our natural tendency is to concentrate power at the top, but Jesus modeled and taught a different way of life.

THE JESUS MODEL: WHAT SERVANT LEADERSHIP IS

Jesus calls for a radical change in leadership models with phrases such as "But you are not to be called rabbi" (Matt. 23:8) and "It will not be so among you" (Matt. 20:26; also Mark 10:43). Far from being swept along by the prevailing currents of greatness, Jesus says we must walk into the force of the gale and not be carried away by it.

The subject of greatness was a topic of discussion among the disciples on more than one occasion. Luke writes, "A dispute also arose among them as to which of them was to be regarded as the greatest" (22:24). *Dispute* literally means "rivalry." It connotes not so much a verbal joust as a habitually contentious spirit. Because of the disciples' fondness for power, they verbally attacked each other, evidently marshaling arguments as to why each should be more honored.

On occasion a disciple moved beyond words to a power play. James and John jockeyed for the top position, preparing to take over the seats of power when Jesus began his earthly reign. Apparently they had an aggressive mother, for Matthew tells us that she was the one who initially approached Jesus on behalf of her sons (Matt. 20:20–28; Mark 10:35–45). Surreptitiously, James and John asked Jesus, "Grant us to sit, one at your right hand and one at your left, in your glory" (Mark 10:37).

It was in this context that Jesus turned the world's view of greatness upside down. First, he redefined greatness. Jesus said:

"Whoever wishes to become great among you must be your servant." (Mark 10:43; also Matt. 20:26)

"Whoever wishes to be first among you must be slave of all." (Mark 10:44)

"Whoever wants to be first must be last of all and servant of all." (Mark 9:35)

"All who humble themselves will be exalted." (Matt. 23:12)

"The greatest among you must become like the youngest, and the leader like one who serves." (Luke 22:26)

"The least among all of you is the greatest." (Luke 9:48)

A direct implication of Jesus' servant stance was his obliteration of titles. What else could Jesus have intended by the following than to wipe out gradations of worth and value? "But you are not to be called rabbi, for you have one teacher, and you are all students. And call no one your father on earth, for you have one Father—the one in heaven. Nor are you to be called instructors, for you have one instructor, the Messiah" (Matt. 23:8–10).

We have refused to take Jesus' words at face value. By dispensing with titles that give people an elevated place in the "pecking order," Jesus' obvious intent was to remove any basis for "lording it over" others. We all occupy the same level ground at the feet of the one Teacher, Jesus Christ. We are not "great ones" or "lords." We are not "fathers" with spiritual authority like Abraham, Isaac, or Jacob. Finally, do not accept the designation "master" or "leader." No human can usurp the position of the head of the body, Christ. In our sinful state, our hearts have a tendency to gravitate toward idolatry, to make someone larger than life. Never forget: Jesus alone is Lord.

Jesus added another dimension to his picture of true greatness with a simple object lesson. He and the disciples were traveling one day, and the disciples were having an intense discussion when they arrived at Capernaum. Jesus asked what they had been talking about. Embarrassed because they had been debating who was the greatest, they remained silent. But Jesus intuited their discussion. To make sure they did not miss the revolutionary nature of kingdom values, Jesus said,

> "Whoever wants to be first must be last of all and servant of all." Then he took a little child and put it among them; and taking it in his arms, he said to them, "Whoever welcomes one such child in my name welcomes me, and whoever welcomes me welcomes not me but the one who sent me." (Mark 9:35b–37)

So servant leadership—true greatness—is demonstrated by a heart for the powerless, unprotected, and exploitable. Through the tenderness of touch and caressing arms, Jesus displayed his care for such as children.

To receive someone into your home meant to embrace them into your life and state that your house was blessed by their presence. To receive means to welcome into friendship and to enfold into your heart. To be great is to make children, the weak, powerless, and needy, the honored guests in your life. Why? Because our Lord's heart went out to these little sheep who needed a shepherd.

The poignant account of Jesus' washing of his disciples' feet appropriately adds the final touch to Jesus' model and interpretation of servant leadership. Jesus had an other-worldly view of power and authority. He is the king who stoops to conquer. Or as someone has said, "Jesus is the king whose scepter is a towel and whose crown is a wash basin."

The lesson of Jesus' model is that servanthood comes out of the security of knowing we are God's children. That security sets us free to be servants. Jesus' strength is that he knows who he is. No one and nothing can take that away. His identity is firmly rooted in his position before the Father. John introduces Jesus' act of servanthood with these words: "Jesus, knowing that the Father had given all things into his hands, and that he had come from God and was going to God, got up from the table, took off his outer robe, and tied a towel around himself" (John 13:3–4). Servanthood, far from being the result of a vacuous ego, is possible only when we are absolutely secure about our worth and value. Jesus embodied "self-emptying" (see Philippians 2:7) because he knew he would never lose his eternal standing before his Father. He was willing to play the role of a household slave, whose task it was to wash the day's grime from between the toes of a master's guests, because his status with the Father could never be shaken.

Afterward, Jesus instructed the disciples on the meaning of what he did. Notice that Jesus returned to the issue of his identity. "Do you know what I have done to you? You call me Teacher and Lord—and you are right, for that is what I am" (John 13:12–13). It is as if Jesus were saying, I have every right to command you to wash my feet because of who I am. But I never have used my position to secure my rights. My whole pattern has been to give up what I could justly claim. "So if I, your Lord and Teacher, have washed your feet, you also ought to wash one another's feet. For I have set you an example, that you also should do as I have done to you" (John 13:14–15).

Only as we know who we are as children of the King can we be secure enough to lead from our knees. People will then recognize an authority that comes from above and will call us "blessed."

Application of the Organism–Servant Model

Having examined Jesus' model and instruction on servant leadership, we must ask, How can this be translated into an organism-servant model of leadership in the church today? Several principles of application emerge from our discussion:

1. People in the highest positions of authority have the greatest obligation to serve. Senior pastors exist to serve associates, the leadership board, and ultimately the congregation. The upper echelon of denominational structures exists for the purpose of enhancing the grassroots ministry of the local church.

2. Servant leadership is rooted in relationship, not coercion. Motivation is generated by modeling and intimacy, not by the force of fear or judgment.

3. Servant leadership naturally seeks to support, not to control. A servant leader is able to come alongside to help others realize their potential, whereas hierarchical leaders attempt to suppress those who might outshine them.

4. Servant leaders shine the spotlight of recognition on those with whom they share leadership. Far from being concerned that they will be diminished if the focus is diverted from them, servant leaders glory in the accomplishments and growth of colleagues.

5. Servant leaders are embarrassed by titles and the trappings of status. They will attempt to remove the hierarchical status language of "senior," "associate," and "assistant" and to put in its place functional language that simply describes what one does (e.g., "pastor for proclamation and evangelism," "pastor for youth," "pastor for senior adults").

6. Servant leaders' authority is recognized on the basis of their character in Christ, not on the position or office that is held. Spiritual authority is reflective of others' awareness of the presence of Christ in the one who is a model. When E. Stanley Jones got it straight who was in fact the ultimate authority, he wrote, "I have resigned as the general manager of the universe."[7] Then Christ's authority was able to shine through.

How then do the principles derived from Jesus' model of servant leadership express themselves through human leaders?

PRINCIPLES OF THE ORGANISM MODEL

The organism model of the church is rooted in a theology of the church as the living, animated body of Christ. The principles for our understanding of the way the organism church functions are as follows:

1. The church functions properly only when Jesus Christ is the acting head of the body. He is not its honorary head; he is its leader. Paul states clearly that Jesus Christ is fully capable of directing the life of his body if we let him (1 Cor. 12). The church must be structured to reflect this truth.

2. The direct relationship that each person has to Jesus Christ enables the church to function as an organism under the direction of the Spirit of Christ. R. Paul Stevens has captured this truth:

> There is a direct and living connection between the Head and every member of the body. . . . No church leader in the New Testament is ever called the head of a local body. That title is reserved for Jesus. The head does not tell the hand to tell the foot what to do. The head is directly connected to the foot. Therefore, people find their ministries not by being directed by the leaders but by being motivated and equipped and directed by the Head himself.[8]

3. These ministries are not discovered in isolation—me and Jesus. They develop within the body. It is within the body that ministry is discovered, affirmed, equipped, and commissioned. Ministry is done within community. This principle is facilitated through "mission communities" where a shared ministry occurs in response to a common call. To keep this principle before us at the churches I have served, we have reduced it to a catchy phrase: "We are to be the people of God as we do the work of God."

4. In the church organism every person makes a valuable contribution to the health of the whole. All service is honorable to the Lord. This being the case, we should avoid positional language that would elevate some and demean others. Using descriptive or functional language gives honor to all the parts.

Team Ministry: Plural Leadership

Biblical ministry is predicated on plural, not solo, leadership. One-person ministry violates the body concept because it views the pastor as the solitary leader. In the Bible, elders in the local church are always referred to in the plural, with the exception of reference to the function and qualifications of a bishop (1 Tim. 3:2; Titus 1:7).

"Although there might have been a presiding elder," David Watson adds, "there is never the slightest hint of a solitary leader (such as the pastor) even in the smallest and youngest churches. Always it was *a shared responsibility,* thereby giving much mutual encouragement, protection and support."[9]

Therefore, I define a leadership team as a group of people working cooperatively to accomplish a common mission through the exercise of their gifts and call in the context of mutual accountability. The assumption is that the whole is greater than the sum of its parts. The wisdom of the group is greater than the wisdom any individual brings to problem solving and vision setting. "In abundance of counselors there is victory" (Prov. 24:6).

Let's examine team ministry from the varied perspectives of authority, accountability, and roles as well as the intangible qualities necessary for a team to gel.

Authority

Pastor, Head of Staff

1. *First among equals.* The organism model features contributions without regard to hierarchical status. The first-among-equals approach places the head of staff in a servant mode with a stress on *equal* rather than on *first.* The head of staff then becomes a servant to fellow servants on a ministry team. Instead of the staff being a leader's alter ego, the head of staff gives his life away to see that those with whom ministry is shared are encouraged to be all they are meant to be. This will require a considerable investment of time by the head of staff in order to know the passion or call of each individual and the gifts God has given as the means to carry out the call. Permission is given in an atmosphere of freedom to pursue the dimension of the call wherever that may lead.

In my previous role as senior pastor, I attempted to live out this "first-among-equals" role in a couple of ways. As I have previously mentioned, when I assumed the lead role, I inherited two associate pastors who had been on the staff for ten years. Besides my strong desire to be affirmed by them, I wanted each to know that it was my desire to work with them to craft roles that were as much as possible an expression of their passions and gifts. Instead of their ministries being static, simply fulfilling job descriptions that ended up being straitjackets, my hope was that we could create an environment where they had the flexibility to explore new frontiers as they were so led and as the church needed.

One of these associates had led the youth ministry during his entire tenure, yet it was evident that it had lost its appeal. He had settled into a routine of rolling out the same program with minor alterations annually. At the same time, we were creating a new position for someone to lead in the areas of small groups and adult education. After a nationwide search, we ended up hiring the "burned out" youth pastor who found his heart gravitating toward this new vision. Our staff worked through a discernment process with him to clarify whether his gifts and call were appropriate to this new role. We jointly concurred that this was the Spirit's growth move for a person whose heart and gifts were known to us.

2. *Leadership.* It is a truism that when everyone is responsible, then no one is responsible. There must be a place where ultimate accountability resides. A ministry team can strive toward mutual accountability, but someone must be designated to hold the group to its shared covenant.

The person who is first among equals must minimally have one or the other of these leadership gifts:

Visionary leadership. Visionary leaders dream dreams or visualize where the church needs to go in the future. James MacGregor Burns, in his book *Leadership,* defines visionary leaders as transformational leaders.[10] Visionary leaders are so able to articulate a picture of the future that others can grasp it and see their part in helping to fulfill it. In a shared-ministry approach, however, vision setting is not the sole province of one person.

The vision of the head of staff can be shaped and qualified in two ways: (1) Once a vision is shared with a staff and leadership board, it should become community property to be reshaped by the wisdom of the whole; people must feel they have a stake in its formulation if they are to put energy into its implementation. (2) The staff, members of the leadership board, and others in the body are invited to contribute and add to the vision of the head of staff. How else could it be if the church is an organism and not just a top-down organization? For staff and leaders to feel fully invested, they must believe that they can affect the direction of the church. Maximizing the tributaries flowing into the vision creates a corporate dream with broad-based ownership.

One of the practices that paid enormous dividends at Saratoga Federated Church was an annual leadership gathering. The staff and elders maintained a list of "influencers" in the congregation whose wisdom was highly valued. At the leadership conference, the staff and elders would share our best sense of the ministry direction and initiatives for the immediate and longer term future. Elders and staff served as conveners of groups of five to facilitate feedback and input into these directions. This served a number of purposes. The leaders had a chance to sense the receptivity to these directions. Were we on the right track? Was our timing appropriate? We also heard what amounted to valuable refinements. This community of leaders was also given opportunity to suggest what they sensed to be the priority issues to be addressed to strengthen the health of the congregation. Finally, a consequential by-product to this congregational consultation was the ability to build consensus as we moved toward a shared community vision.

Administrative leadership. Some lead pastors are not themselves visionary leaders but are capable of managing people resources so that a vision can be drawn from those with whom ministry is shared. An administrative leader creates an environment in which staff and leadership can formulate direction together on a particular ministry.

I observed administrative leadership at its finest during a weekend retreat of our board of elders (the session). An outside consultant had been hired to help the staff and the session work in harmony toward a reinvigoration of purpose, goals, and objectives. The consultant was there, not to set an agenda for the church or to impose his sense of vision, but simply to draw from the twenty participants their sense of the crucial issues facing the church.

Using the nominal-group method, which places each person's concerns on a par, the consultant asked us each to write down the four key issues facing our church. We were instructed to take responsibility for our concerns. We then took several hours for each person to communicate his concerns to the group, posting them for all to see. From there we identified the high-priority items on the basis of their repetition in the lists. We all had the opportunity to influence the group, but we also agreed to submit to the will of the whole. The agenda for the church arose out of a corporate mind, not the vision of a single authority. Moreover, the pastoral staff was included on an equal basis with the board of elders. With this approach the head-of-staff pastor can function as an administrative coordinator, drawing on the vision arising from the group. In essence, the first among equals then becomes a consensus builder.

If visionary leadership gifts are not present, it seems to me that the gift of administrative leadership must be. Otherwise what is left is a caretaker approach to pastoral ministry that sees the church as a family tending to its internal needs but not as a mission that is ever evolving and developing.

There is a need for someone to keep an eye on the big picture and survey the landscape. Staff members and individuals on the leadership board tend to focus on small plots of ground. Often this means tending to their territories without much thought of how it fits into a master plan. In contrast, the head of staff coordinates the whole so that people resources and ministry fit together in a comprehensive direction.

Staff

In the equipping church (the organism model), members of staff with specialized areas of ministry are fully vested with the authority to dream and implement a vision. In the hierarchical model, congregational members look to the head of staff to articulate positions on ministry direction, while the staff acts as "gofers" for his wishes. In our organism model, authority and responsibility are shared, and this creates an atmosphere for staff to grow and evolve. As an associate, I received permission to develop the discipling ministry to the full extent of my dreams. I was allowed to be an experimenter. I was given the opportunity to write a guide for implementing discipling relationships. A test group of "disciples" fed back their observations on both the content and the dynamics of the discipling process. The result was a field-refined tool that passed through the furnace of actual ministry. This created an atmosphere of shared ministry between pastor and people. The dross and impurities were removed in this approach to discipling ministry as the lives of both pastor and disciples were enhanced and enabled by mutual contribution.

Accountability

The traditional hierarchical model is based on a one-way flow of accountability from the top down. But in an organic team ministry, accountability is mutual. Submission is not exclusively up the ladder, but one to another. Heads of staff set the pace. They must strike a balance between, on the one hand, being the one with whom the buck ultimately stops, and on the other, submitting to fellow team members. The head of staff must courageously permit the others to require accountability of him.

Mutual accountability impinges on two areas:

1. *Ministry.* As the team members articulate their desired goals and God-inspired accomplishments in ministry, other team members encourage the fulfillment of these goals and monitor their completion. After a particularly anxiety-producing season of ministry, I decided that I needed a thorough rearranging of my out-of-control schedule with a narrower focus on immediate goals. I submitted a detailed plan to the staff for their information and feedback. Though fellow staff members appreciated the information and were impressed by my self-reflection, I encountered a reluctance to intrude into my life at the level of accountability. I sensed that this was foreign territory to the staff. Our usual approach is to exist somewhat autonomously in our specialized areas, only reporting information to each other but not placing our ministry design on the table for each other's shaping.

To be mutually accountable means to have a stake in the success of fellow partners in ministry. I have had the privilege of being on a couple of teams where I received such encouragement and confidence from respected team members that I discovered potential I had never seen in myself. A dear friend and respected colleague, Darrell Johnson, became my "head of staff" for a brief period of eighteen months. He would say to anyone who would listen, "More than anyone I know (or know of), Greg has grasped and lived the radical implications of the biblical doctrine of the priesthood of all believers. There is much 'talk' about this . . . but little 'walk.' Greg walks every bit of this talk." This book is a direct result of the encouragement of Darrell, who saw in me what I could never have seen in myself.

Mutual accountability is not only encouragement but also correction. This involves speaking hard words to each other. Gordon MacDonald has written, "One solid and loving rebuke is worth a hundred affirmations."[11] Though MacDonald is focusing on the value of rebuke, I like his ratio. A hundred affirmations for every rebuke is just about right. One of the most painful yet fruitful rebukes came through a hard-nosed and thorough review process with the personnel committee that I had the temerity to initiate. At the time, the report seemed thin on affirmation and heavy on criticism. Once I worked through my angry reaction and sat down with those who had authored the report, I could see that they had my welfare and the church's at heart. They called me to be more warmly and relationally connected to the congregation. It was true that I can get so wrapped up on vision and the tasks related to accomplishing that I miss the people in it all. This was a word I needed to hear, and my life and ministry benefited from it.

2. *Personal growth.* In an equipping environment, ministry development cannot be separated from personal growth. To foster personal integrity in Christ, accountability means to open our lives to our teammates. Staff meetings regularly need to deal with questions like, What is the Lord teaching us in our devotional life? What is the cutting edge of our discipleship? How much attention and time are we giving to family? Where is the pressure of the world squeezing us into its mold? and Where are we feeling like a failure in ministry?

I have a tendency to get so wrapped up in what I am doing in ministry that I am not aware of what is going on elsewhere. When that happens, I neglect building relationships with team members. I need to balance task orientation with tending to relationships. In the press of the schedule I can fail to build in the relaxed moments in the office in order to catch a casual conversation or an impromptu dialogue in the hall. I need people to call me away from the treadmill of task and productivity and toward caring for each other.

Time to build relationships is important. So is regular time to review and evaluate goals. I find quarterly two-day retreats a necessity for effective ministry team building. This block of time is essential for building stronger personal relationships and for opportunities to refine the staff's vision and goals. Likewise, our weekly staff meeting at SFC consisted of three elements within a two-hour time frame. The first third focused on spiritual refreshment and personal sharing led by one of the staff on a rotational basis. The next hour was spent tackling one of the annual goals adopted by the staff. Finally, we concluded with sharing important information with each other of what was happening in our areas of ministry. Monthly, we replaced our two-hour weekly meeting with a "focus" day. This was a lengthier time for strategic thinking around one or more of our shared staff goals.

What God's people see modeled in staff relationships will affect the way ministry is fulfilled throughout the church. We decided to organize the staff as a mission community. By "mission community" I mean a group of three to twelve people who share a common heart for ministry. We wrote a covenant together that stated our purpose and the specific activities we agreed to accomplish together. This provided a basis for clear expectations, mutual ownership of ministry goals, and a standard for accountability.

Roles

Roles or job descriptions are fluid in an organism model. Positions are defined on the basis of the spiritual gifts and the call of God on the individual. Unfortunately, job descriptions are often so tightly written that they become a straitjacket. What they provide in clarity they lack in flexibility. They may articulate the church's need for a particular job to be done, but they are not necessarily able to take into account the unique profile of the person who has filled the position. There needs to be room in the job description both to provide for the identified needs of the church and to encourage development of the gifted individual hired to accomplish the desired goals. The person hired should certainly have the abilities required to do the job, but from then on, the church needs to set that person free to arrive at these goals in the way he or she is particularly motivated to carry it out.

Fluidity means not only freedom to carry out a responsibility but also the opportunity to grow into new dimensions of ministry. As people follow their hearts, develop approaches to ministry, and refine the dimensions of their gifts, they discover new vistas. When our discipling network was growing from one generation to another, an inner compulsion began to develop within me that was matched by an outward call to spread the discipling vision. In support of this vision, our leadership team began to set me apart for defined periods of time to take this ministry beyond the church. They also allowed me a three-day block each month to put my vision for ministry on paper. Such a relationship is symbiotic. It is a mutually advantageous sharing of life. It is the church organism acting together in ministry.

Flexibility within staff means that roles are defined among the team according to their giftedness. In the institutional model it is assumed that the head-of-staff pastor will be the primary administrator, visionary, pulpiteer, pastoral caregiver, and so on. Though some abilities are essential to operate as a head-of-staff pastor, the organism model says that the roles on the team should be defined by the gifts each person brings to it. The key role of the head of staff is to make sure the ministry is given away to those who are gifted and in turn to get out of the way so that it can go forth.

Qualities Needed for a Team

We can hold an organism view of authority, accountability, and role definition, but if the intangible qualities of a team are lacking, all goes for naught. These intangible qualities are the glue that holds a team together.

Head of Staff

In my experience the most important quality for a head of staff is personal security. If ministry is shared with others who will receive the spotlight, the senior pastor must not be easily threatened. Insecurity about one's abilities in a leadership position leads to control of the other team members. Ministry jealously guarded rather than graciously given away will stifle associates.

Frank Tillapaugh articulates the internal struggle that will periodically raise its ugly head:

> I thought I had settled the shared leadership issue long ago. Yet all of a sudden I felt this tremendous need to be visibly appreciated. I knew that I was appreciated and people continually expressed their appreciation, but it wasn't enough for my hungry ego. I frequently thought about those pastors who had built their ministries differently and who had received all kinds of trips and material things. I began to dwell on how good those pastors really had it.
>
> A pastor in a shared ministry has a price to pay. . . . When the poor-little-old-me blues strike, you may wish you had done it another way.[12]

When your self-worth is rooted in God's love and acceptance, then you are freed to herald gladly the graces of fellow pastors.

Staff Team

1. *Mutual respect.* One ingredient in the glue for team ministry is the ability to respect the competence of teammates. If you question a team member's abilities to do the job, you may tend to hold back what you give or feel overwhelmed or resentful because you are covering for his deficiencies. This is obviously destructive of the very spirit of trust and interdependence essential for ministry together.

2. *Work ethic.* Properly functioning teams share a similar degree of intensity and work ethic. I once headed a college ministry team of five full-time staff, all of whom had a passionate commitment to reach and disciple the university for Christ. Our staff meetings felt like military strategy sessions plotting a conspiracy to win the war for Christ on campus. It was a supercharged atmosphere with students coming to Christ weekly. We were willing to pay the price of battle because we were equally committed to our goal.

3. *Positions that fit.* A fluid and functioning team will place its members in positions that fit their gifts and calls. When all members are doing what they love, the whole team is energized. Individual satisfaction makes for group satisfaction. If a person is not functioning because he or she does not "fit" the position, the rest of the team will be thrown out of balance trying to cover deficiencies, helping that person to learn or to do the job, or fielding the congregation's complaints.

4. *Servant spirit.* The call to ministry is the call to serve, not to be served. Yet people in ministry who are tempted to be known as "great" servants or superstars stifle community and camaraderie. They engender jealousy and resentment. They fear they will diminish their own stature if they praise the talents of others. In contrast, a genuine desire to see others succeed and become all God intended them to be will foster esprit de corps. What a delight to be a part of a group where you cheer for and rejoice in the way you see God using another! True servants are thrilled by others' successes.

When these qualities of team ministry are combined with an organism understanding of authority, accountability, and roles, the result can be dynamic ministry unleashed and the New Reformation realized in our lives. When it all works, there is a freeing of energy for ministry that makes it feel as if we are working in God's powerhouse.

In the concluding chapter I will address a redefinition of "call" and ordination in the New Reformation conception. If all God's people are ministers, then our exclusive designation of "call" and "ordination" for professional believers needs to be reexamined.

NOTES

1. Although these questions have been addressed in part in chapter 7, this chapter will provide a more systematic look at these questions through the contrasting lens of servant leadership and authoritarian leadership.

2. Philip Greenslade, *Leadership, Greatness and Servanthood* (Minneapolis: Bethany House, 1984), 7.

3. Richard G. Hutcheson, *Mainline Churches and the Evangelicals* (Atlanta: John Knox, 1981), 119.

4. Frank Tillapaugh, *The Church Unleashed* (Ventura, Calif.: Regal Books, 1982), 71.

5. Jimmy Swaggart, as quoted in *Time* magazine.

6. Peter Wagner, *Leading Your Church to Growth* (Ventura, Calif.: Regal Books, 1984), 83.

7. As quoted by Gordon MacDonald, *Ordering Your Private World* (Nashville: Thomas Nelson, 1985), 91.

8. R. Paul Stevens, *Liberating the Laity* (Downers Grove, Ill.: InterVarsity Press, 1985), 36.

9. David Watson, *I Believe in the Church* (Grand Rapids: Eerdmans, 1978), 271.

10. James MacGregor Burns, *Leadership* (New York: Harper & Row, 1978), 4.

11. Gordon MacDonald, *Restoring Your Spiritual Passion* (Nashville: Thomas Nelson, 1986), 191.

12. Tillapaugh, *The Church Unleashed,* 108.

Chapter 10

Call and Ordination in the New Reformation

THROUGHOUT THIS BOOK I HAVE been attempting to hold up before us a picture of the church as organism. Implicit in the discussion has been a critique of our traditional under-standing of call and ordination. How does the truth that all God's people are called to ministry affect our conceptions of call and ordination? Is it fair to assume that if all have a ministry, then *all are called*? And if that is the case, what "rite of passage" might there be for the members of the body that sets them apart for their call?

As has been our approach, we will again explore answers to these questions by contrasting the institutional and organic views of the church.

CALL AND ORDINATION THROUGH THE INSTITUTIONAL LENS

Since the institutional paradigm views the church from the top down, the call has been restricted to a few who go into vocational ministry. Phrases like "heard, sensed, or received a call" automati-cally conjure up images of missionary, pastor, parachurch worker, or seminary professor. Those who receive a call enter some form of pro-fessional Christian service. A private or "secret" call is prerequisite to pursuing a vocation in the church. It is secret precisely because it is known only to the inaccessible heart of the individual on whom God has placed his hand or whose spirit God has quickened.

Thomas Gillespie has captured in his experience how far we have strayed from the New Testament concept of call:

> In our ordinary church parlance, the call of God *is limited to* those among us who bear ordination to professional ministry. . . . I cannot remember ever hearing either an elder or a deacon saying that he or she serves because of the call of God. Neither have I heard a church member say that his or her life vocation is the result of a divine calling.[1]

Our theology of ministry will lead directly to our conception of call and ordination. Gillespie goes on to say that the reason we have limited call to a restricted few is that our starting point for understanding the nature of ministry is wrong. Traditionally, he states, our theology of ministry has begun with a doctrine of ordained offices. This starting point leads to clericalism and therefore to an elitist understanding of call and ordination. Our theology of ministry is off base precisely because our point of departure is wrong.

The inevitable result is a split-level arrangement with the clergy "upstairs" and the laity "downstairs." A theology of ministry turns into a sociology of status. No matter how much we push for the people of God to be engaged as ministers within this framework, they will have second-class status. A "trickle-down" theology in the church, just as in economics, results in the "haves" and "have nots."

Since a hierarchical theology of ministry has been our worldview, we have implicitly operated out of a hierarchy of call. Challenging this corruption of the Reformed tradition, Donald McKim writes,

> The Reformed tradition, it is true, has put some special emphasis on the calling to "Word and Sacrament," to the position of pastor in the church. But it is a perversion of the tradition and diversion from the New Testament if we conclude from this that called Christians who are preachers, or evangelists, or missionaries (or even seminary professors!) are somehow blessed by a special calling that puts them head and shoulders above the rest of the called body of Christ.[2]

The result has been an unconscious hierarchy of call. Where you are in the hierarchy is determined by the seriousness or cost connected to your call. If we were to look at this like a pyramid, the base would be labeled "secular" and its pinnacle would be labeled "sacred." All people could be found somewhere along a continuum of status between these two poles. At the base are those who do not take their faith too seriously. Their vocational pursuits are invested in the temporal. Then as we move up the pyramid, there are those who are just "homemakers"—who perhaps have a little more serious sense of call to the family. Further up are those who go into the caring professions, such as the medical field or some form of "people" work. But serious Christians demonstrate their commitment by becoming professional Christians—that is, pastors or missionaries or seminary professors. Devoting one's whole life to God means passing into the realm of the sacred.

Sadly, we are still dealing with a version of the same issue that Martin Luther encountered in the Reformation that led to the articulation of the priesthood of all believers. In his *Open Letter to the German Nobility,* Luther attacked what he called "the three walls of Romanism." The first was the division in life between the "spiritual estate" and the "temporal estate." The "spiritual estate" referred to the church and to roles such as monk and priest; and the "temporal estate" referred to artisans, farmers, cobblers, politicians, and so forth. If one was truly committed to serving God, one aspired to go into the church as the highest calling.

This division of life into sacred and secular realms underlies our unbiblical, hierarchical view of call. We assume that service to God means entering the sacred sphere.

What is the sacred realm? It is ministry in the church or at least overt Christian activities such as working with youth, teaching Sunday school, going on a short-term mission assignment, and serving in the leadership structure. Yet also included within the sacred are those matters that might be considered the personal or even private life of the individual: family, relationships, values, beliefs, attitudes, assumptions, character, inner motivation and thoughts. Since the sacred is considered personal, family, or church, there is often minimal association of the sacred with our work. A newly converted vice president for NBC television was asked about the impact of his new faith on the moral standards of programming at NBC. Buying thoroughly into the sacred/secular bifurcation, he said, "All it does is give me peace of mind in my personal life. But whether it will affect my programming, it doesn't. It just makes me think clearer, but that just means I will probably think more commercially than I did before. "

Many Christians unconsciously take off their Christian "hats" when they walk through the doorway of their marketplace jobs. We have been taught to believe that the way we view our work has nothing to do with being Christian. There is a different set of rules that we follow in the marketplace that have very little to do with discipleship. If the sacred is the church or private life, then the secular has primarily to do with the public or corporate life of society such as our institutions of business, economics, media, education, and politics.

As long as this is the framework that defines our view of call, we de facto will remain mired in a hierarchical, sacerdotal, and clerical view of call.

This understanding of call is confirmed through the meaning we attribute to ordination. Viewed as the rite of passage into the sacred, ordination not only implies the right of the church to set standards to recognize and order its leadership, but it also conveys a mystical entrance into a realm that is off-limits to "ordinary" Christians. It is not surprising to read the following view of ordination in a report of the Anglican-Roman Catholic International Commission:

> Christian ministers ... share through baptism in the priesthood of the people of God.... Nevertheless their ministry is not an extension of the common Christian priesthood but belongs to *another realm* of the gifts of the Spirit. Ordination denotes entry into this apostolic and God-given ministry.[3]

What is disturbing is that this same language was adopted in *The Report of the Churches' Council for Covenanting,* an alliance of Protestant denominations exploring structural union.

One of the reasons that the priesthood of all believers has not been realized is that we practice a priesthood within a priesthood. On the one hand, we affirm that a "minister" participates as every Christian does in the priesthood of all believers, but in the next breath we list special responsibilities that are marked "for the ordained only." We cannot have it both ways. What is affirmed in one moment, is taken away the next. What is the difference between "the ministry" and "lay ministry"? Ordination. Anthony Harvey asks, "What is it that makes a Christian minister what he is?" His answer: "We shall, of course, regard one qualification as essential. The man [sic] must have been ordained."[4]

Ordination has its sacerdotal perks. First is the exclusive right to preside at the Lord's Supper. What was originally a matter of church order has been turned into a mystical rite for the ordained. In chapter 4 I quoted Thomas Torrance's views regarding the practice of Communion. He sees ordination as not having been completed until the ordinand takes up the bread and wine for the first time, thereby entering into the sphere of the self-consecration of Christ. Deny it as we may, this is nothing less than a New Testament veneer placed over an Old Testament priesthood. We could also question why baptisms, weddings, funerals, preaching, and the like are off-limits to the nonordained.

A few summers ago I was the speaker at a family conference at a retreat center. A man in his early thirties asked if we could have lunch together so that he could process whether he should pursue professional ministry. We continued to converse as we sat at the end of the lunch table with six others sharing the same space. At the time, he was a location reporter for a local television station while taking some seminary courses on the side. He wanted to explore how one knows whether one is called to professional ministry. In particular, he was debating whether he should pursue ordination or if that was even necessary to validate his ministry. I don't recall the specifics of what triggered it in me, but words came from my mouth with an intensity of emotion that even caught me off guard. Before I could reach out and stuff these words back down my throat, I heard myself say, *"Ordination is evil!"* All conversation around us immediately ceased. Dead silence prevailed. Besides startling the young man with whom I was speaking, I startled myself. *Where did that come from? What was that all about?* I thought.

As I have seen ordination practiced, I have watched it create a class distinction or gap of status between clergy and laity that becomes a great divide. John Stott has powerfully stated the corruption that the practice of ordination can create:

> Where this ordering of ministry results in a class or caste system, where it divides the community into "clergy" and "laity," where it separates those who have "a part" in the

ministry from those who have no part in it, there *the theology of ministry authorized by the New Testament is forsaken.*[5]

CALL FROM A "NEW REFORMATION" PERSPECTIVE

I fully concur that engagement in ministry is the result of a prior call of God upon every believer. Yet a hierarchy of call is foreign to the New Testament. Martin Luther challenged the conception of a "special" calling, which had been fully entrenched in the Roman Catholic tradition:

> Monastic vows rest upon the false assumption that there is a special calling, a vocation, to which superior Christians are invited to observe the counsels of perfection, while ordinary Christians fulfill only the commands; but there is simply *no* special religious vocation, since the *call* of God comes to *each* at the common tasks.[6]

"The Report of the Special Committees on the Theology of Call" from the Presbyterian Church, USA, gives us the proper angle to begin our discussion of call: "There is one call of God to all the people of the earth, to the whole Church, and to every member of the Church, to the one ministry of God's word and work in Jesus Christ." Ministry is accomplished through the *whole* church, not just a part of it. To quote Thomas Gillespie again, "The membership becomes the medium of God's ministry. Through the distribution of the Spirit's ministry, every member becomes a co-worker with God. To each for the sake of all."[7]

As I understand it, the Scriptures speak of call in three ways:

1. There is a *primary call* to Christ, community, and transformation to all who are in Christ.
2. There is a *secondary call,* which is the application of the primary call into all spheres of life.
3. Each of us has an individual *heart or purpose call* that is the particular reason that God has placed us on this planet.

Primary Call

Call defines the relationship between God and his people. God calls, and his people respond. The New Testament verb is *kaleom,* meaning "to call, invite, or summon"; the noun is *klemsis,* meaning "call or calling." These ordinary words take on special significance when it is God in Christ who issues the call. Os Guinness stresses the all-encompassing nature of God's claim on us through his call: "Calling is the truth that God calls us to himself so decisively that everything we are, everything we do, and everything we have is invested with special devotion and dynamism lived out as a response to his summons and service." [8] Donald McKim says simply, "God's call is to all who believe *to be* Christian."

This primary call has three inseparable aspects: a call to Christ, a call to community, and a call to transformation in community.

1. *Call to Christ.* A disciple is one who responds in faith to the gracious call of Jesus Christ. The primary call means that we place ourselves under the formative, shaping influence of Jesus in all areas of our life. Being a disciple of Jesus "always implies the existence of a personal attachment which shapes the whole life of the one described as *mathetes,* which in particular, leaves no doubt as to who is deploying the formative power."[9] Jesus said, "If any want to become my followers, let them deny themselves and take up their cross daily and follow me" (Luke 9:23).

This is a call to Christ as Savior and Lord in the context of relationship. Jesus met Simon and Andrew, James and John working as fishermen by the Sea of Galilee. He summoned them to follow him. These disciples left the predictable, secure trades their families had followed for generations in response to the magnetism of the Son of God (Mark 1:19–20). Call fundamentally means to enter into *relationship* with God in Jesus Christ. "God is faithful; by him you were called into the fellowship of his Son, Jesus Christ our Lord" (1 Cor. 1:9).

Jesus came to seek and to save the lost. When the religious leaders questioned him about the disreputable company he was keeping, Jesus said that he came to call "not the righteous but sinners" (Mark 2:17). Paul sketches in broad strokes the panoramic plan of God's eternal salvation. When the plan of salvation intersects individual humans in history, God sends forth an "effectual" call. Paul writes, "And those whom he [God] predestined he also *called*" (Rom. 8:30).

That call has its origin in a call to the person of Christ is made painfully clear to the Galatians, who were rapidly turning from the source: "I am astonished that you are so quickly deserting the one who *called* you in the grace of Christ" (Gal. 1:6). The call of Christ is a claim on us that is so radical and uprooting that it means being called "out of darkness into his marvelous light" (1 Peter 2:9). Christ calls us into a relationship with himself that involves an ultimate shift of allegiance.

2. *Call to community.* Donald McKim has described the church as the *locus* out of which we live the *focus* of our particular call.[10] The church itself is the called community. The *locus* of the church is the base of operations from which our particular ministry is launched. It is the supportive place where we find our identity, nurse our wounds, and are held accountable. A call to Christ is simultaneously a call into community. Is it any wonder that the Greek word for church, *ekklesia,* is derived from the verb meaning "to call forth"?

The Second Helvetic Confession defines the church as "an assembly of the faithful called or gathered out of the world; a communion, I say, of all saints, namely of those who truly know and rightly worship and serve the true God in Christ" (ch. 17, 5.125). Writing to the Corinthians, Paul greets them with this description of their identity: "To the church of God that is in Corinth ... *called* to be saints, *together* with all those who in every place call on the name of our Lord Jesus Christ" (1 Cor. 1:2).

The "called out" people are both a local assembly in a particular locale and the church universal, "in every place." There is no call to Christ without a call to the body of Christ. To be in Christ is to be in the church. Paul substitutes the image of baptism for call in 1 Corinthians 12:13, but certainly "call" is implied in his meaning: "For in the one Spirit we were all baptized into one body." This advice was given to John Wesley before his conversion: "Sir, you wish to serve God and go to heaven? Remember you cannot serve him alone. You must therefore find companions or make them; the Bible knows no solitary religion."[11] The church community is the indispensable *locus* or center. It is within the church that our *heart or purpose call* is discerned, supported, and refined.

3. *Call to transformation in community.* When we respond to Christ, we enter a lifelong process of change. Gordon Cosby describes the call to transformation as a call to inward development: "We are to overcome those obstacles in ourselves which hold us

back and keep us from growing up into the full stature of Christ. The call of Christ is a call to die to the old self in order to become the new creation."[12] Paul states that God has called us "in holiness" (1 Thess. 4:7). Addressing the character and qualities of the Christian community that make for unity, Paul pleads, "I therefore, the prisoner in the Lord, beg you to lead a life worthy of the *calling* to which you have been *called*" (Eph. 4:1).

The Scriptures use a number of different images to capture the goal of transformation. All these metaphors assume that there must be an inward change of heart that will then be reflected outwardly. Jesus taught us that *fruit-bearing* will be the result of our abiding in the life that flows through the vine, an image Jesus uses to describe our relationship with him (John 15:1–11). Good fruit cannot occur unless the tree producing the fruit is also good (Luke 6:43–45). Good works are a product of a changed "inner being." Paul's image of *being led by the Spirit* points to the same reality. Those who relinquish their life to the Spirit's control will produce the fruit of the Spirit as the natural by-product (Gal. 5:16–26).

In another place Paul shifts to the picture of *maturity* as the goal for Christian living: "It is he whom we proclaim, warning everyone and teaching everyone in all wisdom, so that we may present everyone mature in Christ" (Col. 1:28). Though "mature" is rendered "perfect" in the King James Version (*teleios* does not convey sinlessness but is closer to "complete"), a mature Christian is one who has passed through the stages of infancy, childhood, and adolescence and is now an adult. Adult Christians are those who take full responsibility for, and are self-disciplined in, their growth in Christ.

The image that seems to summarize all that has been stated so far is simply that we are to grow to *Christlikeness*. Paul Tournier describes growth in Christ as an increasing congruence between our "person" and our "personage." One result of the fall of Adam and Eve was a disjunction between the inner and outer persons. Clothes covered up the shame of nakedness. Humans were cut off from themselves. The image of God in humans was marred.

When the relationship with God was severed, so was knowledge of self. The "person" is the hidden inner being; the "personage" is the façade or public image presented to the world.[13] When Christ comes to live in us, he begins restoring our fractured inner image. So Paul writes that the goal of salvation is "to be conformed to the image of his Son" (Rom. 8:29). The more we relinquish our life to the indwelling Christ in our person, the more our personage becomes a reflection to the world of a divine life within. "Christ . . . through us spreads in every place the fragrance that comes from knowing him" (2 Cor. 2:14). "And all of us, with unveiled faces, seeing the glory of the Lord . . . are being transformed into the same image from one degree of glory to another" (2 Cor. 3:18).

The primary call of God is a call for our character to be transformed individually and corporately so that we reflect Christ's life in and among us. No one has said this better than C. S. Lewis:

> The more we get what we now call "ourselves" out of the way and let Him take us over, the more truly ourselves we become. There is so much of Him that millions and millions of "little christs," all different, will still be too few to express Him fully. He made them all, He invented—as an author invents characters in a novel—all the different men [and women] that you and I were intended to be. In that sense our real selves are all waiting for us in Him. . . .It is when I turn to Christ, when I give myself up to His personality that I first begin to have a real personality of my own."[14]

The primary call to Christ, community, and transformation places a priority on the inner life of being that undergirds and gives direction to the outer life of doing.[15]

Secondary Call

If the primary call is to come under the formative and shaping influence of Jesus in community, then the secondary call is to live out our new identity in all the spheres of life. The church is the community or crucible of Christian formation and the body from which we are sent into the world. The church is the base camp from which we go into the various realms of our lives. Os Guinness puts it this way, "Our secondary calling is that everyone, everywhere, and in everything should think, speak, live and act entirely for Him."[16] Donald McKim adds the secondary call to the primary call with the addition of the phrase "in all we do": "God's call is to all who believe to be Christian *in all we do*."

From this Guinness draws the conclusion that the Christian can say that being a homemaker, lawyer, or art history teacher is a secondary calling. Paul Stevens refers to the secondary call as our Christian vocation.[17] In our contemporary usage, *vocation* has become equated with "profession" or "occupation." Stevens, on the other hand, uses *vocation* in its historic context to refer to the varied spheres in which we carry out our primary call. *Vocatio* historically refers to the all-encompassing obligation or duty to serve Christ in the various contexts of life. In other words, under secondary call, it is appropriate to refer to many "callings." Mother Teresa had a way of cutting to the core: "The work is not our vocation. Our belonging to Christ is our vocation. People are confused." Our primary call is to belong to Christ. This then gets lived out in the varied venues of life—the secondary call.

For each of us, these callings take specific shape depending on the particular area of our call. Figure 10.1 is an attempt to capture the biblical conception of our secondary call in five spheres:

- The Church
- The World (Diaspora)
- The Ministry of Work
- Family
- Sabbath

Each of these spheres has its own internal design, order, and place in God's scheme. To fulfill the Lord's secondary calling, we must understand the biblical structure of each and its place in God's world. Obedience or living out our secondary call will vary with the sphere in which we function and the stage of life in which we are engaged. For example, parents with three children under ten will experience obedience in the family sphere differently than will an unmarried person or a couple with grown children.

Given the limits of space, I will concentrate my description of secondary call on the emphasis of this book: the church, the world, and the ministry of work. I will leave for others to define the place of family and Sabbath in God's order. These descriptions of secondary call serve as a backdrop to help us understand and listen for a heart or purpose call.[18]

Figure 10.1

CALLED TO MINISTRY
(Sphere of Our Call)

Church: Ecclesia Ministry
"Called Out People"

Shape of Call:
1. Gifts—Ministry abilities
2. Sphere—Particular focus of use of gifts

Key questions:
1. In service where/and when is joy/excitement/energy flowing?
2. What particular concern for or need do you observe in your church?

Family: The Ministry of Home

Shape of Call:
1. Protector—Provide a safe haven
2. Teacher of values
3. Development of self-worth and value

World: Diaspora Ministry
"Sent Out People"

Shape of Call:
1. Witness in word and deed to the kingdom of God
2. Expression of the compassion of Jesus Christ
   a. Ministering to felt need
   b. Standing for justice

Key question:
Where does the compassion of Christ in you intersect the brokenness of the world?

THE CALLED PERSON
"Much of the will of God for us is written in us."

Key questions:
1. What gifts and motivated abilities has God given to you which are an expression of your inner design?
2. What contribution has God given you to make?

Sabbath Rest:
The Ministry of Rest

Shape of Call:
1. Restoration—Refilling the reservoir of joy
2. Worship
3. Recreation

Key question:
What activity restores your soul?

Work: The Ministry of Work

Shape of Call:
1. Inherent identity in the created order
2. A place to express inner design or motivated abilities
3. A place of witness to the kingdom of God

Key question: As you review your life, what achievements have given you the greatest satisfaction?

Call to the Church

The "called out" people, the church, constitute one sphere in which we do ministry. In terms of *primary call,* the call to community is the *locus* of all our ministry. But the church is also the *focus* of ministry. It is the call of every Christian to upbuild, edify (1 Cor. 14:3), strengthen, and work for the common good (1 Cor. 12:7).

How does one know where to place one's efforts to *upbuild, edify, strengthen, and work* for the common good of the church? Our call is discovered at the intersection of spiritual gifts and passion. A fellow teacher in my former church used the following formula to describe call:

Spiritual gifts + need (that I care about) = call

She illustrated this mathematical formula from the physical sciences. In our high school chemistry class we learned that the natural world is made up of elements such as oxygen, hydrogen, and carbon. When atoms become positively or negatively charged, they seek to restore stability by combining with those of the opposite charge. For example, a positive hydrogen atom is naturally attracted to a negative oxygen atom. Their fusion as H_2O produces water. The same is true with us. When our motivated abilities (+) are applied to a need we care about (-), then energy is released in us. What you feel welling up in you is a sense of call.

A generation ago when the spiritual gifts emphasis hit the church, it was taught that all we needed to do was to find out what our spiritual gifts were and put them to use and then we had discovered our ministry. I and many others have come to see the limitations of this teaching. Spiritual gifts are like tools in a workman's kit. Having a bunch of useful tools does not tell us what type of project we are to work on. As I noted in the opening chapter, among the synonyms for spiritual gifts in Paul's parallel structure in 1 Corinthians 12:4–7 is *diakonia.* This word, translated "service" or "ministry," not only tells us the *manner* in which gifts are to be exercised but, following the insight of Ray Stedman, also conveys the idea of *sphere.* The sphere is the particular locale or context within the church where our gifts are best used. Gifts are related to sphere as means are to ends.

Our call to *church ministry* is clarified when we know both our spiritual gifts profile and the place where those gifts are best used.

For example, I may know that I have a gift of teaching, but that doesn't tell me how it is to be exercised. Is my gift of teaching most beneficial to children, adolescents, or adults? Am I to be a classroom teacher, or would I function better in a small-group or discipling setting?

Each of us has a contribution to make in the church. The call is not static. The call God places on our life evolves as we grow in our own gifts and willingness to own what God has placed in us, all of which interacts with the particular needs of a congregation at any given time.

Figure 10.2

Call to the Church

Focus:

1. The exercise of our spiritual gifts
2. A sphere of our call

Discernment questions:

1. Where and when are joy, excitement, and energy flowing in service to the church?
2. What particular burden or concern do you have for the church?

Call to the World: Diaspora Ministry

Martin Luther said that every Christian should experience two conversions. The first conversion is to respond to God's call to come out of the world in the church. The second is to be sent back into the world to penetrate it with the message and model of the kingdom of God.

God's kingdom is an invading force, and we are the shock troops. This kingdom penetrates the darkness. Jesus calls us to pray it into being and to be a part of the answer to the prayer, "Thy kingdom come, Thy will be done, on earth as it is in heaven" (Matt. 6:10 KJV). When Jesus said, "You are the salt of the earth . . . the light of the world" (Matt. 5:13–14), he was speaking of our being infused with life from God as a mark of the kingdom's presence that has come through Jesus. We are penetrating salt and light when we are connected with Christ the King.

As shock troops, we are called to be diaspora—scattered—ministers, sent from the *locus* of the community of believers into the world. In Scripture, *world* is a technical word. It refers to the created order shattered by sin. Humanity's rebellion against God's authority resulted in brokenness. The "world," therefore, is corporate life organized and functioning without reference to God. Jesus calls us to go into this needy, hurting world: "As you have sent me into the world, so I have sent them into the world" (John 17:18). This is the Christian's "second" conversion, the mandate of which Luther spoke.

What is our call to the world?

Figure 10.3

Call to the World

Focus:

1. Declaration of the gospel (witness of words)
2. Compassionate acts of service (witness of deeds)
   a. Sympathy
   b. Outrage

Discernment question:

Where does the compassion of Christ in you intersect the brokenness of the world?

We are to be witnesses to God's invading kingdom of love and justice in word and deed.

1. *Witness of words.* We have been entrusted with the message of reconciliation. The means by which God has chosen to call people to him is our articulation of the gospel. The gospel is the power of God unto salvation. As we faithfully share the good news that God has taken the initiative to reconcile us to him by ransoming us through the costly death of his Son, God's Spirit penetrates the darkness of people's hearts, drawing and wooing them into a life-changing relationship. God has no other plan. He has tied the accomplishment of his purposes to save mankind to our willing cooperation to proclaim the good news that we are the "visited planet." (I refer the readers to the numerous discussions of the biblical imperative for the Great Commission and the tools needed to carry it out.)

2. *Witness of deeds.* We live in a "post-Christian" age in which the Western world is indifferent, apathetic, or hostile to the biblical God. We need other forms of witness to build bridges of contact to the unbelieving world. To be witnesses to the kingdom of God in deed means that we touch people's lives at the point of their felt need. There are gaping wounds in people's lives that need the healing touch of Christ's compassion through the Christian community.

We live in a casualty society. People are weighed down by the baggage of guilt from abortions, the wreckage of divorce, and the aftereffects of alcoholism and substance abuse. The more we can enter into the pain of people's lives, the more we win the right to share the gospel. To be kingdom people penetrating society means that *we enter the spiritual battle against the forces of darkness that oppress and do violence to people's lives.*

Our attitude toward this world can be captured by one word: compassion. As exemplified by our Lord, compassion has two components: sympathy and outrage.

Sympathy. After Jesus had ministered among the villages of Palestine, Matthew recorded the following: "When he saw the crowds, he had *compassion* for them, because they were harassed and helpless, like sheep without a shepherd" (Matt. 9:36). What did Jesus see as he walked among his errant creation? He saw people who were harassed and helpless. These people were living without knowledge of the Father, though they were beings created for fellowship with him. Jesus, the agent of creation, slipped incognito among them. What was Jesus' response? He had compassion.

Our call is to show the lost world the compassion of Jesus. "God so loved the world that *he gave* . . ." (John 3:16). Yet what I often see in myself and other Christians is not a servant spirit of graciousness but judgment and anger toward the world. With red-faced belligerence we castigate the world for having values that are anti-Christian. We seem to build walls, not bridges, to a world in need. We appear more repulsed by the world than compelled by God's great love to show the compassion of Christ.

For our Lord, compassion meant sympathy. Its origin is a Greek word, *sympatheom,* meaning "to feel with." Jesus had a deep feeling for humanity. In the incarnation Jesus identified with us in our weakness. That is sympathy. The letter written to the Hebrews captures the *sympathy* of his compassion:

Since, therefore, the children share flesh and blood, he himself likewise shared the same things, so that through death he might destroy the one who has the power of death, that is, the devil, and free those who all their lives were held in slavery by the fear of death. . . . For we do not have a high priest who is unable to *sympathize* with our weaknesses, but we have one who in every respect has been tested as we are, yet without sin. (Heb. 2:14–15; 4:15)

For Jesus, sympathy ultimately meant he would himself bear the penalty for our sin. His sympathy extended to being our substitute, to stand in the way of and to take the full brunt of God's fury toward sin. Isaiah predicted that a servant was coming who would absorb the wounds and bruises we deserved for our transgressions and iniquities. Our wholeness would come at the price of his punishment; he would be "smitten by God" (Isa. 53:5–6). Os Guinness writes, "As God became man in Jesus, he was no White Hall or Pentagon Chief, making quick flying inspections of the front lines, but one who shared the fox holes, who knows the risks, who felt the enemy fire. Ours is the only God with wounds."[19]

As followers of Jesus into the world, we too are called to identify with the pain. I believe that for the church to restore credibility with the world, we must both be and be seen as suffering servants ourselves. The world is able to recognize that true sympathy is much more like Mother Teresa's service to those dying on the streets of Calcutta than like the showbizzy glitz of some Christian ministries. Our call is to costly service.

Outrage. But we get only a partial picture of compassion if we stop with sympathy. Compassion is sympathy laced with outrage. One of the Greek words that means "compassion" even sounds as if it might indicate righteous anger: *splagnizomai.* The Hebrews thought that emotions emanated from the bowels. When someone was particularly pained by a life circumstance, a person would say, in effect, "you are cutting up my intestines." This is how the father felt when he saw his prodigal son returning in rags. The Scripture says he "had compassion" on him (Luke 15:20 KJV).

It is also Jesus' response to the leper who threw himself at the Master's feet, pleading, "If you choose, you can make me clean" (Mark 1:40). Mark records that Jesus was "moved with pity." The word "pity" in no way captures the intensity of Jesus' emotion. He did not simply feel sorry. His reaction to the leper and the father's response to the broken prodigal is a visceral clutch at the stomach. To have compassion means to simmer with controlled anger against the forces that trap individuals and reduce them to a quality of life far less than God intended. Compassion was Jesus' agonized cry against leprosy: "This is not the way it is supposed to be!"

Another graphic term, though not translated "compassion," reveals Jesus' reaction to the ultimate human enemy. It is used when Jesus stood before the tomb of his friend Lazarus, who had been four days in the grave. Emotions were intensified by the gawking onlookers anticipating Jesus' next move and the grieving of Mary and Martha over the loss of their brother. John says of Jesus, "When Jesus saw her [Mary] weeping, and the Jews who came with her also weeping, he was *greatly disturbed in spirit* and deeply moved. . . . Then Jesus, again *greatly disturbed*, came to the tomb" (John 11:33, 38).

"Greatly disturbed" does not do justice to the depth of Jesus' intensity. This is the same word used to describe a powerfully trained Greek stallion ready to charge into battle. The stallion would rear back on its hind legs with muscles rippling, paw the air, and in controlled fury, "snort" before hurling itself at the enemy. As Jesus stood at Lazarus' graveside, death for him symbolized the zenith of evil, pain, sorrow, suffering, injustice, cruelty, and despair: "This is not the way it is supposed to be!!" As Jesus stood face-to-face with death, he "snorted in spirit" and let loose an inner fury against the final enemy. In compassion, Jesus cried out from the depths of his being, "Lazarus, come forth!"

The compassion of Jesus incarnated in us is *sympathetic identification with and outrage against the corruption of the world.*

Our call to the world is at the intersection of the world's pain.

Call to Our Work: The Cultural Mandate

One of the great legacies of the Reformation was the rediscovery of the dignity of work. Martin Luther stated, "There is simply no special religious vocation, since the call of God comes to each at the common tasks."

Luther identified "calling" with occupation or profession. In his exposition and translation of 1 Corinthians 7:20, he used the German word *Beruf.* "Every one should remain in the state [*Beruf*] in which he was called." Luther assumed this meant vocational immobility. In the highly authoritarian, stratified German society, one's vocation was the inherited family trade and therefore predetermined. Parental authority was to be obeyed. Ironically, Luther did not take his own advice. Hans Luther, Martin's father, wanted him to be a lawyer, but Martin wanted to dedicate his life to God, which in his mind meant pursuing the highest call, being a monk.

Figure 10.4

Call to the Vocation

Focus:
1. Declaration of the gospel (witness of words)
2. Vocation as an expression of our motivated abilities (cultural mandate)

Discernment question:

As you examine your life at various stages, what achievements have given you greatest satisfaction?

Most biblical scholars today believe Luther's interpretation of 1 Corinthians 7:17–24 was off the mark. Paul's concern in the passage was broader than occupation. He instructed the Corinthians not to attempt to change the life circumstance in which they received the gospel. The two life situations he mentions are (1) circumcision/uncircumcision, and (2) slavery/freedom. It makes no difference whether we are circumcised or uncircumcised, or whether we are slaves or freedmen, he says. "However that may be, let each of you lead the life that the Lord has assigned, to which God called you" (v. 17) And "In whatever condition you were called, brothers and sisters, there remain with God" (v. 24). In other words, don't attempt to change your life circumstances, but serve Christ in whatever situation you find yourself. Paul viewed "freedom" as being in Christ.

Calvin's commentary on the same passage speaks of "calling" as life duties that govern our life action. Vocation keeps us from wandering aimlessly through life, he says. Calvin was more flexible than Luther and felt that one's vocation could change: "It would be asking too much if a tailor were not permitted to learn another trade, or a merchant to change to farming."[20]

The important rediscovery of both Luther and Calvin for our purposes is simply, "Work is a place to serve God." Our life situation is the locale of responsible calling. Therefore, work is not merely the way we earn a living, but the way we give expression to our Christian life. Our job, according to Calvin, is "the post at which the Lord has placed us." In other words, vocations are not hierarchically graded on a religious-secular continuum.

We were created in the image of God and delegated the responsibility by God to have dominion over the living things and the created order (Gen. 1:26, 28). Work is a means whereby we live out the dignifying call to be co-workers with God. We are called to serve together in the creative process to structure justice in the social order. Miller and Mattson have said of this role, "What a pleasure it must have been for Adam to cultivate the ground for the pleasure of God."[21]

But the Fall contaminated work along with everything else. Although "creation and order cooperated in pre-Fall days, now we labor as the means to take care of the necessities of life."[22] At its worst, work can become a task to be endured. Yet even under the curse, work can provide an environment to express the creativity God has placed in humans. While work was cursed, it is not in itself a curse. The "Genesis principle"[23] is still in place—the world was created by God as good. Though marred by sin, work is still to be the context for dignifying activity.

The workplace is not just the locale for Christians to witness to the gospel or minister to human need but also an avenue to express our unique abilities. Work is an expression of being. Being good stewards of the abilities God has placed in us is also a fulfillment of the call to work. This is often referred to as the *cultural mandate*. In other words, we are free to seek a vocation that expresses the inner design God has given to us. God receives no glory by our laboring in frustration in jobs that are inconsistent with our motivated abilities. The *cultural mandate* exists alongside the Great Commission.

Although this rediscovery of the value of work can be stated simply, it is no simple matter for Christians. Augustine taught us that Christians are simultaneously citizens of two worlds in conflict: the kingdom of God, whose expression should be most clearly seen in the church (though not to be equated with the church), and the kingdom of darkness, often referred to simply as the "world." These two worlds often collide most clearly in the sphere of work. Our workplace is often the single greatest source of tension in our lives. Dual realities that tug us in different directions converge on our jobs. On the one hand, work is the place where we are immersed in the world; on the other, it is the place where we are called to reflect the light of the gospel and fulfill the cultural mandate. Therefore, work is for many the location of their call to the world. Everything I have written about call to the world often is almost co-terminus with the workplace as the focus of call to penetrate the darkness as reflectors of light. And yet it is also the place where we serve God as stewards of the gifts and design that he has placed in us.

Study after study has shown that human resources are tragically wasted and many people live in frustration because there is a mismatch between their skills and the jobs they hold. Conservatively, these studies show that three or four out of every five people have jobs for which they are not suited. One person expressed his frustration this way: "I think most of us are looking for a calling, not a job. . . . Jobs are not big enough for people."[24] When there is congruence between one's abilities and inner motivation, in a position that facilitates the inner design, calling is a natural by-product.

This book is not the place for an exhaustive theology of work or a thorough discussion of the complexities and tensions of the workplace for Christians in the fallen world. My aim is to focus on work as one place where the call of God to us is fulfilled. For Christians, work need not be only an unwanted job that puts food on the table or a place of evangelizing the lost. Though we recognize that in a fallen world there are no perfect jobs, as Christians we are called to express our individual inner design as a means of producing societal wholeness. The workplace provides the context for this to happen.

The call of God originates in our being. Being precedes doing. Our unique self gives the fundamental shape to our call. What God places in our heart from birth, releases through the grace of Christ, and enhances by the anointing of the Holy Spirit is fundamentally an inside job. So we can say that much of the will of God for us is written in us. Parker Palmer captures the same truth in this book title, *Let Your Life Speak*. The various spheres of church, world, work, family, and Sabbath all have the particular demands of faithfulness I have outlined. These spheres are the context for doing what flows from our being.

Purpose or Heart Call

Is that all there is to call? Is call summed up by a *primary call* to be transformed by Jesus in community and the *secondary call* to be faithful in the various spheres of life? At the core of our being, there is also a particular *heart call* that defines the unique purpose for our existence. It is like a golden thread that runs through the fabric of our lives. It is the story line of our life that provides a sense of continuity and coherence in an otherwise fragmented and confusing world.

There is an essential, unchanging design that forms the fabric of our inner world. This unchangeable you is carried into the various spheres of our call. Far from entering this world as a tabula rasa on which our specific cultural milieu etches its design, I believe that all people are unique and therefore order their environment at least as much as the environs order them.

Any attempt to describe the central motivating thrust of our life remains somewhat illusive. Arthur Miller and Ralph Mattson, Christian vocational counselors, have discovered what they describe as an inner governor, which we might call the "motive" or "will," that gives shape to everything we do. They believe this is part of what it means to be created in the image of God. They conclude that "people begin with a specific design that remains consistent through life and that design cannot be changed."[25]

Contrary to the *me-ism* of our culture that suggests that each day brings unlimited possibilities, we cannot wake up each morning and say, "What do I want to be today?" Overnight the molecules in our bodies do not rearrange themselves so that we greet the new day with a vastly different temperament, set of abilities, and set of desires. This does not exclude alterations in our lives. Skills can be taught; character can be molded. Rather, we are amazingly consistent so that over time others become aware of our unique personality.

What is this consistent inner self of which we speak? It is not just talents and abilities but something that lies behind them.

According to Mattson and Miller, "We seek a description of a central pattern that resides behind a person's talents and determines how and when they are used. We aim at knowing that fundamental part of us that needs to be fulfilled before we can believe our talents have value."[26] This is the stuff of inner drive or motivation—in a word, the will. The will is what Miller and Mattson call "the dictator within"; it gives shape to thoughts, intention, and attitudes. "To know the pattern of motivated abilities is to know the shape of a person's will."[27]

As I look back over almost thirty years of professional ministry, I am amazed by how consistent my own sense of who I am has been. At the heart of all that I do is the desire to *influence,* to leave a transforming mark on people's lives. The role of equipper and trainer has fit me since the beginning of my professional ministry. My desire has been to help others discover the unique contribution they have to make to Christ's kingdom. As I grew in this self-understanding, the image of *coach* became appropriate. The coach designs the strategy for the game and sees how each player can make a contribution to the winning effort. A commitment to be a *discipler* comes out of the desire to influence people's growth in Christ. Finally, as a *teacher* I want to inform minds so that people's views are transformed. All these labels that describe my motivation spring from the same desire: I want to leave an imprint for Jesus Christ on people's lives. That unchangeable part of me directs all the various spheres of my life.

Much of the will of God for us is "written" in us. God has created us to live lives that are complete only when directed by his purposes. Yet in our evangelical subculture, we are often programmed to seek God's will in the outward circumstances of our lives. We tend to equate God's will with the discovery of the right marriage partner or with a career. But the will of God is a far more dynamic, lifelong process of being a steward of our inner design in the context of the specific demands of the various spheres of our call.

Lloyd Ogilvie asks, "What difference would it make if you knew the purpose for which we were made?" Is there such a particular purpose for each of us? I believe there is. It is this heart call that in a sense transcends the particular spheres of church, world, work, family, and Sabbath. Os Guinness says that *heart or purpose call* speaks to that which is deep within us:

Deep in our hearts, we all want to find and fulfill a purpose bigger than ourselves. Only such a larger purpose can inspire us to heights we know we could never reach on our own. For each of us the real purpose is personal and passionate: to know what we are here to do, and why. Kierkegaard wrote in his journal: "The thing is to understand myself, to see what God really wants me to do; the thing is to find a truth which is true for me, to find the idea for which I can live and die."[28]

What are the characteristics of this heart call or life purpose? This is where you can do your own inventory. A purpose or heart call is...

- ◆ Focused on a need you care about
- ◆ A positive burden, a sense of inner oughtness or this I must do
- ◆ Bigger than we can accomplish in our own wisdom and strength
- ◆ Expressed with energy and joy

1. *A call is focused on a need you care about.* The key to a call is to get in touch with a need *we* care about. The needs in this world are endless and can be overwhelming. We can't care about everything or direct our energies to address the vast needs. But what is the need that God has particularly put on *your* heart?

For the sake of simplicity and application, let us look at two of the spheres of secondary call that I have just described as a means of getting in touch with the need you care about.

Church—If your heart is turned toward the church as the focus of your ministry, you would do well to complete this statement: *"My greatest concern for this church is ..."* What needs do you see? God has given you a particular set of eyes. We don't all see the same thing. Our hearts are wired differently. I have often been tempted to illustrate the varied nature of the body of Christ by taking a roving microphone out into the congregation during worship and simply asking people to state their greatest concern for the church. The variety of answers would be astounding. We would hear responses like: a freedom in worship, prayer for healing, helping people grasp the Word, a heart for the lonely and disconnected, middle school youth, health of the family unit, and on it would go. Our hearts are drawn to needs. When we apply our gifts to the need we care about, therein lies an indication of our call.

World—For some of us in this season of life, our ministry is focused beyond the church as our focus to a hurting world. I will never forget the time I was present when a call took shape in Janet's heart. We met to follow up and apply the discoveries of the workshop that was designed to help people discern their heart callings. I asked Janet, "If the fear of failure were removed and you could do one thing for Christ, what would it be?"

Janet lowered her head and got very quiet. When she lifted her head to answer me, tears were already streaming down her cheeks. Gently I spoke, "What's going on?" For the first time she was about to give expression to the call on her heart. She said, "I would have a ministry to at-risk teenagers who might take their own life. I want to work on a lifeline for those who are threatening suicide."

"Tell me about that," I said.

"My sister took her own life when she was a teenager," Janet said, remembering. The pain had become her call. She not only began to volunteer for a hotline, but she went back to school to gain the expertise to have a ministry of her own in this field.

The Lord may be calling or already has called you to a point of intersection with this broken world. The question for you is, *"Where does the compassion of Christ in you intersect the brokenness of the world?"*

What need is your heart drawn to?

William Wilberforce was a member of Parliament in the late 1700s. After his conversion he continued his aristocratic, self-centered lifestyle until he realized that his conversion had not produced a change to a higher purpose. He wrote in his journal, "The first years I was in Parliament, I did nothing—nothing that is to any purpose. My own distinction was my darling object." He asked God for a purpose that would make a difference. On October 28, 1787, he made this notation in his journal, "God has set before me two great objects, the suppression of the slave trade and the reformation of manners (or morals)."[29] This was the need God gave him to care about.

2. The second characteristic of a call is closely related to the first. A call has a feeling of a *positive burden, an inner oughtness, or*

this I must do. The apostle Paul describes the passion of his heart to take the love of Christ to the Gentiles with these words: "If I proclaim the gospel, this gives me no ground for boasting, *for an obligation is laid on me. . . .* I am entrusted with a commission" (1 Cor. 9:16, 17). Paul is saying that carrying the gospel to the Gentiles was not something he chose to do, but something he was chosen to do. He cannot *not* preach the gospel to the Gentiles. He had to because God had taken hold of him. He should not receive a reward because he is doing just what he was made by God to do. He could no more stop preaching the gospel than will himself not to breathe.

In his book *Under the Mercy,* Sheldon Vanauken tells how he came to write his Christian bestseller *A Severe Mercy,* the story of the life he shared with his wife, his passionate love and life partner, Davy. Under the influence of C. S. Lewis, both Sheldon and Davy became Christians while graduate students at Oxford. He walks you through the emotional agony of Davy's untimely death from a fatal disease. Yet from the early 1950s to the mid–1970s after Davy's death, Sheldon meandered away from his commitment to Christ. In January of 1976 his heart was stirring again toward obedience to his Lord. He sat down to re-read the letters C. S. Lewis had sent him that drew him to faith and encouraged him after Davy's death. Then something very unanticipated happened. "At one moment nothing was further from my mind. Thirty seconds later I was going to write a book that was named *A Severe Mercy.* I recall no process of thought or decision, certainly no Voice or Presence. The intention, calm, clear, firm was simply there—a fait accompli—and thirty seconds before it had not been."[30] It had to be done. This was a divine appointment.

When I read this, I openly wept. I thought, "I am not alone; I am not crazy. Someone else has had this experience." In the spring of 1983 I was jogging around a high school track when like a lightning bolt out of the sky I had a picture in my mind of the format of a discipleship tool. I had been involved in one-on-one discipling, assisting others' growth in Christ, but had been frustrated with empowering them to disciple others. As with Vanauken, the epiphany came out of the blue. I remember no conscious mulling over of my frustration in the moment. Suddenly, with no forewarning, it was as if I had been claimed to write this tool, and it must be done.[31] Yet when you are called to do something, you realize that it is simply the Lord choosing to use you to fulfill a purpose. The fulfillment of that purpose is simply something you must do, which gives you no grounds for boasting.

With a call comes the message, *"This must be done and I am the one who has been called to do it."*

3. The third characteristic of a purpose or heart call is that *it is bigger than we can ever accomplish in our own resources.* There is nothing worthy of the name "call" that does not have enormous obstacles connected to it and to which we say, "Who me, Lord? You have got to be kidding!"

The Lord caught up with Moses after he had been a shepherd for forty years in the wilderness. Moses had fled to the wilderness from his privileged position in Pharaoh's household after he had tried to right the injustices against his Hebrew people by killing an Egyptian. The forty years were necessary if Moses was going to accomplish his people's deliverance in God's way. The Lord informed Moses that he had heard the cries of oppression from his people under their taskmasters in Egypt and had now come to deliver them. It was as if the Lord said to Moses, "Moses, guess how I am going to do that? I will send you to Pharaoh."

But Moses spoke the typical reaction to a call from God. "Who am I that I should go to Pharaoh?" With call should come a reluctant response, "Who me, Lord? You have got to be kidding. What am I?"

God's call on us is pushed into the recesses of our inner being because a fearful inner voice says, "I could never do that." For some time I had felt that God had set me apart to influence the next generation of pastors in their understanding of the pastoral role. Each time the thought dared to surface, I would squelch it with an opposing thought: "Who do you think you are?" Two things needed to happen for me to respond to this call: (1) I had to recognize that the accusing voice was the Evil One attempting to cut me off at the source. I am nothing, but the call of God is everything. If God has something for me to do, I am simply the custodian of his purpose; and (2) I had to see that fear is opposed to love. Only when I experienced the love of God poured out in my heart through the Holy Spirit (Rom. 5:5) was I able to embrace the call.

The call of God brings us to the end of our resources so that we must throw ourselves upon the Lord along with other like-hearted people. The call of God is rarely individual. We live out our call with others who share the same heart commitment.

Let's return to the story of William Wilberforce and his call to end slavery in the British Empire. John Wesley's last letter just six days before his death in his nineties was to Wilberforce: "My dear sir, Unless The Divine Power has raised you up, I see not how you can go through with your glorious enterprise in opposing that execrable villainy which is the scandal of religion. Unless God has raised you up for this very thing, you will be worn out by the opposition of men and devils; but if God is with you, who can be against you?"[32] Wilberforce's character was publicly lampooned in political cartoons, yet he was not alone. There was a group of like-minded people known as the *Clapham Society* who sustained each other in this forty-year battle. They sacrificed their resources; they met regularly together for prayer and strategy sessions to bring down this institution of evil. As God would have it, the day in 1832 when slavery was abolished throughout the British Empire was the day of Wilberforce's last breath. A colleague wrote, "It is a singular fact that on the very night on which we were successfully engaged in passing the Act of Emancipation . . . the spirit of our friend left the world. The day which was the termination of his labors was the termination of his life." Life is not usually so tidy. Some of us may live to see our call from God fulfilled, and many will not as is the testimony of Hebrews 11.

4. Finally, the last sign of a purpose or heart call is that there is *energy and joy* that wells up within you when you apply your gifts to a need that you care about. In John 15, Jesus calls us to abide in him as a branch abides in the vine. If we are to bear fruit, which is the goal of our life, then we must remain attached to the vine. Jesus concludes this section by saying, "I have said these things to you so that my joy may be in you, and that your joy may be complete" (John 15:11). What was Jesus' joy? He found his greatest joy in doing the will of the Father. When Jesus hung on the cross, giving his life for us, he said, "It is finished." He had completed what his Father had set before him. How could this be? Only a few people in an inconsequential land had any idea what this meant. Yet the work the Father had assigned him was done. Jesus told his disciples, when they were concerned that he had skipped a meal, "My food is to do the will of him who sent me and to complete his work"

(John 4:34). In accomplishing what was set before him to do there was the deepest sense of satisfaction and well-being.

What does Jesus want for us? That we would have the same joy that he had and that our joy would well up full to overflowing. One of the synonyms for spiritual gifts is the Greek word *energematon*. "There are varieties of *working* . . ." (1 Cor. 12:6 RSV). We could translate this literally, "There are varieties of energizings." When we operate in our call, there is a release of energy. You are at the heart of what you were made for. Functioning in your call is like drinking at the refreshing wells of God's Spirit. It is a welling up. You step into the stream or flow of God's Spirit. This is the opposite of the idea of service that many of us have inherited. Service, by definition, must be something you don't want to do. Ray Stedman has written, "Somewhere this idea found deep entrenchment in Christian circles that doing what God wants you to do is always unpleasant; that Christians must make choices between doing what they want to do and being happy, and doing what God wants them to do and being miserable." When we operate in our call, we tap into an energy that flow and says, "*I am made for this.*"

In summary, the call of God is focused on a need you care about; it comes with "this I must do"; it is bigger than we can do on our own; but it releases energy and joy like a refreshing stream. There is a *primary call* to be transformed into Christlikeness in community, a *secondary call* or callings into the various spheres of our life, and then the *heart or purpose call* that is the expression of our life.

It is this heart or purpose call that all of God's people need to know is available to them. I pray for the day that all of God's people will be able to live the truth that Gordon Cosby describes:

> Vocation [calling] has the elements of knowing that if you respond to the call, you are faithful to your own inner being and you are enhanced by it. Your own awareness converges with some need out yonder and intersects with it in such a way that you have the sense that you were born to this.[33]

Is There a Special Call?

In the New Reformation redefinition of call, I have stressed the primary and secondary call that is incumbent on all the members of the body. Conspicuous in its absence has been any mention of a "special call" associated with ordained ministry. Is there a qualitatively different call to leadership that is of a nature not experienced by the ordinary members of the body of Christ? Or does the New Testament conceive of the call to leadership as a purpose or heart call among other purpose or heart calls? My bias is toward the latter. From within the one body of Christ, some have the function of helping the members of the body discover their ministry to upbuild the church and be deployed to the world. Any view of call that debilitates and devalues the ministry of the whole body of Christ is contrary to the New Testament conception of the church:

> The traditional roles of clergy and laity must be reversed: The laity become the troops in the front lines and the clergy, with the gathered church, help to support *them*. Until this revolution occurs, the Protestant concept of "the priesthood of all believers" remains vague and unrealized.[34]

ORDINATION IN THE NEW REFORMATION

A study in the United Presbyterian Church, U.S.A. raised the pertinent question, "Is ordination, as it is now practiced, consistent or in conflict with the understanding of the common ministry of all Christians?"[35] I have already argued that ordination traditionally serves as the great divide that creates the class consciousness between clergy and laity. It is the "essential difference" between two peoples.

James Dunn proposes a radically different application of ordination: "Until we count 'ordination' of Sunday School teachers and distributors of church flowers as no different in essence from 'ordination' of an elder or bishop, we cannot claim to be functioning as the body of Christ."[36]

Ordination, a setting apart, is conferred through a symbol. If we apply ordination to *all* the ministries within the body, what might be the symbol of an every-member ordination?

My suggestion is that we recover the significance of baptism. As it is now commonly practiced, baptism is an initiation rite into the body of Christ that represents the washing of regeneration and the newness of life in Christ. But who associates baptism with ordination for ministry? I urge a reclaiming of baptism to fill this symbol with content associated with the entrance of all into Christ's ministry.

We can see Jesus' baptism as the prototype. Jesus' ministry was inaugurated in the waters of John's baptism (Matt. 3:13–17). John recoiled at the thought of baptizing Jesus, the Sinless One. Yet Jesus claimed that it must be done to "fulfill all righteousness" (v. 15). In baptism, Jesus was entering into a solidarity with sinners and foreshadowing his redemptive act in the cross. It was not for his own sin that he was being baptized, but for those whom he came to save.

Equally significant in Jesus' baptism, however, is that "he saw the Spirit of God descending like a dove and alighting on him" (v. 16). We cannot miss here the connection between the descent of the Spirit in baptism at the inauguration of Jesus' ministry and the same empowerment received with the descent of the Spirit at Pentecost and its connection to baptism. Peter told those under conviction who had gathered to hear his Spirit-emboldened message, "Repent, and be baptized every one of you in the name of Jesus Christ so that your sins may be forgiven; and you will receive the gift of the Holy Spirit" (Acts 2:38). The Faith and Order Report on "the Meaning of Baptism" states, "The outpouring of the Spirit at Pentecost is the counterpart of what happened to Jesus at his baptism. . . . The same Spirit who remained on Jesus for his messianic ministry has ever since Pentecost dwelt in the church, which is the temple of his body."[37]

The apostle Paul also makes a connection between the Holy Spirit and baptism as a sign of entrance into ministry of the whole body. In 1 Corinthians 12 he wrote that the Holy Spirit apportions gifts of ministry to the whole body for the building up of the church: "For in the one Spirit we were all baptized into one body" (v. 13). It is this baptism of the Spirit that inducts a person into the one ministry of Jesus Christ.

Historically, our emphasis in baptism has been on the benefits received and not on the claim of Christ on the one baptized. We have stressed our entrance into the covenant community of God's people and the forgiveness of sin and cleansing from guilt symbolized in the water, but we have failed to instruct the candidate for baptism that in that rite, the Holy Spirit empowers us to give our life away in service to Christ. Every service of baptism should be a service of ordination for ministry and an opportunity for the gathered people of God to recommit themselves to living out the implications of their baptismal vows.

Therefore, whether or not we believe in the rite of ordination to a "special" ministry for pastors, we must not forget that there is only one people of God—all are baptized Christians. All have the same identity in Christ no matter the particular form of ministry to which we may be called. This means that ordination should never create a class distinction where a group of people is set apart *from* and *above* the rest of the members of the body. Leaders from *among* the body are set apart from *within* and *for* the body, to equip them so that the body may arrive at the fullness of its ministry.

Ordination of the Membership

Instead of limiting ordination to a few, a more fruitful approach consistent with the church as organism is to conceive of ways to affirm the calls within the body. George Peck opens up our thinking by proposing a five-step process whereby ministries can be confirmed.[38] To have a ministry means we are:

1. *Called*—have a sense of God's hand upon us for a particular task
2. *Prepared*—enter a regimen of training necessary to carry out this task
3. *Recognized*—be affirmed publicly by the congregation and appointed for a ministry
4. *Supported*—serve in the context of community, rarely in isolation
5. *Held accountable*—submit to a standard established by the community

This pattern could function for those called either to a specific ministry within the church or to the world. For example, in our church, small-group leaders are recruited (1) from within the existing groups after demonstrating gifts to lead a group and passing through a discernment process to test call. There is a course of training (2) that includes formal classroom sessions and on-the-job apprenticeship. There is a means to publicly recognize (3) their role in the church. A small-group leadership team meets regularly to provide relational and prayer support (4) and to uphold the standards of accountability mutually agreed upon (5).

Peck urges a similar model for vocation-call as Christians respond to serve where they are planted in the world. Why do we not have structures of support and accountability for Christian doctors, lawyers, nutritionists, builders, social workers, and the like?

The traditional view of call and ordination restricts ministry to a few. But the New Reformation view throws open the door of call to all who have responded to the summons of Jesus Christ. There are not a few who have important things to do for God's kingdom, but it is the privilege and responsibility of all to cultivate God's voice in order to hear the inner promptings of the Holy Spirit. What ministry could be released if only we believe in the full empowerment of all of God's people!

NOTES

1. Thomas Gillespie, "The Call and Ordination in a Reformed Theology of Ministry" (Unpublished paper), 10–11.

2. Donald McKim, "The 'Call' in the Reformed Tradition" (Unpublished paper), 7.

3. "Anglican–Roman Catholic International Commission, Final Report" (CTS/SPC, 1982), 36.

4. Quoted by James D. G. Dunn, "Ministry and the Ministry: The Charismatic Renewal's Challenge to Traditional Ecclesiology" (Unpublished paper), 11.

5. Quoted in Gillespie, "The Call and Ordination," 10 (emphasis mine).

6. As quoted in Roland H. Bainton, *Here I Stand: A Life of Martin Luther* (New York: Mentor, 1950), 156.

7. Gillespie, "The Call and Ordination," 7.

8. Os Guinness, *The Call* (Nashville: Word Publishing, 1998), 4.

9. Gerhard Kittel, *Theological Dictionary of the New Testament,* vol. 4, trans. Geoffrey W. Bromiley (Grand Rapids: Eerdmans, 1967), 441.

10. Donald McKim, "The Call in the Reformed Tradition" (Unpublished paper), 7.

11. Paul Stevens, *The Other Six Days* (Grand Rapids: Eerdmans, 1999), 63.

12. Gordon Cosby, *Handbook for Mission Groups* (Waco, Tex.: Word, 1975), 27–28.

13. Paul Tournier, *The Meaning of Persons* (New York: Harper & Row, 1957), 9.

14. C. S. Lewis, *Mere Christianity* (New York: Macmillan, 1952), 189.

15. This balance is captured by the title and is the subject of Elizabeth O'Connor's book *Journey Inward, Journey Outward* (New York: Harper & Row, 1968).

16. Guinness, *The Call,* 31.

17. Stevens, *The Other Six Days.*

18. For a more in-depth and cogent treatment of call intertwined with the church, work, and world, see Paul Steven's *The Other Six Days* and Os Guinness' *The Call.*

19. Os Guinness, *The Dust of Death* (Downers Grove, Ill.: InterVarsity Press, 1973), 387.

20. John Calvin, *Institutes of the Christian Religion,* trans. John McNeil (Philadelphia: Westminster, 1936).

21. Arthur F. Miller and Ralph T. Mattson, *Finding a Job You Can Love* (Nashville: Nelson, 1982), 46.

22. Ibid., 46.

23. Ibid., 47.

24. As quoted in Frank Tillapaugh, *The Church Unleashed* (Ventura, Calif.: Regal Books, 1982), 199.

25. Arthur F. Miller and Ralph T. Mattson, *The Truth About You* (Old Tappan, N.J.: Revell, 1977), 17.

26. Ibid., 19.

27. Miller and Mattson, *Finding a Job You Can Love,* 97.

28. Guinness, *The Call,* 3.

29. Garth Lean, *God's Politician* (Colorado Springs, Colo.: Helmers and Howard, 1987), 47.

30. Sheldon Vanauken, *Under the Mercy* (Nashville: Nelson, 1985), 102.

31. This book is now published with InterVarsity Press as *Discipleship Essentials* (1998).

32. Lean, *God's Politician,* 58.

33. Cosby, *Handbook for Mission Groups,* 28.

34. Ernst Klein, "A Christian Life Style in the Modern World" (Unpublished pamphlet).

35. *Report of the Task Force to the General Assembly Mission Council Executive Committee,* 1978.

36. Dunn, "Ministry and the Ministry," 26.

37. From the Faith and Order Report on "the Meaning of Baptism," in *One Lord, One Baptism* (London: SCM Press, 1960), 53ff.; as quoted in *Theological Foundations for Ministry,* ed. Ray S. Anderson (Grand Rapids: Eerdmans, 1979), 432.

38. George Peck and John S. Hoffman, eds., *The Laity in Ministry* (Valley Forge, Pa.: Judson, 1984), 88–89.

Index

We want to hear from you. Please send your comments about this book to us in care of zreview@zondervan.com. Thank you.

ZONDERVAN™

GRAND RAPIDS, MICHIGAN 49530 USA

WWW.ZONDERVAN.COM